Native Plants in the Coastal Garden

A Guide for Gardeners in British Columbia and the Pacific Northwest

Native Plants in the Coastal Garden

A Guide for Gardeners in British Columbia and the Pacific Northwest

By April Pettinger

Edited by Elaine Jones
Reviewed by Douglas Justice
Copy-edited by Elizabeth McLean
Proofread by Peggy Trendell-Whittaker
Line drawings by Kathy Thomson
Landscape design by Martina Voss
Site plan drawings by Patricia Piwowar
Cover photograph by Patrick Morrow/First Light
Cover design by Steve Penner
Interior design by Margaret Ng
Typeset by Margaret Ng

Printed and bound in Canada.

Canadian Cataloguing in Publication Data

Pettinger, April.
　　Native plants in the coastal garden

　　Includes bibliographical references and index.
　　ISBN 1-55110-405-9

　　1. Native plant gardening—Pacific Coast (B.C.). 2. Native plant gardening—
　　Pacific Coast (U.S.). I. Title.
SB439.26.N77P47 1996　　　635.9'51795　　　C95-911142-5

**To Cik, Jenny and Ben
and to Barry,**

with love

Contents

✻✺ Acknowledgements ✺✻

Before I began this project little did I realize that the best way to tap the milk of human kindness is to write a book. I have been overwhelmed by the thoughtfulness and generosity of the many individuals who have been eager to assist me in spreading the word about native plants. Perhaps it is the nature of the subject which causes those involved to share so willingly; whatever the explanation, I am deeply indebted to the following generous, knowledgeable people.

Throughout this project Brenda Costanzo, assistant curator of the University of Victoria Herbarium, has been a vital source of information, encouragement and support; I am particularly grateful for her contribution to the propagation section of this book. I also wish to express my appreciation for the encouragement and support I have received from members of the Victoria Horticultural Society Native Plant Study Group, of which Brenda is the present chairperson.

Many thanks are due to Dr. Robert Ogilvie, former curator of botany at the Royal British Columbia Museum, for his time and consideration in reading a portion of the text and for answering some difficult questions; to John Pinder-Moss of the Royal British Columbia Museum, for reading and advising on a large portion of the text; and to Jim Rainer, a Pacific Northwest field editor for *Wildflower* magazine, for

reading and commenting on the complete manuscript.

Thank you to Jill Stewart-Bowen for always being there to answer questions, read excerpts and lend encouragement, and to Jill and to John Ewing of the newsletter committee of the Victoria Horticultural Society.

I am particularly grateful to Dr. Hans Roemer for his contribution on meadows and rock gardens; thanks also to William MacGillivray, site manager of the Swan Lake Christmas Hill Nature Sanctuary, for his generous donations of literature, suggestions and encouragement.

My friends Karen Woodland and Joel Ussery have been gratifyingly interested in this project since its conception, and I thank Joel for his invaluable contribution on the topic of meadows, and Karen for her background information on the subject of the lawn.

I also extend my gratitude to the following: Dennis Demarchi, habitat classification specialist in the Wildlife Branch of the British Columbia Ministry of Environment, for information and materials; David DeShane and Gerald Fleming of the Municipality of Saanich Parks and Recreation Department for helpful information; Dave Fraser of Arenaria Research and Interpretation and Fraser's Thimble Farms on Salt Spring Island, for information and plant lists; Andy MacKinnon, Manager of Forest Ecology Reserves, British Columbia Ministry of Forests, for helping me define the region; Rod Silver, Program Manager of Naturescape British Columbia, for his support and permission to use portions of that program's materials; Charles Thomson, Professor of Landscape Architecture at the University of Manitoba, for materials, and for his enthusiastic response to my ideas; and the Canadian Wildflower Society and the editors of *Wildflower* magazine for permission to print their "Gardener's Guidelines."

The following friends and acquaintances provided encouragement, support and information: Joanne Acampora; Simon Bunn; Dr. Adolph Ceska; Nancy Fields; Caroline Herriot; Lowell Hinrichs, Dawn Loewen; Agnes Lynne; Diane Pierce; Carol Rossell; Karen Skowron; Helen Stewart; and Dr. Nancy Turner.

I would also like to pay my respects to the memory of Mrs. Wilma Vincent, who enthusiastically shared anecdotes about her beautiful wildflower lawn.

I owe special thanks to the talented women who have contributed their work to this book: Trish Piwawar for her clear, precise site plans, Kathy Thomson for her brilliant art, and Martina Voss for her splendid landscape designs. Thanks are due as well to Des Kennedy for his foreword to this book and to the pleasant, supportive people at Whitecap Books.

Above all I thank my husband, Barry, who has given me his full support in every sense of the word, and without whose partnership this work could not have been completed—or even begun.

Foreword

The explosion of interest in gardening that has reverberated across North America in recent years has exposed all manner of horticultural propensities, some more preposterous than others. At the less intelligent end of the spectrum is the unfortunate phenomenon called power gardening. Here the attraction seems to lie in pillaging the garden of its magic, dragging it into the marketplace and selling it as a status symbol. Combining the outlandish with the vulgar, this cult will inspire adherents to pay $10,000 for a sterling silver spade from Tiffany. Its self-indulgence mistakes the garden for a fad, a craze, a capricious fancy picked up because "everybody's doing it."

Meanwhile, many miles away, another contemporary theme is emerging with far greater promise: the evolution of what's being called "the natural garden." Its parameters are not entirely nor precisely defined, but its spirit is instantly recognizable. To garden naturally—in a saner age the term would be redundant—means to touch the earth with dexterity and affection and with a keen awareness of the primacy of nature's part in the lovely *pas de deux* that is gardening.

Collaborating with nature involves designing planting schemes in harmony with the characteristics of the site and reflective of the natural growth patterns of that particular area. Wherever possible it employs native local materials for structures and features, thereby knitting the hardscape into the regional topography. It encourages wildlife by creating habitats that provide food, water, and shelter for a diverse range of organisms. Ideally it connects naturally to adjacent wildlife areas and corridors. It features plants that are naturally adapted to local growing conditions, requiring a minimum of maintenance from external sources. Among its highest achievements is the use of indigenous plants in associations that emulate nature's own impeccable flair for design.

This latter element is the focus of April Pettinger's *Native Plants in the Coastal Garden*. In it she writes: "Native plant gardening has come into its time." The same might be said for her timely and comprehensive guide.

I believe there has been, until quite recently, a general sense that no great skill is required in cultivating native plants. After all, they grow perfectly well on their own, without any fussing or fiddling from us. A more traditional garden, which often served to show off the horticultural expertise of its owner, had precious little room for plants that appeared to require no such expertise. Common, they were called, with just a bit of a sniff. Gardeners who were observed cultivating workaday natives might be dismissed as well-intentioned crackpots, the way people who shopped at health food stores used to be.

Nothing, as we now realize, could be farther

from the truth. Natural gardening generally, and native plant gardening specifically, requires both skill and a high level of interest.

Wisdom and humility are the hallmarks of the native plant gardener. The meek may or may not inherit the earth, but it's the humble who are wise enough to understand that any small patch of ground we claim as "our" garden is in reality a place where we exercise—even should we remain there throughout our lives—a fleeting steward-ship. The garden is no more mine than are the clouds that float above it on a changeable May morning. This sense of the gardener as dutiful steward, one who takes delight in an enterprise that transcends the individual, is a particular strength of *Native Plants in the Coastal Garden*.

The successful native plant gardener needs to be prescient enough to understand something of the ecosystem in which the garden exists, and humble enough to intuit how profoundly we fail to understand that ecosystem completely. The forestlands of the Pacific Northwest are a living web of such astonishing complexity, beauty, and diversity, most of us can only hope for a small insight into its workings.

Those who seek to emulate nature in their gardens spend as much time rummaging around in ecology as in botany. Their interests extend beyond individual plants into elements of con-nectedness among different plants and animals and microorganisms. Their passions stir at the mere mention of myccorhizal fungi.

Native plant gardeners suffer no illusions that they're gardening in Edwardian England or Renaissance France or Imperial Japan. They're firmly rooted in the Pacific Northwest coast in the twilight of the twentieth century, when most of the region's great forests have been felled, when many of its native plants and creatures are pressed to the brink of extinction. And yet where still remains an opportunity to preserve significant components of a bioregion that's among the most impressive on earth. They strive to understand the soils and plants, the winds and weather patterns, and the creatures that comprise this lovely portion of the planet. *Native Plants in the Coastal Garden* offers page upon page of insight into this exhilarating quest.

Those who garden with native plants open themselves to an awareness that each of our small gardens is a tiny fragment of the Global Garden, that our gardens, like our lives, flow out from across their boundaries, connecting and interlocking one with another, and with nature's own splendid wild gardens. Ultimately they rec-ognize that gardens, like the wild places of nature, are the premises of transcendence, the haunts of magic plants and creatures that only those blessed with wisdom and humility are privileged to encounter.

—*Des Kennedy*
Denman Island

Introduction

Astonishment provided the initial impetus for writing this book—my astonishment at discovering the abundance of indigenous flora in coastal British Columbia and the Pacific Northwest. When I moved here, it was the ocean that lured me, but the first time I visited Pacific Rim National Park on the west coast of Vancouver Island, it was the rainforest that filled me with awe. Not only the majesty of the forest itself, but the ferns, lichens, wayside wildflowers, and acres of actual hedges of salal (*Gaultheria shallon*) astonished me. My eyes were opened to the beauty of our wild vegetation in this horticulturally bountiful region, and I began to see it even in urban areas. Victoria, for example, where I now live, has a number of parks which annually present a dazzling display of springtime beauty with their carpets of native wildflowers, often spread out under a canopy of Garry oak (*Quercus garryana*).

Our ancestors, of course, saw such displays all around them, in all regions of the continent. One reads, in Sarah Stein's inspiring book *Noah's Garden*, of the multitude of species which have now disappeared completely, recorded by a Mrs. Dana in the last century. And just the other day I was told of a whole meadow of the rare and beautiful native orchid *Calypso bulbosa* a short distance from my own home, in a field now overrun with intrusive imported weeds. How nice it would be, I began to think, to participate in the restoration of some of these wild plants to their rightful domain.

The increasing awe with which I regarded our west coast vegetation, combined with my interest in gardening, spawned a growing curiosity about native plants, which in turn led to a stubborn determination to pierce the mystique that seemed to surround this form of horticulture. As I became mildly intrigued, then fascinated, then committed to the concept of native plant gardening, I began to ask myself some questions.

O With more than 250 species of native plants appropriate for garden cultivation within our horticultural region, why do we find so few in our gardens?

O In this climate of rapidly increasing global concern with ecological issues and awareness of the environmental crisis threatening our forests, what can each of us do on a local, individual basis, to help restore plant, animal, bird and other wildlife habitat?

O Why is it so rare to find native plants in local nurseries? Is it because we are not demanding them? Why not?

O Why is there such a mystique surrounding the subject of native plant gardening?

Pondering these questions, I became convinced that the answer to all of them was the same: we do not have enough information. Many gardeners are intrigued by indigenous

The Pacific coastal region

The plants and gardening procedures discussed in this book apply to the region that stretches from southeast Alaska in the north to approximately Eugene, Oregon in the south. From east to west it extends from the coast of the Pacific Ocean to the Coast mountains in British Columbia and the Cascades in the United States. The region includes the Queen Charlotte Islands and Vancouver Island, and encompasses the rainshadow belt of Mediterranean climate and dry habitats found on southeastern Vancouver Island, the Gulf and San Juan Islands, the eastern Olympic Peninsula, and in the Willamette Valley.

For the purposes of this book, I refer to this area as the Pacific coastal region, although it covers only a section of the Pacific coast.

plants, but uncertain about which plants to use and how to garden with them. If this is your situation, this book of basic guidelines is designed to help you, whether you wish to incorporate a few natives into your mixed border, establish a flowering meadow, or develop a completely wild garden.

Gardening is a thoroughly engaging, soul-satisfying activity. Now that I have been studying and participating in native plant gardening for a few years, I find it ideally suited to the time and place in which we live, and a fascinating addition to a gardener's repertoire. I hope this book will help you arrive at the same conclusion, and enhance the enjoyment you derive from all your garden activities.

1

Native Plant Gardening: Dismantling the Mystique

"Nothing, not even fairyland, could have been so lovely as our lily field. The wild lilies blossomed in April or May but they seemed to be always in the field, because, the very first time you saw them, they did something to the back of your eyes which kept themselves there, and something to your nose, so that you smelled them whenever you thought of them. The field was roofed by tall, thin pine trees. The ground underneath was clear and grassed. The lilies were thickly sprinkled everywhere. They were white, with gold in their hearts and brown eyes that stared back into the earth because their necks hooked down. But each lily had five sharp white petals rolling back and pointing to the tree-tops, like millions and millions of tiny quivering fingers. The smell was fresh and earthy. In all your thinkings you could picture nothing more beautiful than our lily field."

Those are the words of Emily Carr, writing in *The Book of Small* of her childhood home in Victoria, in an area that is now densely urbanized. Most of us have childhood memories of fields and forests and wildflowers that we seemed to know intimately, back then. Sadly, many of us have become somewhat distanced from these once-familiar plants. But we can rejoice; they are coming back into our lives, this time in the form of newly popular garden plants. Now we find ourselves, having forgotten those intimacies of childhood, asking the question: what is native plant gardening all about?

Any obscurity attached to this gardening concept is unnecessary; native flora are those very plants we grew up with: the wildflowers we found in woods and fields, the catkins we collected, the wild berries we enjoyed. Essentially, native plant gardening is about creating a garden that respects the natural environment.

The terminology describing this way of gardening seems to reinforce the mystique; it varies from region to region and even from gardener to gardener. A whole new gardening lexicon is developing, including such terms as *habitat restoration*, *xeriscaping*, *biodiversity* and a vast array of unfamiliar botanical names. We suddenly find ourselves encumbered with a new horticultural style while we are still trying to grasp the fundamentals of organic gardening. Now there is a new code to break. Where do we start?

Perhaps the best way to begin is to ask the meaning of words. In this book terms are generally used in the widest and most popular sense. The following pages contain some terms that provide a key to understanding native plant gardening. (See the glossary for more terms, largely botanical, which are used throughout this book.)

○ What is a native plant?

It is a plant species that occurs naturally in a specific geographical area. That area, or range, could be a few square miles or a major portion of the globe. In North America we consider a native plant to be a species that has existed in a given area prior to European settlement. Although a distinction is sometimes made between the terms *native* and *indigenous*, in this book the two are used synonymously. An indigenous, or native, plant is by its nature hardy to its own environment.

Every species started out, at some time and in some form, as a native plant somewhere in the world. An *exotic* is a plant not of local origin; it is imported from elsewhere, and grown outside its native range. When a plant native to our region is grown in another area it is usually called an *exotic* (or *introduced*, or *alien*).

All the plants listed in this book are native to the Pacific coastal region defined in the Introduction. Well over 250 kinds of plants native to the Pacific coastal region are known to be adaptable to garden cultivation, under the appropriate conditions.

○ What is the difference between a native plant and a wildflower?

Strictly speaking there is no difference. A wildflower is a native herbaceous plant (not a tree or shrub). Depending upon your source, however, the term *wildflower* can have diverse meanings—not all of them completely accurate. Sometimes we see the term used commercially—and inappropriately—on packages of imported flower seed mixtures which, we are told, will produce beautiful wildflower meadows. These cannot be wild, or native, if they are imported! The most common and correct use of the term wildflower is in reference to a native plant that has an attractive blossom; in our region, it refers to native plants (often bulbs) that flower in open fields or slopes, such as in oak meadows. It is often incorrectly used to describe an introduced species that has naturalized in a particular area —adapted so well to its new surroundings that it now grows wild. Some commercial sources and even garden writers have used *wildflower* to refer to any small flowering plant that adapts well to a meadow or other open site, and others

use it to refer to flowers which are native only to grassland terrain.

If this is getting just a little too confusing, simply think of a wildflower as a flowering native plant.

○ What is a naturalized plant?

A naturalized plant is an introduced, non-native species that has spread and now grows in the wild without cultivation; naturalized plant populations are self-established and self-maintaining. Plants can naturalize in gardens as well as in the wild. An example is the English daisy (*Bellis perennis*).

Another term for a garden-cultivated plant which has become established in the wild is *escapee*. Some escapees that have become naturalized in the wild, such as Scotch broom (*Cytisus scoparius*) and purple loosestrife (*Lythrum salicaria*), become problem invaders.

○ What does ecology mean?

Ecology is the branch of biology that deals with the relations between living organisms and their environment. Plant ecology is particularly concerned with relationships between plants and their environment: discovering what types of environments plants live in; how they interrelate with the environment and with each other; and how environments and plant communities change with time.

○ What are ecosystems?

Each ecosystem is a basic unit of nature made up of a community of animals, plants, bacteria, and the interrelated physical and chemical environment. Ecosystems provide a way of looking at our environment not as made up of many separate entities but as a complete, integrated unit.

What is meant by the term biodiversity?

Biodiversity simply means biological diversity, or the diversity of living organisms. It encompasses genetic, species, and ecosystem resources. It is inspiring to know that, in terms of species, British Columbia is the most biodiverse province in Canada. However, the ongoing depletion of wildlife habitat threatens that diversity.

Does the term habitat simply mean home?

Yes; the environment in which a unit of wildlife (plant or animal) lives is called a habitat. Each habitat is a particular combination of physical, environmental, and biotic factors (those factors related to other living organisms). It includes substances such as water and soil; the forces of wind and gravity; conditions such as temperature and light; and other organisms—among them animals, insects, and microorganisms.

What is xeriscaping?

Because a native plant has adapted to the conditions of its natural environment and receives no artificial maintenance in the wild, it requires little maintenance—and this includes little or no watering—once it is established in a garden site with conditions similar to those of its natural habitat. The most popular term to describe this use of plants for low water-maintenance is xeriscaping, a word which has been bandied about a lot recently. Derived from the Greek word *xeros*, meaning dry, it means landscaping for dry regions. Introduced by the Denver Water Board in the 1970s, the word first gained popular usage in the arid southwest and high plains regions of the United States. In that dry, desert terrain where drought is a common occurrence, the plants used were extremely drought-tolerant (requiring less than 14 inches/350 mm of rain yearly).

Obviously this is not the case in our comparatively lush zones. Plants that are drought-resistant in our region cannot tolerate such low yearly rainfall levels—but they need not. They receive over 30 inches (750 mm) yearly, even in those areas that experience the summer droughts of a Mediterranean type of climate. (In some parts of this region the annual rainfall is over 200 inches/5,000 mm.) If we match the conditions of our plants' wild homes, our native plant gardens will require little watering. In our climate, rather than use the term xeriscaping, it seems more appropriate to refer to such gardening as water-wise, water-saving, drought-resistant, drought-tolerant, low water maintenance, or water conservation gardening. Whatever the terminology, however, and wherever you garden, the principle remains the same: use plants (native or introduced) whose water requirements equal the rainfall in your climatic zone.

What is the difference between native plant gardening, habitat restoration, and naturalistic landscaping?

Creating a garden using at least some native plants is called *native plant gardening* in this book, but this way of gardening involves more than simply the use of certain plants. The basic principle of native plant gardening is choosing plants whose needs are closely met by the conditions in their landscapes. Some ways of meeting these requirements are discussed in chapter 3. Because it considers the needs of the plants, the methodology of native plant gardening will benefit any type of garden.

A well-developed native plant garden creates its own biodiverse ecosystems and, as well as restoring the natural habitats of plants, provides food and shelter to wildlife. Consequently, one of the many characteristics of such a garden is that it becomes home to a range of wildlife species, fauna as well as flora. For this reason, native plant gardening is often referred to as *habitat restoration*; in fact, the two terms are frequently used almost interchangeably. A variation—actually an extension—of this type of garden is a wildlife habitat garden, or backyard sanctuary, which is developed with the primary purpose of attracting and nurturing wildlife. Chapter 5 deals in some detail with the subject of wildlife in the garden.

The term *naturalistic* is not a description of a gardening style or plant materials; it is a landscape term. A naturalistic (sometimes called *natural*) garden is one in which the arrangement of plants is similar to arrangements in nature; nature is the inspiration for the design. A naturalistic garden emulates a particular habitat; for example, a natural shade garden can be modelled on a woodland habitat. The effect can be achieved either with the use of native plants, or by conventional gardening techniques using introduced species. A naturalistic garden, therefore, is not necessarily a native plant garden.

✹   ✹   ✹

The principles of native plant gardening have a logic that applies to any kind of garden. We all have our favourite gardening styles and our favourite plants, native and exotic, and it is quite probable that, for various reasons, you may not wish—or be able—to fill your entire garden with indigenous species. You may decide on a mixed garden, which combines native plants with exotics, or you may add native plants slowly, over a long period of time. Whatever your style of garden, it will flourish when you observe the tenets of native plant gardening.

2

WHY?

A Native Plant Imperative

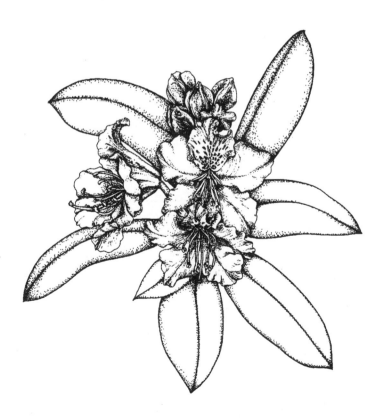

Why, after all these years of cultivating exotics, are so many gardeners turning to native plant gardening? Why would you choose to garden this way?

Each of us who desires to move in this direction has a particular set of reasons: aesthetics, improved gardening methods, personal philosophy, pure enjoyment or a combination of these. The arguments in support of native plant gardening form a compelling imperative.

The Historical Imperative

Throughout history, there has been a direct relationship between gardening and political, philosophical, and cultural fashion. The earliest gardens we know of reflected the prevailing characteristics of their cultural environments. For example, the Romans successfully introduced ornamental pleasure gardens into Britain during their occupation of that country in the first century A.D. The enthusiastic response by the Celts to this new cultural form was indicative of the acceptance of a general refinement of style and ease of living introduced to Britain by the Romans.

Later, in Europe during the Dark Ages, gardens became the preserve of monasteries and were enclosed by them. This was a tangible symbol of the introspective nature of the era, the need for protection during politically and economically unsettled times. In that uncertain world the garden offered peace and order when chaos ruled elsewhere, and life was nasty, brutal and short.

This enclosed form of the garden did not change until Europe began to experience political stability, and the whole of society became infused with the spirit of adventure that characterized the Renaissance during the fourteenth, fifteenth and sixteenth centuries. Now, as the cultural focus moved from inward to outward, the garden was built to surround the house, rather than be enclosed by it. It was during this time that European powers began to embark on voyages of exploration and discovery. On an increasingly larger scale, botanists on these expeditions collected plants from all over the world, and European gardens displayed correspondingly greater numbers of exotic species.

In the seventeenth century, during the reign of the Sun King, Louis XIV of France, formal gardening styles all over Europe expanded from classical gardening concepts, which had originated in Italy, to reflect the swelling ostentation and pomposity of the Grand French Manner. This trend eventually permeated all cultural characteristics and activities of the age. Formal gardens fashioned after the Versailles model remained the style of choice for the next 100 years.

With the approach of the eighteenth century, gardens symbolically began to burst their constrained, symmetrical bonds and open up to stretch from the house to the horizon. The revolutionary eighteenth-century Landscape Movement, which turned gardens into "natural" romantic parks, was the most glorious reflection of the cultural tastes of the age. The English landscape garden represented a whole philosophy intimately connected with literature and painting, in which the leaders were the intellectuals and the aesthetes.

With the industrial revolution a new middle class emerged and the prevalent philosophy was characterized by industry, education, self-improvement, moral self-righteousness and economic prudence. The Victorian garden, accordingly, became a centre of education and usefulness, characterized by rigidity of design, garish planting and the mass use of new exotics. This style softened during the elegant Edwardian period, when William Robinson and Gertrude Jekyll, with their cottage gardens and perennial borders, encouraged the spreading reaction against the formal rigidity of the Victorian garden.

As in Europe, garden development on other continents mirrored prevalent cultural characteristics. Early Egyptian records indicate that garden styles reflected the rigid social structure of this early culture. Scrolls depict the grand, extensive gardens of the temples, the villa gardens of the wealthy, and the small gardens of the middle class.

The gardens of Islam are superb illustrations of gardening style as a reflection of the cultural climate. Islamic garden design has been strongly influenced by the teachings of the Koran, and has developed following a model which fuses the strong influence of religious principles with the practicalities of everyday life. Through history, the Islamic garden has sought to represent the nomad's dream of cool shade, abundant fruit, scented beauty, and running water (the Muslim symbol of purification and life itself) inside protective walls—the earthly foretaste of the Koranic promise of paradise for those who follow the word of the prophet.

The traditional Japanese garden remains today as one of the most beautiful demonstrations of a place designed as a sanctuary, a response to the turbulence of the surrounding environment. Many Japanese gardens, particularly the sand and rock gardens of Zen temples, are places for meditation and discipline, and symbols of Zen thought. However, the Japanese garden goes beyond being merely a response to the social climate. For the Japanese, there is a strong cultural connection with the elements of

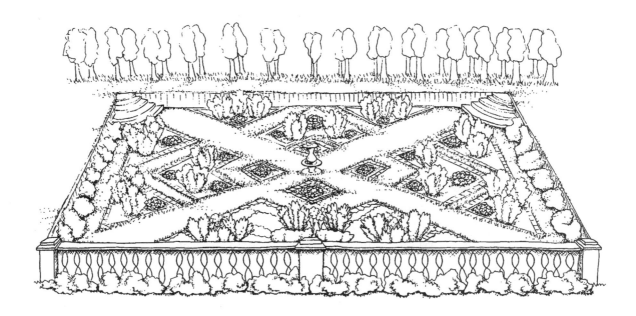

nature. Each plant, each rock—in fact, every feature of a Japanese garden—symbolically represents some aspect of Japanese philosophy, so that the garden itself becomes a cultural metaphor.

During the twentieth century, instant global communication has allowed us to see or experience cultures from around the world, and this is reflected in our gardens, which borrow from many cultural styles. Among other experiments and adaptations of garden styles we have witnessed the spread of small suburban residential gardens; the use of gardens as public space; the multiplied use of shrubs in the garden; and the adaptation into landscape design of the tenets of modernism as introduced by the Bauhaus school. The cataclysmic social change precipitated during the last century by the industrial revolution influenced many of these trends; the loss of a domestic labour force and the expansion of leisure pursuits have had an enormous influence on the state of gardening in the western world. The activities that occur in the suburban garden, for example (lawn games, lounging, barbecuing, and intense gardening activity), are indicative of the large amount of new leisure time that has been allotted to the middle class during the twentieth century.

As we enter the third millennium, ecological concern is developing as a leading social, political, and philosophical influence in our lives. We are beginning to recognize the fragility of the natural environment, and to realize that we must learn to live to a greater degree in harmony with nature. As with any other cultural attitude, this understanding, if we are committed to it, will be reflected in the way we think and feel; the way we work, play, and carry out our daily lives; the way we handle our economy; the way we create art, music and literature—and the way we garden.

Native plant gardening has come into its time.

The Geographic Imperative

The Pacific coastal region in which we are so fortunate to live and garden is one of this continent's most favoured in terms of indigenous floral bounty and ecological diversity. Our water system forms one of the most biologically rich marine elements in the world, and our forest ecosystems are world-famous for their abundance and beauty.

Our good fortune in being surrounded by all this natural beauty has long been recognized by gardeners from all over the world. Our botanical resource is the envy of many gardeners in England, for example, where so much of the existent flora is introduced. The abundance of true native plants in our lush forests, coastal plains, mountainsides and meadows demonstrates options that are rare in the gardening world—yet we often fail to recognize the potential that native plants offer. A large number of our taken-for-granted natives are cultivated and highly valued on other continents. In fact, our native plants have been replenishing European gardens for several centuries. Red-flowering currant (*Ribes sanguineum*), for example, is a popular ornamental in gardens throughout England and continental Europe, and our odoriferous skunk cabbage, or swamp lantern (*Lysichiton americanum*), is a much sought-after and prized rare exotic in England. As long ago as 1919, our native orange honeysuckle (*Lonicera ciliosa*) received an award of merit at a British garden show. We often hear stories of visiting English gardeners who are amazed at our attempts to imitate British gardens with perennial borders or the English cottage garden look. They cannot understand why, when we are so fortunately favoured with our own horticultural abundance, we choose to borrow the plants of another continent and the gardening style of an earlier era.

Effective and enduring garden design demonstrates a true sense of location, which explains why the designs of the legendary Gertrude Jekyll were so brilliantly successful. She designed each garden to relate to its house and natural setting, and her achievement was the composition of an organic, integrated whole. Jekyll conceived the definitively prototypical English garden, splendidly appropriate for a British country house at the end of the nineteenth century—but perhaps not the most suitable style for a twentieth-century west-coast setting. With her brilliant sense of time and place and her instinct for the appropriate, if Jekyll were to find herself gardening in the here and now with our wealth of native vegetation at her disposal, she might well devise a true habitat restoration, or native plant garden.

Native plant gardening seems perfectly suited to our place and time. It offers both a unique alternative and an addition to the more traditional styles of gardening; blending natives with exotics, for instance, can result in a beautiful mixed garden.

Commercial outlets are making indigenous plants increasingly available, expanding our opportunity to become familiar with them and to learn to garden creatively with them. Through gardening with native plants we may perhaps acquire a wider understanding and deeper appreciation of the natural beauty that surrounds us.

The Ecological Imperative

"What we seem to forget is that, yes, the sun will continue to rise and set and the moon will continue to move across the skies, but mankind can create a situation in which the sun and moon can look down upon an earth that has been stripped of all life."

—*Dr. Albert Schweitzer, in his Declaration of Conscience speech, 1957*

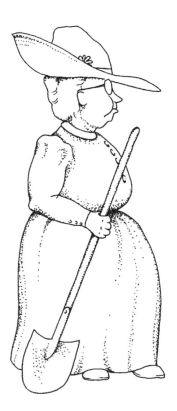

Four decades ago little heed was paid to such a voice as Dr. Schweitzer's, but today there is growing concern over the threat to all forms of life on this planet. Much of this concern is focused on the destruction of wildlife habitats: of the entire range of activities which daily jeopardize the diversity of our ecosystems, the most threatening among them is habitat destruction. Since 1991 the British Columbia Conservation Data Centre has documented over 600 rare, threatened, or endangered plants in British Columbia. Scientific forecasts predict catastrophic species loss in fish indigenous to western North America. There is also concern—although less pressing—for the preservation of our outstandingly rich, varied and diverse animal population. Our birds, as well, are in a perilous situation, particularly forest birds, whose habitats are constantly diminishing due to urban development and forestry practices.

Although the problem sometimes seems hopelessly vast, we can reduce it to smaller proportions by tackling it within our own backyards. Acting individually, we can help reverse environmental destruction in urban and suburban areas and contribute to the replenishment and restoration of wildlife habitat by gardening

with native plants. Our backyards are potential habitats for many wild creatures. Indigenous wildlife is irresistibly lured (for food and shelter) to garden plants, natives providing some of the most popular attractions. Even standing alone, many native plants, especially shrubs, are wonderful food providers for wildlife—look at the way robins and thrushes flock around salmonberry bushes (*Rubus spectabilis*). However, a single food-providing plant is not the main attraction of a native plant garden, nor is the provision, important as it is, of water and shelter. It is the diversity of interdependent species that can make our gardens genuine

homes to wildlife, by re-creating the habitats found in nature.

Not everyone is excited about the idea of having a garden full of insects, frogs, newts, bats, raccoons, rabbits and deer—often understandably so! However, the alternative, as developed areas continue to expand into wild terrain, may be the disappearance of some of these species. We may feel disinclined to give our entire gardens over to the animals, but perhaps we can accept the idea of sharing yard space with them. As Sara Stein points out in her ground-breaking book *Noah's Garden*, it is astonishing to consider what a small proportion of our residential gardens we really use. In Stein's model, the perimeters of yards are corridors used by animals in their travels between wild areas, leaving the rest of the garden for human pursuits. This wonderful and creative suggestion is explored further in the design section of chapter 3.

The full implication of native plant gardening is perhaps beginning to look rather formidable. It is true that anyone who gardens with native plants will be encouraging some wildlife, but it is up to you to decide to what degree you want to involve yourself. The decision to include a few native plants along with the exotics in your border, for example, is not a commitment to a full-time job as a wildlife custodian.

We see environmental destruction accelerating daily, and we blame most of it on development: forests being torn down, chemicals in the water and air, acres of concrete, and relentless suburban expansion. However, as gardeners we must also be aware of another destructive element: the presence of invasive exotic plants. The fragile ecosystems of our natural world have difficulty withstanding the effect of these invaders, and many of our native species cannot compete for ground space with them. Scotch broom

(*Cytisus scoparius*), for example, not only moves in and takes over the habitat of our native plants; once established, it can destroy the entire ecosystem it has invaded. The presence of broom chemically alters the soil on the site, making it unsuitable for some indigenous plants. So when we speak of restoring habitats, we include the effort to rid them of their exotic invaders.

By maintaining biodiverse ecosystems in our gardens we are providing a natural balance of biological predators and environmental enhancers; not only our flora, but also our fauna benefit greatly from this protective environment, and we gardeners benefit as well because of reduced maintenance requirements. Whether or not we are able to find a place in our hearts (and our gardens) for wild animals, we must face the fact that what we have in common with all other living creatures on this planet is that our existence depends on theirs.

This is the strongest argument for native plant gardening. Each of us who plants a biodiverse garden takes a small step toward protecting all species, including our own.

The Aesthetic Imperative

An argument that is sometimes levelled against native plant gardens is that they are unattractive: messy, weedy, dry, and—amazingly—colourless. In some regions of this continent, native plant gardens, based on the xeriscaping concept, are dry, and, at certain times of the year, of a subtle palette, but there is much beauty in the bold sculptural form of a cactus, or in golden clumps of waving autumn grasses.

Perhaps we must expand our criteria of beauty to include the raw, rugged, or monochromatic, in order to appreciate some wild landscapes. But in our coastal region with its multiplicity of bioregions, beauty can be seen in every aspect, in every season. Masses of dazzling pink blossoms of Pacific rhododendron (*Rhododendron macrophyllum*) surprising us in a shady forest understory; hosts of white *Trillium ovatum* lighting up a woodland glade; brilliant rose-pink bursts of shooting star (*Dodecatheon hendersonii*) or sea-blue clouds of camas (*Camassia quamash*) adrift in an open meadow; the slender red trunk of a red osier dogwood (*Cornus stolonifera*) brilliantly outlined against the greying winter sky; the startling discovery of a fresh green carpet of vanilla leaf (*Achlys triphylla*) spread across the forest floor, illuminated by the watery light filtered between massive trunks of the western red cedar (*Thuja plicata*); the breathtaking sight of a lone hairy manzanita (*Arctostaphylos columbiana*) growing out of the barren rock face of a cliff overhanging the blue waters of the Pacific: we are privileged indeed to have opportunities to replicate this splendour within our own personal realms.

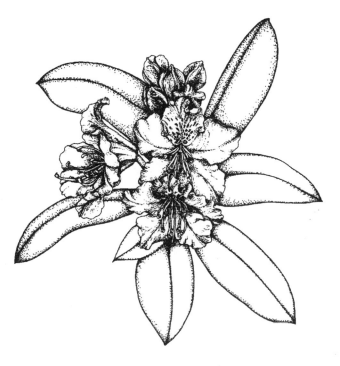

The Pragmatic Imperative

Whether your plant material is native, exotic, or mixed, a landscape using native plant gardening methods will become, once it has matured, a low-maintenance garden.

There are some distinct benefits to incorporating at least some natives into the garden scheme. For example, we have information as to native species' cultural requirements close at hand; simply by observing a plant in its nearby natural surroundings we can learn the conditions that suit it best. Also, native plants are not only water-conservative when planted appropriately, they eventually require little maintenance of any kind. Longevity is another factor to consider: many native plants, cultivated under appropriate conditions, have the potential for a surprisingly extensive life span.

The real advantage to this kind of gardening, however, is that it can be applied to all garden species, native or introduced. Learning to garden with native plants means gardening site-specifically, an approach that is ultimately water and time-efficient. This gardening method is discussed more thoroughly in the following pages. It is a time-honoured approach that happens to be particularly appropriate for a garden that includes indigenous species.

Native plant gardening—when applied to any plant material—simply makes sense.

3

❧ HOW? ❧

Understanding the Basics

It is reassuring to know that in order to embrace the concept of native plant gardening, there is no need to throw out all our previous gardening knowledge—along with wheelbarrow-loads of garden exotics that have taken years to establish. Native plant gardening is not essentially different from conventional gardening, but in the long term it does become simpler in that it provides an alternative to the labour-intensive approach of altering the garden site and amending the soil to suit the plant material. As you follow the principles of native plant gardening you will find that they are fundamental tenets of good garden practice and, as such, depend largely on that most important garden tool, common sense.

Growing Native Plants

The overriding principle of gardening with native plants is really a rule of thumb which should be observed under any gardening circumstance: choose plants whose needs are closely met by the conditions of your garden site.

The first step is to identify your site's environmental characteristics and habitat type by familiarizing yourself with its features. Some elements to observe are local climate; temperature; amount of light; rainfall; soil type and ability to retain moisture; topographic conditions including water; and other plants on the site. Further on in this chapter, the section "Working with the site" examines these factors and the information they give us.

The second step is to select plants on the basis of their suitability to the site characteristics and habitat types you have identified in your garden. This means that you will need to become aware of the characteristics of plants' wildlife homes. To help you recognize which plants belong in your particular environment, chapter 4 describes typical plant communities and their habitats.

Finally, grow your plants in groups of species requiring similar site and soil conditions, whether they are all native plants or a mixture of natives and exotics.

When you think about it, this kind of gardening really makes sense. It is simply a matter of finding the right plant for the right place. Successful gardeners have been gardening with consideration of their plants' needs for years. Perhaps it is our renewed appreciation of wild things, bringing about an awareness of the way plants exist in nature, that is rekindling our appreciation of this type of gardening.

Native plant gardeners are not the only horticulturists taking the new common-sense approach to planting: the concept of selecting appropriate plants for the site is acquiring world-wide appeal, under various guises. In England, which North Americans still seem to regard as the seat of all garden learning, this approach to gardening has been introduced as "natural garden design" by the eminent British garden writer and lecturer Stephen Lacey, who has borrowed it from a German method being introduced to North American gardeners in a book entitled *Perennials and Their Garden Habitats* by Richard Hansen and Friedrich Stahl. And the universally popular English landscape gardener John Brookes has veered so far from traditional landscaping concepts as to introduce his latest publication, *Planting the Country Way*, with this statement: "I have become increasingly more uncomfortable with what might be called 'the manicured garden.'" He then goes on to commend the principles of gardening described here.

As we see, not only does this site-specific style of gardening make sense, it is gaining universal popularity. In our region, however, we are able to carry this gardening methodology one step further. In a talk he gave to garden enthusiasts while visiting this area, Stephen Lacey revealed that the English and German gardeners who work with this gardening system must "scour the globe" for appropriate plants for their sites. Here at home, however, we need not look beyond our own horizons, as our stock of indigenous flora includes over 250 species suitable for garden cultivation. We are uniquely fortunate in having within our own region native plants suitable for every type of local garden site. One of the most important advantages of gardening with natives is that we are able to observe the plants in their nearby natural surroundings; when using introduced species we must rely on secondary sources for information about required conditions.

❧   ❧   ❧

Although the advantages of using native plants vastly outweigh the disadvantages, there are a few negative aspects to consider.

Most of the colourful display from native plants occurs in the spring because that is when the largest number of them—particularly the more commonly known species—bloom. Once you become familiar with native plants, however, you will discover many lesser-known wildflowers that bloom in other seasons. There are also displays of vibrantly colourful foliage to be seen at any time of year. In winter, shrubs such as the red osier dogwood (*Cornus stolonifera*) sport wonderfully colourful bark, and fall brings the brilliant colour of countless native berries. Many native plants offer the further attractions of fascinating architectural form and interesting textural qualities.

Another drawback for some gardeners is that many natives take longer than introduced species to establish themselves in the garden. This is because they are not bred for cultivation. But once a native plant is established, you may have it for life. Under appropriate conditions, native perennials live a long time, and healthy native annuals will go on self-seeding indefinitely.

A mature native plant garden is well worth waiting for because it is almost self-sustaining. Once established, native plants are exceptionally insect- and disease-resistant and require little or no upkeep other than very occasional watering. This ease of maintenance is seen by many to be the strongest attraction of gardening with natives.

A third drawback is that native plants are difficult to obtain. Until recently the only nurseries that carried native plants were specialist outlets, and only a few at that. Now, however, more and more mainstream nurseries and garden centres are stocking natives, and gardeners can do much to stimulate the increasing commercial popularity of native plants by demanding them of retailers. In this way we can all help each other have wider access to native stock. However, it is a good idea to inquire where the plants were propagated in order to ensure that you are receiving them from an ethical source (not removed from the wild).

Because of the difficulty in obtaining some native species you may want to start your own plants: see the propagation section of this chapter for some basic directions.

For your information

When buying a native plant at a nursery, be sure to acquire a plant that is true to the species by purchasing only non-patented plant material. (Cultivars, hybrids and varieties of plants may be patented; species may not.)

Ethics Guidelines

In case all this has been enough to propel you into the woods and meadows in a gleeful fit of horticultural fervour, a word of warning is necessary: removing a plant from the wild and disturbing its natural home is not condoned unless the plant is threatened (see #8 in the "Gardener's Guidelines" below). You should also be aware that some plants thrive only in the wild and will not survive under cultivation, so native seeds must be selected with great care. It is an objective in gardening with these plants to increase— not decrease—their populations.

When you do collect plant material, keep in mind that you are not the only person collecting in the wild; without consideration on the part of collectors it will not be long before a plant population becomes decimated—as has been the case with a number of indigenous species. It is crucial to leave enough seeds and fruit for a plant to self-propagate and feed wildlife. And never remove any plant material unless you know definitely that you are going to use it.

The best situation is to collect seeds from the plants in a friend's garden—if you are fortunate enough to have a friend with a native plant garden—or obtain them through a seed exchange. (See the Resource Guide at the back of this book for a list.)

In British Columbia three plants are protected by law: western flowering dogwood (*Cornus nuttallii*), Pacific rhododendron (*Rhododendron macrophyllum*) and western trillium (*Trillium ovatum*). You cannot remove any part of them from the site.

Any collecting is prohibited in all public parks. This applies to all plant material, as small as an acorn or as large as a tree.

In other situations, there are strict regulations we should always follow when working with the fragile and often endangered plant species of the wild. The following "Gardener's Guidelines," developed by the Canadian Wildflower Society and made available to the public through the pages of *Wildflower: North America's Magazine of Wild Flora*, is a code of ethics which should be observed by all who garden with native plants.

1) Do not disrupt native plant communities.
2) Acquire native plants from seed, garden or nursery.
3) Buy only wildflowers and ferns certified by the vendors as "Nursery Propagated".
4) Use plants and seeds which have originated in your immediate bioregion. Such plants and seeds are best adapted to the local climate, soil, predators, pollinators and disease.
5) Give preference to bioregionally native plant species in your garden, rather than naturalized or exotic species. The latter group may escape to wild habitats and interfere with the growth and spread of native flora and fauna.
6) Promote the cultivation and propagation of bioregionally native plants as an educational

and conservation measure to supplement the preservation of natural habitat.

7) Keep accurate records of any bioregionally rare flora which you are growing, to increase our understanding of the biology of the species.

8) Transplant wild native flora only when the plants of a given area are officially slated for destruction, eg: road construction, subdivisions, pipelines, golf courses, etc. Obtain permission before transplanting.

9) Collect no more than 10 percent of a seed crop from the wild. Leave the rest for natural dispersal and as food for dependent organisms.

10) Use natural means of fertilizing the soil, controlling predators and eliminating weeds, rather than synthetic chemical means.

11) Consider planting native species attractive to native fauna, especially birds, butterflies and moths uncommon to your bioregion.

12) Exercise extreme caution when studying and photographing wildflowers in order not to damage the surrounding flora and fauna.

13) Cooperate with institutions like: arboreta, botanical gardens, museums and universities in the propagation and study of rare species.

14) Openly share your botanical knowledge with the public but ensure that native plant species or communities will not be damaged or endangered in the process.

🌿   🌿   🌿

To obtain lists of endangered wildlife species for this region, contact:

○ British Columbia Conservation Data Centre
Wildlife Branch, Ministry of Environment, Lands and Parks
780 Blanshard Street

Victoria, BC, V8V 1X4
Telephone: (604) 356-0928

○ Natural Heritage Program
Washington Natural Heritage Department, Department of Natural Resources
P.O. Box 47016
Olympia, WA, 98504-7016
Telephone: (360) 902-1340

○ Department of Agriculture
Mount Hood National Forest
2955 NW Division Street
Gresham, OR, 97030
Telephone: (503) 666-0771

Native Plant Propagation

Although they are becoming easier to obtain commercially than ever before, acquiring native plants is not always as simple as dropping in to your neighbourhood garden centre, so you may want to learn an alternative way to obtain them. To many gardeners the idea of propagating plants is somewhat daunting, but gardening with natives may provide the motivation to learn a few basic propagation techniques. There are definite economic advantages to being able to propagate your own plants, and, because the basic methodology for propagating all plants is the same, acquiring these skills will certainly enhance your general gardening proficiency.

A great number of our indigenous plants have become rare, many to the point of extinction. Removing plants from the wild is not an ethical practice, nor is it practical, as wild plants have a limited chance of surviving transplantation. Collecting seed from wild plants is an ideal way to increase plant stock, as long as we follow the 10 percent guideline. For cuttings and root divisions, garden or nursery stock are the appropriate sources.

Growing from seed

Growing from seed is the least expensive and easiest way to propagate native plants, although it is admittedly a slow process (some species will not be ready for transplanting to the garden until several years after seeding). Many of the finest native species can be obtained only in seed form. Some grasses and annual wildflowers are commonly grown from seed. It is a very satisfying experience to collect, plant and nurture seeds and observe them as they develop, over time, into mature and healthy plants.

Seed collection

Some native plant seeds are available commercially or through plant societies and organizations; see the Regional Source Guide at the end of this book for a list of seed exchanges. Seeds of some plants are only available by collecting from the wild. Gather them as soon as they are ripe; this means when pulpy fruit have turned their full colour (no green remains) and when capsule fruits are brown, dry and papery but not completely split open. Collection time varies depending on the species; it is just before the plant would naturally disperse the seed.

Remove the seeds from pulpy fruit such as Saskatoons (*Amelanchier alnifolia*) and huckleberries (*Vaccinium* spp.) by mashing the fruit by hand or in a blender, and floating off the seeds. Spread them to dry on paper either outside in the sun or in a cool, dry place that is not subject to temperature and moisture fluctuations.

For dry capsules, shake the seeds from the capsules into a paper bag or envelope and remove stems and capsule bits. You may want to gently crush smaller capsules to separate the seeds from other matter.

Store the seeds in film canisters or envelopes labelled with seed collection date and the plant name. Keep seeds in a cool, dry place with low humidity.

Seed sowing

Sometimes, particularly when we are not sure of a plant's requirements for germination, the easiest way to treat the seed is to plant it directly into the garden and trust that its dormancy will eventually be managed by natural processes. This is often the case for large, tough seeds with simple dormancy mechanisms. Otherwise, seeds can usually be sown in flats or small pots, and placed in a cold frame over the winter. Make sure all pots are sterilized and rinsed clean.

A good soil mix for seed-starting is: 2 parts loam (or potting soil), 1 part peat moss (dampen first), and 1 part sand (or perlite). Place soil mix into pots and pack down firmly. Lightly cover the seeds with fine sand (use pea gravel for larger seeds). This will help with drainage and prevent damping off. Label the pots with the date and plant name. Use only one species per container. Use pencil or a waterproof and sunproof felt marker on labels.

Gently water the pots and keep them moist, but not soggy.

Seed stratification

Some seeds need a period of cold dormancy, or stratification, to help them germinate. These are often seeds of plants that have learned to survive in cold climates. Examples of species in our region that germinate faster with cold stratification are tiger lily (*Lilium columbianum*), bunchberry (*Cornus unalaschkensis*), *Erythronium* spp. and *Brodiaea* spp.

To stratify seeds, place cleaned, dry seeds in moist peat moss or sand, in plastic bags or containers, and store them in a refrigerator (not a freezer) for one to three months. You can also layer the seeds between moistened paper towels, and place in plastic bags. Keep the containers moist but watch for mould and drying-out while in the fridge. Start the stratification in the fall and remove the seeds by February, when you can sow them directly into flats or pots, as described above, and place them outdoors in a cold frame.

After germination

In the spring, transplant seedlings that have their first true leaves into individual 2- to 3-inch (5- to 8-cm) pots using the soil mixture described above or sterilized potting soil. Plant one seedling per pot. Prick out each seedling with a small stick and hold it by the leaves, not the stem, as it can be easily damaged. Make a small hole in the potting mixture and bury the stem a little deeper than it was before. Tamp the soil around the stem. Water from below or mist carefully with a gentle spray. Protect the seedlings from sun and wind within a shelter such as a cold frame with lathing. Keep them watered but do not allow them to get soggy. The pots can be plunged into sand, chips or mulch to keep them upright and moist. You may also want to fertilize with a weak solution.

In the fall, seedlings that have developed good root systems may be potted up into 4- to 6-inch (10- to 15-cm) pots and held over outdoors; or to give them a little more protection, overwinter them in a cold frame or cool greenhouse.

A cover of hay or burlap sacks covered with leaves for insulation can also be used for protection. By the following spring or fall the seedlings may be large enough to transplant into the garden. (The seedlings of herbaceous perennials will die back over the fall and winter, so be sure to label them with indelible markers.)

Plant out the strongest seedlings by late in the following spring, making sure the garden site has been prepared with the correct soil mixture. Keep the seedlings watered, paying particular attention to their moisture requirements during the critical period of the first few weeks. You may want to mark their place in the garden to locate them the following year.

It is advisable to keep records of the sowing, transplanting and planting dates, along with the numbers of seedlings and flowering dates of each species. This will be a helpful guide for future sowing.

Taking cuttings

Cuttings are taken from trees and shrubs. Most cuttings you take will be softwood cuttings: the cuttings are taken from deciduous or evergreen trees or shrubs when the wood is green and bendable, in either late spring (when leaves expand) or late summer. Hardwood cuttings are collected from some deciduous trees and shrubs and from some evergreens, including conifers, in fall or winter when the plants are dormant. Hardwood differ from softwood cuttings in several ways: hardwood cuttings are woody rather than green and pliant, usually have no leaves attached, and have buds already formed for next spring's growth. Put more simply, softwood cuttings are taken from the current season's growth, hardwood cuttings from the previous year's.

Softwood cuttings

To take a softwood cutting, cut small branches approximately 12 to 18 inches (30 to 45 cm) long, which you can later cut to 3- to 8-inch (8- to 20-cm) sections. Place the cuttings in plastic bags and keep them moist. Remember to label the twigs as you collect them, and keep species separate. Next, with a pair of sharpened clean secateurs, make a cut just below a leaf node. For most shrubs, about 6 to 8 inches (15 to 20 cm) is a good stem length. Remove two or three lower leaf nodes so that they will not end up under or near the soil surface. You may wish to cut several sections at a time, so it's a good idea to have a container of water into which you can place the cuttings. If you are taking multiple cuttings from one stem, cut the bottom end at a slant and the top end square so you can tell which end is which.

Immediately before planting the cuttings, remove any terminal buds as well as any flower buds which have developed. This will encourage root development. Have prepared a moistened mix of equal parts of peat and perlite (or sand), and fill 2- to 6-inch (5- to 15-cm) pots. Fill the pot to within approximately 3/4 inch (2 cm) of the rim. Tamp the mix down firmly.

You may want to use rooting hormone, which comes in three strengths: softwood, semi-hardwood and hardwood cuttings. Dip the cutting into the hormone powder before inserting into the mix. Make holes for the cuttings and bury them to a depth of about one-third their length. Place the cuttings around the edge of the pot. Pack the mix around the cuttings to keep them upright. Label the pot with the plant name and cutting date.

Here on the west coast we can keep cuttings in a cool greenhouse or even outside, in an area that is not too exposed to the elements. If you are worried about harsh weather and choose to keep your plants indoors, cover the pots in a clear plastic bag for the first two weeks to keep the humidity high. However, watch for mould and too much condensation. Open the bag for a day if this occurs. Keep the pots out of direct sun or wind, and remember to keep them moist.

The cuttings may lose their leaves, but this does not necessarily mean that they have not rooted. At approximately six weeks, tug gently on a twig; if you feel any resistance it probably has rooted. Or scrape the twig to see if the underlying layer is green, which indicates the twig is still alive. When the twig produces new leaves it has definitely rooted.

The following spring, the cuttings can be transplanted into individual 4-inch (10-cm) pots (or 3-inch/8-cm pots for smaller cuttings). Use a soil mix of three parts compost to one part each of peat and sand. Keep the pots out of direct sun and wind. To harden off the cuttings over the summer, gradually expose the transplanted cuttings to more sun each day.

In the fall, those seedlings that have good root development can be transplanted out or moved to 6-inch (15-cm) pots for planting into the garden the following spring. Plant deciduous cuttings before the buds swell.

Hardwood cuttings

The treatment of hardwood cuttings is somewhat different from that of softwood. In the fall or winter, select sprigs of the previous season's growth and cut to a length of 6 to 8 inches (15 to 20 cm). Dip the bottom end into rooting hormone, bundle the cuttings with string, and place them in a moist medium of sand or wood shavings, then pack them in boxes that are set a little way into the ground in a cool place outdoors. Store them here throughout the winter, keeping them moist and safe from freezing. In colder climates, where freezing is more of a threat, store them indoors in an unheated garage or basement.

In early spring, open the bundles and set each cutting upright into a pot of a good rooting mix (the compost mix described above, or a perlite and peat mix), or into its permanent spot in the garden. The cuttings will form roots first, then shoots. Be patient: some hardwood cuttings take up to two years to be ready for transplanting into the garden.

Root divisions

Some plants that form spreading clumps, or plants that have rhizomes, such as Oregon grape (*Mahonia* spp.), can be propagated from pieces of their spreading, horizontal roots. In the spring, before the plants begin active growth, look for pencil-thick roots. Being careful to disturb the plant as minimally as possible, cut pieces 2 to 6 inches (5 to 15 cm) long, noting which end of the piece was nearest the centre of the plant. Bundle the cuttings and store for several weeks in a cool, moist medium, as you would for hardwood cuttings. Plant the cutting by setting it vertically.

Divisions can also be taken from plants like trailing raspberry (*Rubus pedatus*) and red osier dogwood (*Cornus stolonifera*), which have creeping runners, or stolons. Simply remove small rooted sections of the runners and replant them.

Layering

This is a very simple propagation method. Using a bendable stem growing from the bottom of the parent plant, weigh it down with a rock and cover it with soil or compost. It may take one or two years to become rooted. Once rooted, cut the new plant from the parent and pot up, or place in the ground.

Red-flowering currant (*Ribes sanguineum*) and red osier dogwood (*Cornus stolonifera*) are examples of natives that propagate well from layering.

Other methods

Once you have mastered some of these basic propagation techniques, you may want to try some variations on them, or some more advanced methods for starting your own plants. Two basic garden books that may stimulate your appetite for more propagation experience are the Sunset New Western Garden Book, *and* The Pacific Gardener, *by A.R. Willis. Another source of quite technical, well-illustrated information is the* UBC Guide to Gardening in British Columbia. *Useful not only for propagation but for all aspects of gardening is Hugh Johnson's comprehensive book,* The Principles of Gardening.

Propagation techniques for specific plants can be found in the plant listings in chapter 4.

Fern propagation

Ferns can be propagated from their spores, a process that requires its own technique. In his classic work, *Gardening with Native Plants of the Pacific Northwest*, Arthur Kruckeberg tells us that the procedure is lengthy but rewarding. He recommends using glass-covered dishes placed under artificial light for eighteen hours per day. The spores are sown on the surface of moist sterilized soil. The first sign of life is *gametophytes*, tiny heart-shaped flecks of sex-cell-bearing green tissue. These must reproduce sexually in the dish to become young fern plants, or *sporophytes*. Two or three months later the young plants are ready for pricking out. In another six months to a year, they can be planted in pots or directly into the garden site.

As Professor Kruckeberg points out, an easier and quicker propagation method is division of clumps or rhizomes. If this is done carefully, it is not necessary to remove the parent plant from its growing place.

A few ferns

Here is a quick list of some of the more common and garden-appropriate indigenous ferns. Consider them for garden use as individual ornamentals and also as splendid ground covers.

Dry conditions

○ Parsley fern, or rock brake (*Cryptogramma crispa*)—Evergreen. Low-growing, densely tufted, grows on rocky sites.

(More ferns for dry places are listed in the rock garden section of this chapter.)

Moist soil

(The following ferns, all shade-tolerant, are available at specialist nurseries.)

○ Maidenhair (*Adiantum pedatum*)—Deciduous. Delicate and lacy; shiny black stems. Prefers damp shade.

○ Lady fern (*Athyrium filix-femina*)—Deciduous. Dense clumps. Large, graceful fern with lacy, bright green fronds.

○ Deer fern (*Blechnum spicant*)—Evergreen, dark green fronds. Drought-tolerant when planted in shade.

○ Spiny wood fern (*Dryopteris expansa*, also known as *D. austriaca*)—Semi-evergreen.

Vigorous. Triangular-shaped fronds.

○ Oak fern (*Gymnocarpium dryopteris*)—Deciduous. Dainty and lacy. Grows in small patches. Prefers shade.

○ Licorice fern (*Polypodium glycyrrhiza*)—Sometimes summer deciduous (dormant in summer, green in winter). Grows on wet, mossy ground and on trees, often on bigleaf maple (*Acer macrophyllum*), stumps, rocks and rock walls. Rhizomes have a sweet licorice taste.

○ Sword fern (*Polystichum munitum*)—Evergreen. Dense clumps. Glossy, dark green, leathery fronds. Can handle full sun. Magnificently ornamental.

○ Giant chain fern (*Woodwardia fimbriata*)—Evergreen, but not hardy throughout its range. Large, handsome, grows in a clump. Erect, arching, dark green fronds.

○ Bracken (*Pteridium aquilinum*)—Deciduous. This fern will thrive in almost any soil and contains chemicals that make it insect-resistant, but be careful; it can be invasive! (Care is also recommended when handling this fern; it is not safe for consumption.)

Weeds or wildflowers?

Why does the definition of the word *weed* present such a problem to the world of horticulture? Almost every gardening book has its own definition; whole chapters are often devoted to grappling with this apparently elusive subject. Whoever came up with the description of a weed as a plant that is growing in the wrong place had the right idea: weeds are unwanted plants, and I would be happy to leave it at that. However, there seems to be a confusion of weeds and wildflowers that needs untangling.

Weed is not synonymous with *native plant*. A large number of the weed species we know in North America arrived here with the earliest settlers. Some of the weeds these Europeans brought with them are dandelions, quack grass, Queen Anne's lace, sow thistle, groundsel, dock and chickweed, to name a few: many weeds are introduced species. Weeds are also the first plants to move in and take over land disturbed by humans: they are invasive. Weeds compete with more desirable plants for cultivated space: they are intruders. Weeds sometimes take on the physical characteristics of the plants they are pushing out, thus making themselves difficult to detect and eradicate (greater plantain, for example, is difficult to detect in a hosta bed): weeds are imposters.

Weeds are imported, invasive, intruding imposters. However, looking at them from another point of view we can identify some good points. For instance, weeds move in to initiate the first step in healing disturbed or unused land.

Some weeds also provide valuable food for animal life. For example, the seeds of lamb's-quarters are favourites of songbirds such as the house finch, which also likes chickweed, knotweed and smartweed. Thistles are favoured by butterflies and goldfinches, and the seeds of the common, or bull, thistle are very attractive to a number of birds, as are the seeds of the field chickweed (*Cerastium arvense*), a native plant. Goldfinches, along with pine siskins, are also attracted to dandelions. Milkweed is a real butterfly favourite; in fact it provides the only known sustenance for the monarch butterfly in its caterpillar form. And many beneficial garden insects are drawn to the garden by Queen Anne's lace.

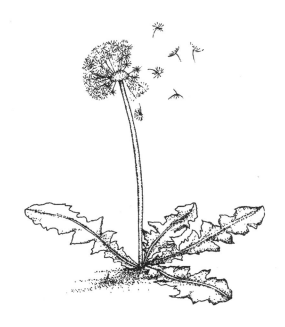

Weeds can also provide information about the soil they inhabit: nettles indicate rich, moist soil; dandelions indicate compacted soil; horsetail indicates acidic soil; and the Canada thistle indicates clay soil.

You can decide for yourself how you feel about weeds, but to most of us they represent an unwanted nuisance and hours and hours of hard work. The one thing you can be sure of is that most of them are not valued and desirable native plants.

Weeds do take a great deal of water from the soil and compete with landscape plants. When establishing your garden you will want as clean a soil bed as possible; if there is ever a time to remove weeds this is it. Unfortunately, there is no way to eradicate dormant weeds and seeds without working the area fallow (allowing the weeds to start growing and then removing them). The most effective method of removing weeds is good old-fashioned hard work. You can hoe an uncultivated area, but hand-pulling weeds is definitely safest for your established plants. (It goes without saying that the precepts of native plant gardening do not include the use of chemicals.)

Once the plants become established, there will be fewer weeds; then you can pull them out as soon as they make an appearance; try to catch them before they come to seed. Spreading a mulch around your plants in appropriate areas is helpful in controlling weeds.

Enhancing the soil

In the wild, leaves and dead plants fall to the ground, rotting where they fall, and eventually creating humus. Soil in developed areas has often been laid bare and depleted of nutrients. These can be replenished by the addition of organic matter which breaks down and forms nutrient-rich humus.

Mulch

When an established native plant garden requires maintenance, it is usually minimal; mulching is probably the most important—and often the only—maintenance required. In any garden, mulching is arguably the most beneficial care you can give your soil and your plants.

There are many advantages to using a mulch. It retards weeds, conserves moisture by minimizing evaporation, and releases nutrients to the soil. Mulch keeps soil cool in summer and warm in winter. It increases soil depth and protects soil from erosion. It improves bacterial

action, encourages earthworms, and increases aeration. A good mulch cover protects ground-cover plants and keeps fruit and vegetables clean by protecting them from splashing rain.

Strictly speaking, a mulch is a layer of material placed on the soil surface. Organic humus is the preference of native plant garden-ers. Good mulch materials are compost, decay-ing leaves, well-rotted manures, sea kelp, mush-room compost, seedless hay or straw, shredded prunings, natural wood chips, grass clippings and evergreen needles and cones. Commercially available screened bark—usually referred to as bark mulch—has little to offer other than its abil-ity to conserve water; it has no nutritional value and in fact depletes the nitrogen in the soil.

When spreading mulch, don't pile it too close to the stems or trunks of plants. If you are using compost as a mulch, spread it about 2 to 3 inches (5 to 8 cm) deep. Other materials may be applied to a depth of 3 to 7 inches (8 to 18 cm).

Mulch is an insulator that helps the soil maintain its condition at the time of application. It is therefore important for the soil to be warm and moist, never cold and dry, when applying mulch. The standard time is mid to late spring.

If you do any weeding, disturb the mulch as little as possible. It is better to pull weeds than hoe them. In well-established, mulched plant beds almost no weeding should be necessary, other than the occasional removal of weeds that grow from air-borne seeds or seeds from lower layers of the mulch. Disturbing the mulch can actually cultivate the bed for weed seeds.

A word of caution: mulching, like any other garden practice, should be approached with moderation and a good deal of common sense. Be careful not to smother your plants; this has been known to happen after a few years of mulch layers have been applied. A good number of native plants do not require mulching. Many spring-flowering bulbs, for example, are accustomed to the exposed, summer-dry conditions of an open meadow and dry, shallow soil. They do not require soil enrichment or moisture retention, and therefore are inappropriate candidates for mulching. Once again, it is a matter of knowing your plants' requirements.

Leaf mould

Leaves, particularly oak leaves, are rich in nitrogen and carbon, and partially decayed leaves make a humus-rich, fertile mulch. The popular assumption that oak and arbutus leaves don't rot is quite illogical, but they will break down faster—as will any leaves—if you crush them first.

To make a simple leaf mulch, gather your leaves in the fall and bundle them into plastic garbage bags which have a few holes poked into them. Add a shovelful of soil, then put the bag in an out-of-the-way spot. By spring the leaves will have rotted to about half their volume, and you will have acquired some wonderful leaf mould. (To accelerate the process, add a handful of a high-nitrogen organic lawn fertilizer.)

Compost

Compost can be thought of as a mulch *extraordinaire*. If you have not kept a compost pile, now is definitely the time to start. Many municipalities have programs to teach and encourage the use of compost bins for recycling the nutrients within vegetative waste. Visiting one of these centres could be your first step in using compost in your garden. After learning about its many benefits, you will probably become convinced that no garden is complete without a compost pile.

Through composting, the natural process of decomposing organic material is accelerated by the soil-processing activity of bacteria, fungi, mites, beetles and earthworms. Household and garden waste is transformed to a rich, crumbly, fertile humus which can be returned to the soil. The composted material enhances soil by providing a balanced source of nutrients. It also improves the soil's texture and water-retaining properties.

A fascinating aspect of compost is that during the course of the composting process, many organisms live out their complete life cycles. The minerals recycled from vegetative matter are augmented by the nutrients from the bodies of these little creatures.

Compost can be made in any type of compost bin, or even in a pile without any container. Fencing wire rolled into a circular cage, concrete blocks, even hay bales, will work as enclosures. The bin should be big enough to accommodate large amounts of material. Most gardeners who have been using compost for awhile find that they need at least two bin sections to have compost piles operating at different stages of the process. Some municipalities have bylaws prohibiting the use of certain types of compost containers so it is wise to be aware of your own municipality's composting guidelines.

One of the most efficient styles of compost bin is a three-bin model constructed of wood pallets. An earthworm compost for kitchen waste is convenient when a small container is desired. Composting centres or nurseries can give you information about these and other types of composting systems. Your municipal offices should be able to tell you about local compost programs. Some municipalities sell compost bins to residents at cut-rate prices.

Compost materials

An efficient compost pile contains a balanced combination of ingredients. Many gardeners use a wider range than suggested here, and I have heard one garden expert say that anything is fair game for the compost pile, but I tend to be somewhat cautious. Here are my suggestions for safe, appropriate compost materials.

○ Kitchen vegetative wastes, including fruit and vegetable parings, eggshells (rinsed out and crumbled up), coffee grounds, and left-over vegetable cooking water (but not used dish-water, which has too much grease and soap chemicals).

○ Grass clippings. (Note that foodstuffs and grass clippings decompose more rapidly than most other compost materials.)

○ Leaves (because they are sometimes tough and fibrous, you may wish to hasten the rotting process by shredding before adding them to the pile).

○ Garden prunings (no more than 1/4 inch/ 1 cm thick or 2 inches/5 cm long).

○ Livestock manure.

○ Weeds (experts say the heat of the composting process is enough to break down weed seeds, but it seems risky; I let my weeds rot for awhile in the sun in a black plastic bag so that by the time they are ready to add to the compost they are already in an advanced state of decomposition).

○ Shredded, uncoloured paper products, such as brown bags.

○ Thin layers of clean wood ashes, but not barbecue ashes or coal.

○ Sawdust and thin wood chips (you may wish to exclude these as they can take years to fully decompose).

Exclude the following materials from your compost pile.

○ Diseased material, such as rose leaves with rust or black spot. However, the fear that mildewed leaves will somehow harm your compost pile is unfounded; the damaged leaves will rot away and decompose in the compost heap just as they do in nature.

○ Material that could possibly contain disease organisms, such as kitty litter.

○ Anything synthetic that will not break down.

○ Dairy and grain products and meat wastes, which will rot, smell, and attract animals and rodents.

Building the pile

You may have the impression that there is a rigid scientific methodology to making compost. Although it is true that there is a technical explanation of how and why the process works, you will discover when you try it yourself that making compost is quite a straightforward procedure: simply arrange different organic materials in layers to encourage quick decomposition.

There are many layering theories, and every gardener seems to have a preferred method. Popular opinion suggests that as long as you have the right base, the order of the layers can be arbitrary. You will probably develop your own system, but here is a very simple layering method.

○ Start with a well-worked floor of soil so that soil organisms can work their way up into the pile.

○ As a base coat, put down about 5 to 6 inches (12 to 15 cm) of some of the coarser materials, such as garden prunings. Another option is dry leaves. The spaces between pieces of matter help the circulation of air. An excellent material for this aerating function is the long fibre of the stinging nettle (*Urtica dioica*). To handle this stinging plant, cut it down, then wait fifteen minutes; it will wilt and the potency of the stinging acid will diminish.

◯ Now introduce the green material: fresh grass clippings and garden debris, then kitchen vegetable waste.

◯ Next add a thin layer of rich earth or completed compost. Manure could also be added here.

◯ Add a sprinkling of water and continue the layering until the pile is about 4 feet (120 cm) high.

Tips

◯ Occasional sprinklings of water help to keep the compost moist, although it should not be soggy. To ensure moisture retention while keeping out excess moisture, cover the pile loosely with canvas, a tarp, or black plastic.

◯ Air circulation is required, so it is important to have openings on the sides.

◯ If you are fortunate enough to come into possession of a chipper or shredder, it can be very helpful in breaking up some pieces that are too large for the decaying action of the compost.

◯ A degree of partially rotted material remaining in the finished compost is good for your soil, but if you want to make your compost a little finer for some parts of the garden, you can sieve it through a 1- to 2-inch (3- to 5- cm) screen.

◯ A good hot compost will be balanced with nitrogen (green materials, such as grass) and carbon (brown materials, like leaves). Too much grass in your compost will give you a slimy, oozy mess.

◯ Many gardeners use additives of fish meal or blood meal for enrichment, or sprinklings of dolomite lime to deter wildlife.

Within a day the pile will start to heat up. Within several days it will reach a temperature at which it begins its transformation to compost. After a few weeks the pile will have cooled down considerably and should be turned over with a spading fork or a pitchfork and allowed to heat up again. Turn the pile every two or three weeks. The process will be complete in about two to four months. The compost is ready when it is dark and crumbly. It will have a fresh earthy fragrance and bear no resemblance to the original materials.

Now you can apply this beneficial elixir to your soil. It is a wonderful mulch for any time of year, and can be worked into the soil at planting time. The benefits of compost are numerous. It contains elements that stimulate plant growth, retain moisture in the soil, and prevent weeds from germinating. As well, compost has a neutralizing effect on soil toxins: it stabilizes iron and aluminum, and it keeps soil acidity levels balanced. Another benefit is increased disease-resistance resulting from the activity of the multitude of microorganisms contained in composted material.

Composted soil remains friable and well-aerated, as earthworms and other compost organisms cycle the vegetative material deep into the soil. Using compost as a mulch moderates changes in soil temperature, which has the added benefit of insulating the living creatures who are so busily processing the soil, enabling them to continue their beneficial activity throughout most of the year.

Water-wise gardening

You don't have to be a purist native plant gardener to design your garden to become water-efficient or drought-tolerant. Water shortage is a legitimate concern for all gardeners. Even within the region covered in this book, with an average

A few plants for dry places

The following drought-tolerant trees and shrubs are all described in detail in chapter 4. For more plants that can withstand dry conditions, look at the suggestions for dry scree in the rock garden section of this chapter, or for wildflowers preferring dry summers, see the grasslands plant list in chapter 4.

Trees
○ Arbutus (*Arbutus menziesii*)
○ Garry oak (*Quercus garryana*)

Shrubs
○ Hairy manzanita
   (*Arctostaphylos columbiana*)
○ Kinnikinnick (*Arctostaphylos uva-ursi*)
○ Oceanspray (*Holodiscus discolor*)
○ Oregon grape (*Mahonia* spp.)
○ Mock orange (*Philadelphus lewisii*)
○ Red-flowering currant
   (*Ribes sanguineum*)
○ Evergreen huckleberry
   (*Vaccinium ovatum*)

annual rainfall of 40 to 200 inches (100 to 500 cm), in many areas dry summers are a typical occurrence.

By observing some or all of these water-saving tips, any gardener will reap many auxil-iary benefits: fewer weeds, improved soil, happier plants and an easier summer. This quick list summarizes many of the ideas suggested throughout this book.

The right plant for the right place
○ Use appropriate plants. The basic principle of native plant gardening is equally fundamental to water-saving gardening: choose plants whose needs are closely met by the conditions of the garden site. These plants not only have a very good chance of thriving even during unexpected periods of drought, they also require little maintenance to keep them looking robust.

Water-wise plants to try are natives, which are adapted to local climatic conditions; species from low-rainfall areas that prefer dry summers but can tolerate our wet winters; plants that require little water; plants that normally prefer a generous amount of summer water but can tolerate a diminished supply of water when absolutely necessary, after they are well-established (for example rhododendrons and azaleas, except those planted in the shade of especially thirsty trees); plants that go dormant during summer (as you might expect, this includes many of our spring-flowering bulbs); and shade-loving plants for northern exposure, sun lovers for south-facing.
○ Group plants together according to their moisture requirements.
○ Plant thickly. Cover the ground completely with plants. Establish them early, before the dry weather, and prepare soil by incorporating compost or other humus before planting.

Lawn considerations
○ Observe appropriate lawn maintenance. Take care of the lawn you have with a good lawn maintenance program. For example, if you dethatch and aerate your lawn, water can seep

into root zones more easily, promoting healthy, deep roots. The way you mow your lawn will also affect its water requirement. Try letting it grow a little longer and mowing it about half as often as you normally would, and you will be surprised at the results. Your grass will start coming in more thickly, its weed population will begin to diminish, you should no longer need to fertilize, and it will require less water. However, to establish a truly water-wise garden, keep lawn size to a minimum.

O Use vegetative ground covers in place of lawn.

O Consider alternative ground covers, such as stones, rocks and pebbles to create an attractive foil for plants.

O Grow a vegetable garden; organic vegetables are a more rewarding crop than grass clippings!

O Plant a tree—or a grove of trees. Keep in mind that there are many attractive and appropriate native species to choose from.

O Use some of the lawn space for a pond. Nothing adds ambiance like the sound of water trickling over rocks. Water-loving plants will thrive on pond edges and birds will flock to your garden.

Soil improvement
O Establish soil that is rich in humus.
O Use mulches.
O Control weeds. Weeds take a great deal of water from the soil and compete with landscape plants.

Effective irrigation
O Water carefully.
O Check soil moisture levels early by digging to the full depth of your shovel blade, in order to start watering at the appropriate time.
O Water when the sun is low, preferably early in the morning.

O Use micro-heads and soaker hoses rather than overhead sprinklers.

O Save household water (used for cleaning vegetables, etc.) for garden use.

O Use rainwater collected in a barrel.

O Incorporate water savings into planning and design. By installing a good water-management program or repairing an old, inefficient system, you can often realize an immediate reduction in water consumption.

Design Considerations

As with all garden ornamentals, landscaping with native plants involves an element of design. Plants are chosen not only for their functional appropriateness but also for such features as form, colour, texture, shape, scale, volume and unity. In all garden design, perhaps the most significant factors in determining the character of the landscape are the gardener's aesthetic judgment and personal style.

Working with the plants

Understanding the logic of natural processes always makes it easier to apply good common sense when we are working with those elements. Before you begin to design a garden incorporating native plants, become aware of the way plants grow together in natural settings. The various species in a plant community interact with each other in balanced relationships that have evolved over thousands of years. By observing which plants thrive together in these partnerships we obtain valuable clues for achieving a similar balance in designing our gardens. Nature has done the planning for us.

Plant succession
Plant communities change over time. Some of the changes are permanent; others temporary.

The more permanent change in plant communities is called *plant succession*. Plant communities within an area are gradually replaced until a community develops that is stable and self-maintaining and in dynamic equilibrium with the surrounding environment.

A habitat will usually go through a predictable series of community stages (called *seral stages*), until the *climax stage,* or self-maintaining community, is reached. The climax community can maintain a stable habitat for a long period—sometimes thousands of years. This type of succession, which occurs very slowly, is called *primary succession.*

The process that takes place after an environment is disturbed (as when a forest is clear-cut or fire kills the vegetation) is called *secondary succession.* Shorter than primary succession, it occurs as the community evolves from open field to forest, and can take place during a fifty- to three-hundred-year period. Sometimes disturbances recur regularly before the climax community is reestablished, preventing the climax stage from developing. In our region, some stands of Douglas-fir (*Pseudotsuga menziesii*) are examples of secondary succession. In drier habitats of the coastal forest, a history of fires has increased the occurrence of the highly fire-resistant Douglas-fir, at the expense of such species as western red cedar (*Thuja plicata*) and hemlock (*Tsuga heterophylla*). In these habitats, under fire management, some of the Douglas-fir stands will eventually undergo succession to the climax growth of cedar and hemlock.

Understanding the principles of plant succession can help you design your native plant garden. For example, if you cut down ancient trees around your house to develop a flowering meadow where a forest originally stood, you are establishing an early successional stage within the forested environment. Your meadow will have increasing difficulty withstanding the continual—and natural—encroachment of the surrounding woods. If, on the other hand, you establish a plant environment that is the climax community for your biosite (which in this case would be a woodland garden), it will be stable and easy to maintain.

Plant interactions and plant community composition

We can learn much about plants just by looking at them. Take a stroll through a wilderness conservation area—a forest, meadow, bogside or riverbank—and observe how the the plants grow in relationship to each other. Move in among the plants: touch them; observe leaf shapes and configurations; get down on the ground and see how the plants grow out of the soil; look at the composition of the soil itself; and take note of the way the plants influence each other in their growing patterns.

Biotic interaction refers to the way plants respond to one another. Each wild plant effects dramatic responses in its neighbours by creating shade, extracting moisture and nutrients, and controlling local temperatures. Awareness of these plant-to-plant interactions can lead you to inspirational choices in your selection and placement of plants.

Plants in any natural community form a predictable structure. The *canopy layer* is composed of the dominant plants of the community —frequently its tallest plants; the subdominant plants of the *substory* (often shrubs) usually grow in the middle layers; and *ground layer* plants are the lowest vegetation layer of the community. (Sometimes the substory is called *understory,* or the substory and ground layer may collectively be referred to as understory.) This structure is further described in the forest section of chapter 4.

Plan your garden to imitate the natural patterns and relationships that plants form in the wild. Consider the eventual spacing of the mature plants, allowing ample room for trees and shrubs and a suitable ground-level habitat for shade-tolerant herbaceous plants and ground covers. Think about vertical relationships as well as side-by-side ones. Sometimes the effect of a mature canopy tree, such as arbutus (*Arbutus menziesii*) or western red cedar (*Thuja plicata*), can adversely affect the understory, robbing inappropriately placed ground-cover plantings of light, moisture and nutrients. In the same way, tall herbaceous plants, placed inappropriately in a garden border, can block smaller plants from sunlight, or tall grasses can outcompete flowering species in a meadow.

Be aware of these negative influences as well as the positive effects plants can exert on each other. The term *allelopathy* refers to the inhibiting effect of one plant's chemistry on another plant's growth. Some natives that demonstrate how allelopathy works are vine maple (*Acer circinatum*), western red cedar, (*Thuja plicata*), hairy manzanita (*Arcostaphylos columbiana*) and arbutus (*Arbutus menziesii*). They give off waste substances through their root systems or the decomposition of their leaves, which makes it difficult for many plants to grow near them, and can inhibit the growth of adjacent young plants.

A technique you can borrow from nature is to plant the dominant species first. It is surprising to see how this affects environmental dynamics, which gradually alter the habitat and make it more suitable for later planting of the other members of the community. Once the site becomes more diversely vegetated, the dynamic of the biosystem will rapidly accelerate.

Working with the site

To garden successfully, you must know your site—its soil, moisture, light, temperature and terrain. In any garden there are probably several small-scale microclimatic environments. Following are some critical elements to consider when assessing your garden site.

Soil conditions

Soil characteristics such as texture, water-holding capacity, and fertility can vary widely from one site to another. Although native plants do better with adequate soil nutrients, many are able to tolerate relatively poor soil conditions.

The type of soil you have—sand, clay or loam—refers to its texture and structure, which is chiefly determined by the size and form of the mineral particles it contains. It is a sandy soil if it feels gritty to the touch and will not hold together well when you squeeze a handful. Sandy soil is relatively low in nutrients. It has large particles, water drains very rapidly from it, and it tends to be dry.

If it feels slick and smooth and holds together in a clump when you squeeze it, your soil has a high clay content. Clay soil is composed of tiny compressed particles, and it drains very slowly. If you have a heavy clay soil you will be able to see water standing in puddles for a long time after a rain, literally drowning the roots of your plants. Although clay is nutrient-rich, it lacks both the organic matter necessary to keep the soil loose and active microorganisms that make nutrients available to plants.

With a texture between clay and sandy soil, loam is the ideal medium. It holds together when squeezed but not as stiffly as clay. The texture of loam is moderately gritty and when it is dry you can feel the small, different-sized particles of silt it contains. It possesses a good level of fertility, holds moisture well, and at the same time drains readily.

The pH level

If you have rocks on your site, they will give you an indication of your soil's pH level: generally speaking, limestone indicates a neutral-to-alkaline soil; sandstone and granite indicate acidic soil. The surest way to determine your soil's pH balance, however, is to do a simple soil analysis with a kit from local nurseries, or send a soil sample to a professional soil analysis lab. You may be fortunate in having a lab near you at a local university, government ministry or agricultural research station. If not, you can find soil-testing labs in the Yellow Pages under Laboratories—Testing. On a 0-14 scale, here is what the pH test results will indicate:

> pH 8 and over = strongly alkaline soil
> pH 7.5 - 8.0 = alkaline
> pH 6.5 - 7.5 = neutral
> pH 6.0 - 6.5 = slightly acidic
> pH 5.5 - 6.0 = moderately acidic
> pH 5.0 - 5.5 = strongly acidic
> pH 4.5 - 5.0 = very strongly acidic

Certain types of soil demonstrate particular infertility problems: peaty soils are usually strongly acid; sandy soils are low in nutrients and in many cases will need the addition of organic matter. Note, however, that some plants prefer such conditions as poor, sandy soil.

If your garden demonstrates a soil acidity or pH levels less than 7.0 (it could possibly test as low as 4.5), you have an acid soil, which usually means that it is low on nutrients like calcium and potassium. Some plants that do well in acid soils are salal (*Gaultheria shallon*), huckleberry (*Vaccinium* spp.), kinnikinnick (*Arctostaphylos uva-ursi*) and arbutus (*Arbutus menziesii*).

If the acidity level of your garden is too high (low pH level) for the plants you want to grow there, it can be improved by adding lime to the soil. When pH level is too high you can add iron sulphate or aluminum sulphate, or preferably organic matter such as peat moss. However, you should find gardening on your site easier and more satisfying if you select plants according to their compatibility with the soil's natural conditions, instead of concentrating your efforts on altering the characteristics of the site.

Drainage

Well-drained soils tend to be arid in the summer. Soil that is wet in spring but dry in summer (which is not an uncommon situation in much of the southern area of this region) is preferred

Beyond the basics

There is a great deal of information to be gained by looking closely at your soil's composition, texture, density, fertility, and other factors. For example, how deep is your topsoil layer? Is your soil peaty, humic or gravelly? What is the composition of the subsoil layer? Comprehensive gardening books for our region will inform you of more than just the basic essentials for working with your soil and improving its conditions. The UBC Guide to Gardening in British Columbia *gives much detail on many soil subjects. Other sources of relevant information are* The Pacific Gardener *by A.R. Willis and* The Sunset New Western Garden Book. *Another helpful little publication, but not specific to this region, is* The Bio Friendly Gardening Guide, *by Dr. D.G. Hessayon* by many of our native flowering bulbs, such as camas (*Camassia* spp.) and shooting star (*Dodecatheon hendersonii*). Other than wetland plants, most of our natives like good drainage, which is provided by coarse-textured, loose, sandy soil and free drainage in the subsoil, which means no under-the-surface hardpan. Gardens on sloping terrains are usually well-drained—if your garden is level, you may experience drainage problems. Another factor that affects moisture is wind: soil on a windy site can be subject to severe moisture loss.

Light and shade

All green plants require light, but they differ greatly in the amount they need. Look at a plant's natural habitat to ascertain its light requirements. Natives of such open habitats as oak meadows and rocky outcrops will probably demand full sun, while forest floor species will be shade-tolerant. A sunny, open, sunny location, for example, would be inappropriate for such a shade-loving plant as vanilla leaf (*Achlys triphylla*).

Full sun usually means eight hours a day or more of sunlight; partial sun means six hours a day; partial shade means three hours of sun a day and indirect or filtered light the rest of the day; and deep shade means no direct sun at all.

When observing your garden's light and shade situation, consider topographical variations and pay attention to the location of such shade-casting elements as hedges, walls, fences, large trees and buildings: the shadow of a tall building can create a shady, cool habitat. Note the path the sun takes during the day and how it changes through the year.

Terrain

If you are fortunate enough to have topographical variation in your garden site, you have a wide selection of habitats to develop. Slopes, rocky outcrops, hills and valleys all provide their own interesting microclimates and environments to work with. Terrain is a significant factor to consider when gauging sun and shade; changes in the topography of your site will quite likely produce some climatic variations within your garden. Valleys are cool, hilltops are hot, and even a slight dip in the landscape will be shadier than the top of a hillock. A rock will provide sun on one side, shade on the other, and the area around the rock will be a warm microclimate because the rock will absorb heat during the day and release it at night.

Indicator plants

If any native plants already exist on your site, they are the most important clues you have to your garden's preferences. Plants are indicators of the conditions of their natural site, and will tell you which other plants would naturally occupy the same habitat. (The habitat descriptions and lists in chapter 4 should help.) Finding a hardhack shrub (*Spiraea douglasii*) in a damp part of your garden, for example, will indicate that other wetland plants are appropriate for that spot.

The information that plants can provide is varied. For example, it is not unusual to find bracken fern (*Pteridium aquilinum*) springing up in healthy clumps all over the garden. If this is the case in your garden, the news is good: bracken fern is particularly sensitive to air pollution, so it is telling you that pollution is one factor you need not worry about in your part of the country.

Usually the dominant plants in a community, trees are frequently the only natives left on a site that has been developed and are therefore helpful indicator plants. If your home is ringed by western red cedar trees (*Thuja plicata*), you can guess that your site was once a forest, and shade-loving woodland plants will be happy under those trees. (Coniferous trees are frequently associated with moist, acid soil; deciduous trees are sometimes indicative of drier conditions.)

Do not be confused or discouraged if you are in the unusual situation of finding a broad range of plants growing naturally on your garden site. Rich biodiversity is the optimum situation for any piece of land: it indicates a healthy, balanced, relatively problem- and weed-free environment, and cause for much rejoicing.

Putting the knowledge to use

In assembling all this information you have been learning your garden's secrets. What is it telling you?

Topographical variations can sometimes cause problems. If you have a steep unplanted slope, for example, you can be assured that you will have some erosion problems—so plant one of the tough native ground covers to hold the soil and stabilize the slope. Salal (*Gaultheria shallon*), not usually thought of as a ground cover, serves admirably for this purpose. Some of the many other native plants that have been used by landscape engineers for slope stabilization in local land reclamation projects are oceanspray (*Holodiscus discolor*), wild rose (*Rosa nutkana*), Sitka alder (*Alnus sinuata*) and willows (*Salix* spp.).

Soil factors, too, will influence how you plant your garden. Instead of adding lime to raise your pH level, follow the dictates of the land: learn which plants require acid or alkaline soil, and put them in their preferred locations.

The same principle applies when assessing your soil's drainage capability. If you have a boggy spot, instead of struggling with major landscape overhauls, place moisture-loving plants there; they will be happy and you will

avoid many hours of labour. Of course, this does not mean that once your plants are in place you will ignore their needs completely. Applying mulch around the base of a plant to prevent loss of moisture is beneficial, and may be absolutely necessary in the case of a plant growing on a windy site.

Under normal weather conditions native plants are winter-hardy in their accustomed environments. When it comes to such factors as rainfall levels, use common sense and practical gardening principles. If you live in an unusually rainy area, why try to accomplish the impossible with plants that want dry conditions? Select your plants based on your garden's biozones and microclimates, and your plants' natural habitats.

We are unusually fortunate in being able to find, in our own region, a wide selection of natives for various garden conditions. The habitat descriptions and plant lists in chapter 4 include the soil, moisture and light requirements of plants in their respective habitats.

Landscape styles

Using native plants expands the ways you can garden. The potential for bringing these intriguing wildlings into your landscape is unlimited. Here are a few approaches you can take to landscaping with native plants.

A mixed garden

Natives and exotics can look wonderful together in many kinds of landscape. You can plan your garden in zones, with the formal areas close to and at the front of the house, and the more wild areas farther away, as landscape designers often suggest; or you can mix the plants together in as free-floating a form as you wish. Just remember the cardinal rule: group plants according to their soil and moisture requirements. A garden grown this way can be fascinatingly varied and bear a very individual stamp.

An evolving native plant garden

You can add natives to your garden incrementally, gradually moving from an exotic to a native plant garden. This is a very common strategy (as it was in my own garden) when the gardener has developed a conventional garden, or a fine traditional garden, then later becomes interested in natives but does not want to destroy the work already done.

A more deliberate evolution from exotics to natives is another approach.

It is no secret that developing a native garden from scratch can be very expensive, especially if there are no natives originally on the site. Although propagating them yourself is a good idea, it is a slow process, so consider a garden that moves through stages from exotic to native, gradually adding indigenous species as time and your budget allow.

A naturalistic landscape

Naturalism is the name given to a landscape style which seeks to emulate—in a cultivated form—the appearance of a wild area, borrowing design ideas from natural landscapes. Although the plant material is not necessarily indigenous, this is certainly a beautiful way to design a garden. It makes sense, when working with native plants, to consider the appropriateness of this landscaping style and its techniques. Three excellent books on the topic are *Northwest Landscaping* by Michael Monro, *Landscaping with Nature* by Jeff Cox, and *The Natural Garden* by Ken Druse. (It is interesting to note that in his more recent book, *The Natural Habitat Garden*, Ken Druse has moved from the concept of naturalistic gardening to the idea of gardening with plant material that is primarily native.)

An urban wilderness garden

A popular movement in the United States and in Europe, where it originated, this trend has caught on like wildfire in some cities; in Canada, Toronto is the centre of this movement. One of the original pioneers of urban wilderness gardening in Toronto, Karen Skowran (Parker), has now moved to Victoria, British Columbia, where she is cultivating a small garden demonstrating the principles of urban wilderness gardening. Tucked away behind a green gate, Karen's garden is a delightful surprise: a quiet green sanctuary in an urban setting.

Referred to in Britain as the City Green Movement, this style symbolizes a departure from conventional landscaping, an effort to move away from the overly manicured look. Although it can involve the use of native plants, it does not exclude introduced species. The idea is to have a comfortable, relaxed environment rather than an impressive horticultural showcase. Here the grass can remain unmown and unwatered, and the gardener can enjoy the setting of a tranquil, welcoming oasis. Anything that might help to bring an element of the country into the city is welcome in this naturalistic habitat, and wildlife is avidly wooed with feed stations, birdbaths and thoughtfully selected plant material. (See chapter 5 for information on designing a garden primarily for wildlife habitation.)

A true habitat restoration

To some gardeners there is a compelling attraction in the vision of a garden filled only with native plants. You may find that a purely native garden appeals to you for a variety of reasons: the symbiotic dynamic of many native species growing together; the food and shelter potential for wildlife; the eventual ease of maintenance; and the undiluted beauty of a truly natural

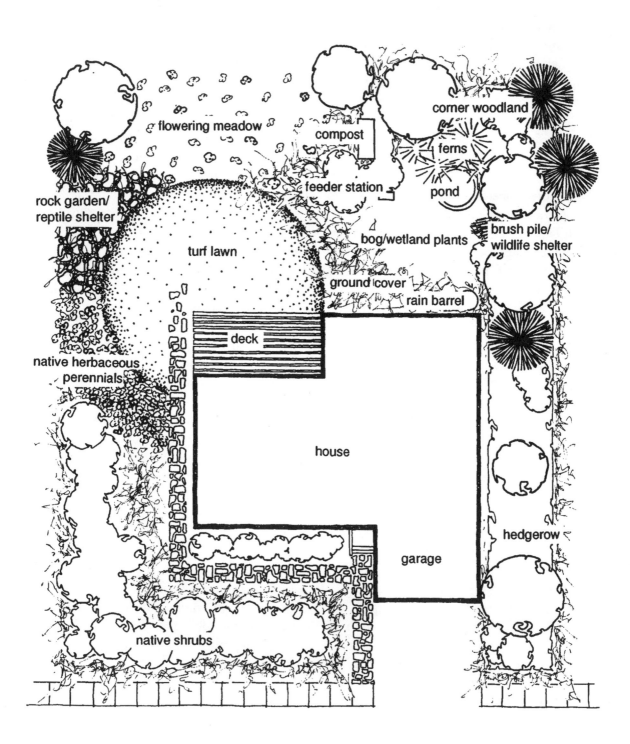

flowering meadow

corner woodland

compost

ferns

feeder station

pond

rock garden/
reptile shelter

bog/wetland plants

brush pile/
wildlife shelter

turf lawn

ground cover

rain barrel

deck

native herbaceous
perennials

house

hedgerow

garage

native shrubs

Site plan 2 (See page 44)

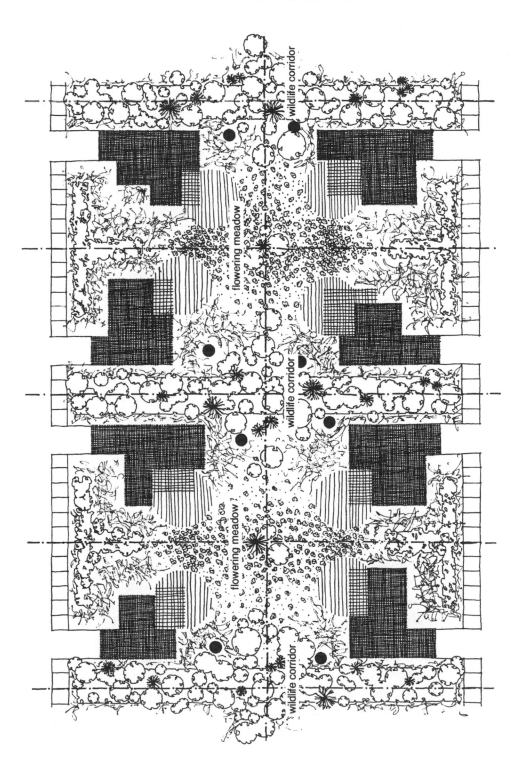

setting, to mention a few. To create such a purely natural environment, carefully observe the principles of native plant gardening. Become familiar with the biosite you are working in, recognize your garden's natural and appropriate horticultural type, and know what kind of wild flora and fauna would naturally belong there.

"Working with the site," earlier in this chapter, describes how to assess your site's natural horticultural conditions by studying such features as indicator plants, soil, and terrain. You can learn more about your garden's location, from a historical and geographical point of view, through reading and research. Provincial, state and municipal offices are treasure-houses of information about local properties and land areas. Personal observations of such early explorers as Captain Vancouver and Archibald Menzies contain some delightful descriptions of the land we now live in.

Once you have determined the original characteristics of the site you are now cultivating, you can begin to restore the conditions of the soil and topography to its approximate natural state. Amend the soil, remove undesirable plants, reestablish a wetlands area, or uncover a rocky outcrop. This sets the stage for the next step: re-introducing the plants native to the original habitat.

A new garden

You may be one of the fortunate few in the enviable position of building a home on undeveloped land. If so, you may be interested in some of the common-sense ideas presented in *A Guide to Backyard Water Conservation*, a publication sponsored by the Greater Victoria Water District and the Swan Lake Christmas Hill Nature Sanctuary in Victoria. This pamphlet takes an environmental perspective in suggesting that you locate the house carefully, both to protect and to enjoy the wild habitat, and that you rope off designated natural areas. Discuss your goals in detail with your contractor, if you are working with one, and continue to protect the site by monitoring the building process.

The site plan

Good design is said to be the key to a successful garden, and in the early stages of the design process a garden plan is invaluable. It is particularly helpful in identifying biosites and microhabitats for planning the locations of specific plants.

Developing the plan

A garden plan can be drawn up by a professional landscape architect or a garden designer— or you can do it yourself. Garden professionals recommend starting with a base map of the property. To help keep it to scale, use graph paper. For a clear and uncluttered plan, use a moderately large scale, for example 1/4 inch = 1 foot, or 1 cm = 1 m.

Indicating accurate dimensions, show the location of your house and any other buildings or structures, and such features as decks, patios, driveways and underground sprinklers. Include neighbouring buildings, roads, trees and other features on adjacent properties that affect yours.

Indicate existing grades, including any areas of steep slope and the direction of drainage. Examine your soil and note areas where soils or topography change. Use heavy arrows to show the direction of the sun shining from south to north, and indicate shadows with shading. Record wet areas, ponds and streams, slopes and wind patterns. Use these indications to identify the various microhabitats on your site.

Show location and approximate spread of existing trees, shrubs, lawn and other vegetation. Note any plants that affect energy conser-

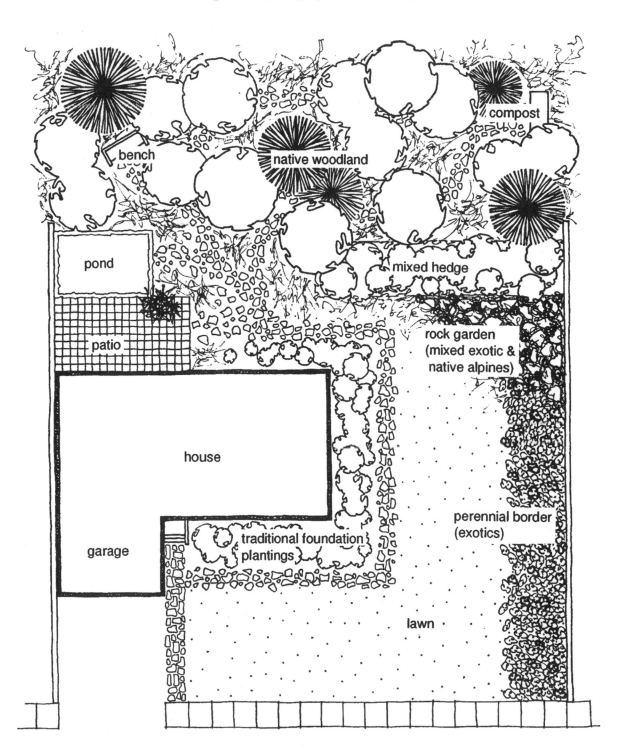

bench

native woodland

compost

pond

mixed hedge

patio

rock garden
(mixed exotic &
native alpines)

house

perennial border
(exotics)

garage

traditional foundation
plantings

lawn

vation—summer shade, winter sun, shelter from wind. Show any diseased or problem plants. It will be of particular interest to the habitat restoration gardener to mark the locations of special wildlife features. Include tree cavities, nesting areas, bird perches, drinking and feeding areas and travel corridors.

The next step is a schematic plan of your proposed garden, drawn on tracing paper laid over your base map. The use of bubble diagrams is an easy drawing device: sketch in broad areas of interest and potential by drawing circles around activity areas, ignoring details of shape. Starting with loose preliminary sketches, develop a succession of these plans.

Next, on a fresh overlay, add any proposed buildings, garden structures, walls or fences, and any hard surfaces such as driveways and paths that you want to add. Develop several bubble diagrams leading to the final plan.

Your task now is to select your plants, considering the characteristics of each species based on the information in chapter 4. Paying attention to the sun, water and soil needs of each plant, develop lists which group the plants according to these requirements. Label each list according to its appropriate microhabitat, matching it to your plan.

In selecting your plants consider, as well, such features as height and spread at maturity, time of bloom, fall colour, and the shape and structure of each plant. Consider plant properties such as shading from summer heat, letting in winter sun, or protecting from prevailing winds. Note any special problems some plants might have, such as messy fruit, peeling bark or invasive roots.

Now turn your bubble diagram into a specific landscape plan by adding details of plant materials and their exact locations and dimensions. The microhabitats marked on your plan will indicate where to group various species according to their requirements.

*   *   *

These are very simple and basic suggestions for designing a garden plan. Many general gardening books include sections on garden planning and site design. A book devoted completely to the subject, *The John Brookes' Garden Design Book,* has extensive, comprehensive details. The backyard wildlife program called Naturescape offers a package which includes creative suggestions for site design for wildlife gardens. Directions for contacting this program are at the end of chapter 5.

Sample plans

The simple site plans shown here are meant to generate ideas and help stimulate your own creative impulses. They illustrate very general approaches to designing for the inclusion of native plants in some common garden situations. Your own site will determine how you use the ideas presented here.

Sara Stein's book *Noah's Garden* is an inspiring work, and has been credited with revolutionizing the way we garden. In this wonderful book Sara Stein presents a landscape plan which she, in turn, borrowed from the northwest gardener, Michael McKeag. This plan has caught on all over the continent as a model for native plant gardens, and Site Plan 1 is an adaptation of it—with a few added features for attracting wildlife. It is a flexible plan which can be adapted to most sites and to the desires of most gardeners. It would be easy to incorporate a vegetable and herb garden, for instance, in a sunny area near the herbaceous perennial plantings. Herbs and natives have a strong alliance; many popular garden herbs are, in fact, locally indigenous. Some common examples are *Angelica*

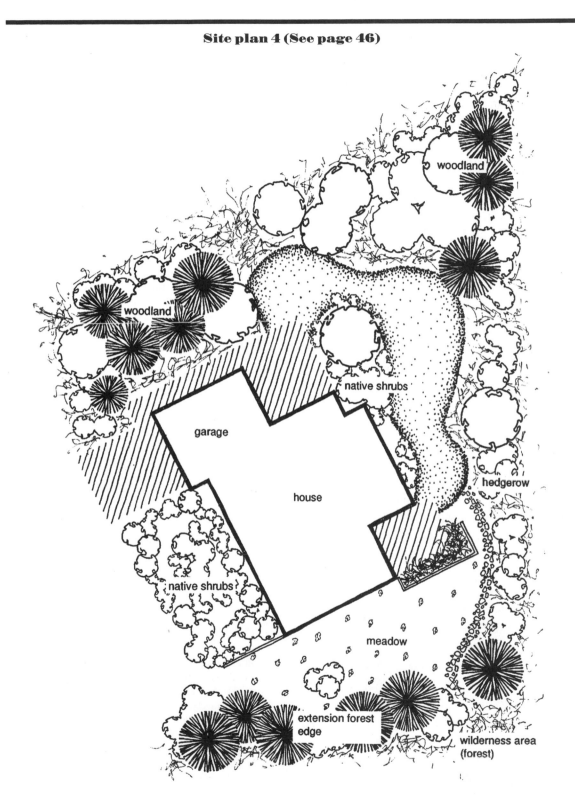

woodland

woodland

native shrubs

hedgerow

garage

house

native shrubs

meadow

extension forest edge

wilderness area (forest)

spp., salad burnet (*Sanguisorba* spp.), lovage (*Ligustichum* spp.), field mint (*Mentha arvensis*) and wild chive (*Allium schoenoprasum*).

To adapt this plan to your own garden, consider the characteristics of your site ahead of the plan. The plan includes several native plant habitats, so select those suited to your site. For example, unless you have a warm, sunny microclimate in at least part of your garden, a flowering meadow would not be appropriate.

The innovative beauty of this plan is that it can be incorporated with neighbouring gardens to fuse a community together into its own small bioregion, with small swaths of flowering meadows and wildlife corridors. Such a project would involve a degree of neighbourliness which you may not have yet experienced. Right now you may be feeling somewhat alone with your wild natives, but take heart; there is every indication that using native plants to some degree is the garden style of the future. When your neighbours see the attractive results of your efforts, you could convert the whole neighbourhood. Site Plan 2 shows what can happen when a cluster of adjoining gardens is designed to merge into one integrated system. If developers were to embrace this new concept, imagine the change of complexion we would see on the face of suburbia!

❦ ❦ ❦

To gardeners who have spent years of devoted labour establishing a traditional garden, the idea of incorporating natives is, to say the least, discouraging, if it means pulling out plants on a large scale and drastically altering the results of previous work. This, of course, is not necessary —or even desirable. Site Plan 3 demonstrates one very straightforward way in which a conventional garden, rather formally laid out with exotic borders in straight lines and geometric patterns, can incorporate native plants with little

Plant listings for site plan 5

Entrance plantings

Trees and shrubs
  western flowering dogwood (*Cornus nuttallii*)
  black huckleberry (*Vaccinium membranaceum*)
  vine maple (*Acer circinatum*)
  tall Oregon grape (*Mahonia aquifolium*)
  mountain hemlock (*Tsuga mertensiana*)
  Pacific rhododendron (*Rhododendron macrophyllum*)

Ground cover species
  bunchberry (*Cornus unalaschensis*)
  vanilla leaf (*Achlys triphylla*)
  western bleeding heart (*Dicentra formosa*)
  wintergreen (*Gaultheria ovatifolia*)
  kinnikinnick (*Arctostaphylos uva-ursi*)
  inside-out flower (*Vancouveria hexandra*)
  western red columbine (*Aquilegia formosa*)
  goatsbeard (*Aruncus sylvester*)
  various ferns

Overall site

Ground cover species
  mitrewort (*Mitella ovalis*)
  yerba buena (*Satureja douglasii*)
  wood sorrel (*Oxalis oregana*)
  fringecup (*Tellima grandiflora*)
  twin flower (*Linnaea borealis*)
  dull Oregon grape (*Mahonia nervosa*)

Woodland slope

Forest trees and shrubs
  western hemlock (*Tsuga heterophylla*)
  Douglas-fir (*Pseudotsuga menziesii*)
  Saskatoon (*Amelanchier alnifolia*)
  highbush-cranberry (*Viburnum edule*)
  twinberry (*Lonicera involucrata*)
  oceanspray (*Holodiscus discolor*)
  red-flowering currant (*Ribes sanguineum*)
  baldhip rose (*Rosa gymnocarpa*)
  Nootka rose (*Rosa nutkana*)
  ninebark (*Physocarpus capitatus*)

Ground cover species
  kinnikinnick (*Arctostaphylos uva-ursi*)
  dull Oregon grape (*Mahonia nervosa*)
  salal (*Gaultheria shallon*)
  western red columbine (*Aquilegia formosa*)
  western bleeding heart (*Dicentra formosa*)
  woodland strawberry (*Fragaria vesca*)
  fawn lily (*Erythronium* spp.)
  paintbrush (*Castilleja* spp.)
  wild lupine (*Lupinus* spp.)

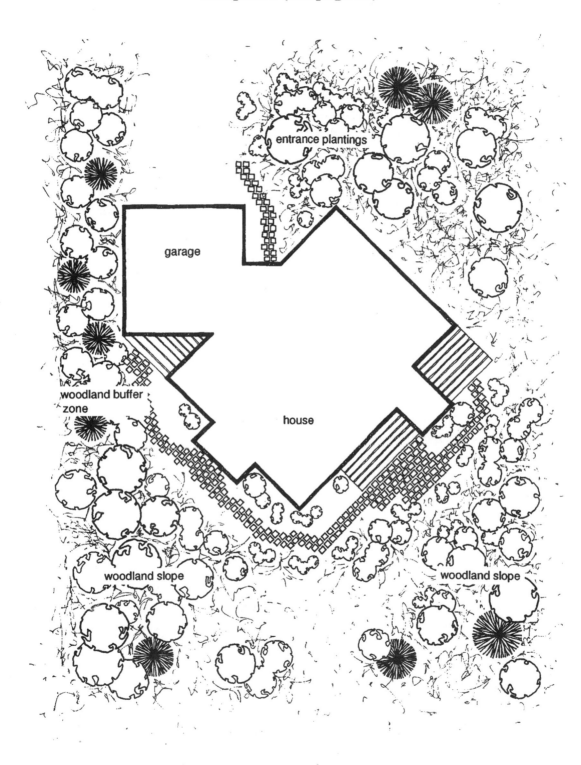

entrance plantings

garage

house

woodland buffer
zone

woodland slope

woodland slope

disruption to the rest of the garden. A woodland garden of native plants has been established at the rear of the property, divided from the rest of the garden by three features which incorporate both wild and formal gardening styles: the rock garden, a time-honoured feature of traditional gardens, but the perfect place to include native alpine species; the pond, which has squared-off, formal lines but is softened on the woodland side with native ferns and grasses and attracts wildlife; and a mixed hedge which includes both exotic and native shrubs. The garden plan is pulled together by the winding stone path which moves through the garden from the formal area to the woodland copse.

(The more popular method of incoporating natives into a traditional garden is to mix them with exotics in appropriate parts of the garden.)

❧   ❧   ❧

Site Plans 4 and 5 were designed by a professional architect for specific clients, and are therefore examples of gardens that have been planned according to the requirements of the site. Site Plan 4 is a wonderful example of a garden in which the naturally defined areas are reinforced

Native plant landscaping principles

Here is a summary of guidelines found throughout this chapter.

○ *Garden site-specifically: choose plants whose needs are closely met by the conditions of your garden site. (Know your site, know your plants, and know your plants' natural habitats.)*

○ *Use original plants on the site as indicator plants.*

○ *Maximize undisturbed areas.*

○ *Preserve existing indigenous trees and other plants, particularly the dominant plants.*

○ *Leave ground-covering mulches in place.*

○ *Achieve a natural effect in your landscape by the use of mass plantings.*

○ *Plant for diversity and try to imitate natural patterns and structural complexity.*

○ *Plant according to design principles and nature's logic: put in dominant or canopy layer plants first to accelerate the ecosystem dynamic, then add substory plants, and finally the ground layer.*

○ *Pay attention to the edge vegetation: use appropriate edge plantings to avoid abrupt boundaries between natural and cultivated areas.*

○ *Avoid rigid pruning.*

○ *Limit lawn area.*

○ *Plant thickly; cover the ground completely with plants.*

○ *Provide opportunities for viewing wildlife.*

○ *Rather than converting your whole garden at once, garden in small ecosites.*

○ *Try to adapt a relaxed attitude to gardening; for example, rather than becoming concerned about insect damage, remember that leaf-eating caterpillars will soon become butterflies.*

by the use of native plants. Site Plan 5 demonstrates a thoughtfully designed garden that considers the needs of the plants and of the people living with them. This plan includes lists, compiled by the designer, of the specific plants used in each area.

Some Elements of a Native Plant Garden

A native plant garden can contain several landscape elements, or it can be composed of a single element: a woodland, for example, or a flowering meadow. The following pages suggest a few ideas for bringing some of the more popular garden elements into your native plant garden.

Turf or alternatives?

Is the lawn still with us, or is it—metaphorically speaking—dead? In horticultural circles this issue is turning into the debate of the decade. Experts from all callings—biology, botany, ecology, horticulture, agriculture, sociology, philosophy, history—are lined up on both sides of the garden fence while we gardeners flounder in the middle, hanging on to our lawnmowers with one hand and our bark mulch with the other.

Of course, as a native plant gardener, I am in favour of reducing the lawn, but I do see that this is not a stance to be taken lightly. Even removing a tiny section of the front lawn can involve some trauma; after all, lawns are part of our cultural heritage.

There are two sides to every argument, and the question of keeping the lawn intact has its pros and cons.

In favour of the lawn
O   Functionally speaking, the turf lawn is a very successful ground cover; it can cover an area of almost any size, no matter how large or small.

O   Lawns provide the tranquility of open space for visual enjoyment and relaxation.

O   Lawn can withstand foot traffic and be used as paths or space for children and adults to play games.

O   A lawn provides a pleasant visual foil for flowers, shrubs and trees, combining handsomely and easily with other garden textures and colours, and lending unity to the whole garden.

O   Turf grass gives off oxygen as part of its photosynthetic process. Other green plants do this, too, but grass is particularly efficient because of its abundance. As part of this process, it helps cool the atmosphere.

O   Its capacity to cover large areas of ground reduces dust in the air, which benefits the atmosphere.

O   Grass is an effective noise insulator.

O   The acquisition of a lawn does not involve much effort in creative planning.

O   The lawn provides the romantic appeal of tradition, a link to bygone times. (Although which bygone times, it is hard to say. It may evoke the soft grassy undulations of the eighteenth-century landscape, or perhaps it takes us back, in our collective memory, to an earlier time in mankind's history. In his book, *Second Nature*, the much-quoted Michael Pollen describes the Savanna Syndrome: "Encoded in our DNA is a preference for an open grassy landscape resembling the shortgrass savannas of Africa on which we evolved and spent our first few thousand years.")

Lawn cons
O   Establishing a smooth, uniform lawn can sometimes involve extreme measures: bulldozing the earth; compacting the soil; rerouting natural drainage areas; and hauling in new topsoil and spreading, flattening and seeding it.

○ Lawns require gallons of water. Large lawns place an inordinate demand on our water supply.

○ The turf grasses which make up our lawns have been introduced to our region: they do not grow here naturally, and hence, despite the loud denials, take a great deal of care and attention to maintain. As well as that never-ending cycle of watering, upkeep can involve mowing, weeding, de-mossing and fertilizing.

○ Lawn care often includes the application of environmentally destructive noxious chemicals. Run-off from high-nitrogen fertilizers can adversely affect plants and water.

○ On a large scale, lawn eats up not only time, but also money: herbicides, hoses, sprinklers, mowers, weedeaters and all that water. (And one of the items we pay for is gasoline, which is harmful to the environment.)

○ Turf grass sucks up hugely disproportional amounts of moisture and nourishment from the earth's surface. This is primarily because there is so much of it.

○ During water restrictions a lawn depletes moisture in the garden, causing other plants to suffer more than necessary.

○ Aesthetically speaking, to most eyes there are many landscape forms more attractive than a large mowed lawn, particularly during water restrictions, when the overcultivated lawn can become a brown and barren wasteland.

○ From an environmental perspective, the most critical argument against the lawn is that it continues to usurp the diversity of native species which have, over thousands of years, adapted to the particular climate, soils and topography of our region.

The compromise

With compelling arguments on both sides, a compromise may be the answer. Today, the preference of many gardeners is for a moderately scaled, easily managed lawn. After all, a lawn does not have to be big to look good or be useful. Small lawns, in fact, can have a stronger total visual impact than large, expansive ones.

This is a common-sense solution that satisfies most of us. Even for a native plant gardener who would like to establish a wildlife habitat garden, a small patch of lawn is desirable, because humans, too, are part of nature's scheme. It seems a bit pointless to go to the trouble of developing a beautiful backyard sanctuary for wildlife if you cannot enjoy it yourself.

For those who are irrevocably attached to a handsome sweep of turf, there remains the question of managing large lawns. There is a new ethic afoot that encourages us all to mow, water and fertilize less. Perhaps if we relaxed our standards of lawn beauty, we could let it grow a little longer and accept a colour—in the summertime, at least—that is less relentlessly green. Watering less frequently but more deeply will encourage your grass to grow deeper roots, making it a healthier lawn for all seasons.

If you presently have a large lawn and want to remove it or reduce its size, this is your opportunity to establish a garden burgeoning with robust native flowers, trees and shrubs—and perhaps even a few eye-catching clumps of native grass. Ground-covering plants provide one of the best alternatives to a lawn.

Native plants as ground covers

The term ground cover can refer to just about anything that covers the ground. Because it covers so effectively, grass has become, in a manner of speaking, the ultimate ground cover, but there are many options.

Mulch-like materials are the best ground covers for providing benefit to the soil. Bark mulch is popular, which is unfortunate, as commercially available bark mulch is not only lacking in nutritional value, it robs the soil of nitrogen. For an area where plants will not be grown, try instead loose pebbles or river stones, which make attractive non-vegetative ground covers in a naturalistic landscape.

As a substitute for green, growing grass, the ideal plant would generally be low-growing; a good spreader (but not to the point of being invasive); have attractive foliage; preferably, but not necessarily, be evergreen; and, because it may be covering large areas, possess a certain hardiness and ease of maintenance.

This is a lot to ask of a little plant—but not impossible to find. Many species of plants native to our Pacific coastal region perform excellently as ground covers. These plants often have the useful ability to spread and fill in the spaces between newly set plants. Most have attractive foliage and some have beautiful flowers. The selection is diverse, with a wide range of plant heights, foliage textures, flower colours, site preferences and growing requirements. Many of us have difficulty finding the right plant for shady parts of the garden, and this is where native ground covers shine.

Concerning maintenance, consider these advantages of ground covers in general: unlike flowers, ground covers do not need to be staked, cut, watered, or fertilized; and you will find that, once established, most ground covers resist weeds well. Ground covers also work well in problem areas. Steep slopes, for example, are subject to washouts in heavy rains. Ground covers—those with deep roots—can be used to hold the soil in place. For areas that are too moist, too dry, too shady or too rocky for grass or other plants to do well, there is almost always a ground-cover plant that can provide a solution.

Planting and maintenance
The first consideration in selecting ground-covering plants is, of course, to choose plants suited to the site conditions. If the area is small, a uniform planting of a single variety may be all that is necessary. For a larger area, consider planting groups of several varieties together for eye-pleasing variations in height and form, and leaf size, shape and colour. Always look for plants whose needs are compatible.

When setting out your plants, the main objective is to cover the area, spacing the plants closely together so as to shade the ground and prevent weeds from competing. For aesthetic reasons, plant in groups of the same species. It is beneficial to mulch around the plants at first to keep the soil moist, encourage spread and discourage weeds. Once the plants have become established and dense enough to fully cover the ground, they should require only occasional top-dressing and weeding.

Keep foot traffic off the plants by designing paths and stepping-stones through a ground-covered area so that you can use and enjoy it.

Plant lists
Here are a few suggestions for native ground covers for various garden sites.

Full sun
❍ Common juniper (*Juniperus communis*)— Low-growing shrub, very cold-hardy, blue-grey foliage. Needs good drainage and deep root-run. Propagates easily from heel cuttings.
❍ Partridgefoot (*Luetkea pectinata*)—Evergreen, low-growing, mat-forming semi-shrub; performs excellently as a ground cover. Thick basal tufts of dissected rosettes of fan-shaped leaves. Dense terminal clusters of small white flowers on upright stems 6 inches (15 cm) high. Propagates easily from seeds or rosettes on rhizomes. Needs moist, acid soil.

Full sun to partial shade

○ Coltsfoot (*Petasites palmatus*)—Tall for a ground cover (4 to 20 inches/10 to 50 cm), but an excellent solution for a seasonally damp spot. Large, deeply-divided basal leaves. Very attractive to goldfinch and a beautiful sight in the spring garden when the yellow birds light on the pale pink flower heads. Grows from rapidly spreading rhizomes, dies back over winter.

○ Kinnikinnick (*Arctostaphylos uva-ursi*)—Broad-leaved evergreen; cold hardy. Leaves leathery green, sometimes turning red in winter. Spring flowers, white or pink, followed by red berries. Good plant for a dry bank, or allowed to cascade over walls. Needs good soil drainage.

Partial to full shade

○ Coastal strawberry (*Fragaria chiloensis*)—Evergreen, grows to about 6 inches (15 cm) high. Thick leaves, prominently veined, dark green, taking on reddish tints in winter. White flowers about 1 inch (3 cm) in diameter. Prefers a good, moist, well-drained soil in partial shade; will tolerate sun if irrigated. An annual springtime mowing will keep it neat and attractive and force new growth.

○ Cutleaf goldthread (*Coptis laciniata*)—Tiny (no more than about 2 inches/5 cm tall), evergreen perennial. Glossy, dark green leaves deeply divided. Small white flowers are rather insignifi-

cant, but intriguing seedheads make this a very attractive ground cover for damp areas in the southern parts of our region. Another species to try is fern-leaved goldthread (*C. asplenifolia*).

○ Twinflower (*Linnaea borealis*)—Charming low evergreen ground cover about 1 inch (3 cm) high. Tiny evergreen leaves. Two small trumpet-shaped pink flowers opposite each other on a 6-inch (15-cm) stem. Spreads by stolons.

○ Inside-out flower (*Vancouveria hexandra*)—Deciduous ground cover. Dull, apple-green leaves. Good under deciduous trees in the mulch created by the falling leaves.

Shade

○ Fairy lantern (*Disporum smithii*)—Deciduous ground cover, good under deciduous trees. Grows to about 15 inches (38 cm) tall. Leaves about 2 inches (5 cm) long; smooth, bright green, parallel-veined, on branching upright stems. Long white flowers are followed by red berries in summer to fall. Spreads and fills in by rhizomes. A taller (about 30 inches/ 75 cm high) species is fairy bells (*D. hookeri*).

○ Wild ginger (*Asarum caudatum*)—Evergreen perennial growing 6 to 10 inches (15 to 25 cm) tall. Leaves heart-shaped, lustrous dark green, 2 to 6 inches (5 to 15 cm) across. Flowers maroon, cup-shaped, each with three long tentacles. Can accept average soil conditions, but thrives in a rich, moist, organic soil. Spreads by very healthy rhizomes; can become rampant. Makes an excellent ground cover in a spacious woodland setting.

○ Another ground cover for shade is oak fern (*Gymnocarpium dryopteris*), described earlier in the propagation section.

🌿 🌿 🌿

The following plants are also excellent ground covers. They are all described more fully in the

forest habitat section in chapter 4, with the exception of false lily-of-the-valley (*Maianthemum dilatatum*), which is found in the wetlands habitat section.

○ Bunchberry (*Cornus unalaschkensis*)—Partial to full shade.

○ Dull Oregon grape (*Mahonia nervosa*)—Full sun/partial shade.

○ False lily-of-the-valley (*Maianthemum dilatatum*)—Shade.

○ Vanilla leaf (Achlys triphylla)—Shade.

○ Wood sorrel (*Oxalis oregana*)—Shade.

Meadows

The vision of a flowering meadow seems to hold us all entranced. In fact, I suspect that for most people the term *native plant garden* conjures up a meadow. Nothing seems easier than the charmingly random arrangement of pretty wildflowers and attractive grasses. The truth is, establishing a native plant meadow is an extremely difficult proposition.

Most of us imagine acres of long swaying grasses gracefully intermingled with myriad colourful wildflowers. In the words of Des Kennedy in his book *Crazy About Gardening*, "In its highest form, the wildflower meadow features a barefoot young woman who looks like Elvira Madigan running perpetually through it." This universal image appears to be a cross between a tall-grass prairie and a California hillside—not the kind of meadow found in our coastal region.

A number of our west coast meadows are plant communities that were formed when accidents of nature (such as trees falling) created sunny openings in a forest or woodland. They are in a transitional state; that is, they have not reached their climax, or self-maintaining stage of development. Trees and shrubs bordering these meadows gradually encroach upon them; in time, they would reclaim the meadows. Much of our meadow community has an open-canopy cover of trees. Other meadows in our region inhabit rocky coastal outcrops. These all constitute a very different type of landscape from that which the word *prairie* describes; a true prairie has no tree cover and is found in more interior regions of the continent.

Our meadow areas are scarce and fragile; so disturbed by human intervention, and so intermixed with introduced species that it is difficult not only to find, but to discern, the true regional grasses. A definitive field guide for our region, *Plants of Coastal British Columbia*, by Jim Pojar and Andy MacKinnon, tells us that "grasslands in our region were originally dominated by native perennial grasses, but are now dominated by Eurasian annuals and seedy grasses. These grasslands also retain many native plants such as fireweed (*Epilobium angustifolium*), lilies, and various shrub species." According to Pojar and MacKinnon, there is one well-known example of natural coastal prairie in this region, on the Olympic Peninsula, in the rainshadow of the Olympic Mountains.

Our region does contain a few smaller grasslands communities. These remnants are far closer to the definition of meadow than of prairie; that is, they contain some trees, well-spaced and open-canopied. The Garry oak (*Quercus garryana*) meadow system, for example, is familiar on southern Vancouver Island and south into Washington and Oregon.

From the Queen Charlotte Islands south, there are small patches of meadow-like Douglas-fir-onion grass (*Pseudotsuga menziesii-Melica subulata*) communities, sometimes mixed with some fescue grasses (*Festuca* spp.) and flowering plants such as broad-leaved shooting star (*Dodecatheon hendersonii*), snake root (*Sanicula marilandica*) and large-leafed sand-wort (*Moehringia macrophylla*).

From the Strait of Georgia in southern British Columbia, through the Puget Trough area, into the Willamette Valley of Oregon and southward, we can find small remnants of bunchgrass (*Festuca idahoensis*) communities at the margins of oak meadow areas, on rocky terraced ridges and on hilltops. Bunchgrass is an attractive short grass species, often mixed with a few flowering plants. Another grassy community found on rocky outcrops is the dryland sedge (*Carex inops*) growing with such flowering plants as camas (*Camassia* spp.) and annual sea blush (*Plectritis congesta*).

Another type of flowering meadow found in this region is the lush coastal mountain meadow. The dazzling photograph of lupines, paintbrush and fleabanes on the cover of this book is an example of a beautiful sub-alpine meadow.

Creating a meadow

A surprising number of gardening books include descriptions, in varying levels of detail, of how to create a meadow. Many contain directions for extensive landscape preparation, which begins at stripping down to bare soil and follows through to such extreme maintenance measures as control by annual fires (an excellent land management technique in large areas when used appropriately and under stringent control). In the face of such major enterprise, I have discussed the subject with agriculturalists, horticulturists, environmentalists, botanists and meadow-owners, and their advice has been consistent —and much less intimidating. Here are their suggestions.

❍ At least initially, avoid taking such drastic measures as ripping out your whole lawn and starting again from scratch. Every site is unique and you won't know, until you've tried, how well your own site is suited to the new vegetation. What if the new seed turns out to be a mistake?

❍ Start on a modest scale. Working a small area you can afford to be experimental.

❍ Go slowly. Before expanding, closely observe the progress of your new plants. A meadow system takes a long time to develop. Be patient and give the plants time to progress at their own pace.

❍ Set realistic goals. This refers to the size of your project and the type of plants you choose. In our region a flowering short-grass meadow is the most common indigenous type of grassland community. Because of this and because native wildflowers are much easier to obtain than native grasses, the appropriate choice in creating a meadow here is a flowering short-grass meadow that contains more flowers than grasses: a flowering meadow-lawn, in fact. Not only is it the most practical choice; because it belongs here, it is the most beautiful.

Flowering meadows

A Garry oak or two in your yard should be an indicator that the area was once a meadow. Arbutus (*Arbutus menziesii*) or Douglas-fir (*Pseudotsuga menziesii*), snowberry (*Symphoricarpos albus*), Oregon grape, (*Mahonia* spp.), some annual grasses and maybe some moss are other possible indicators of former meadow colonies. The site should have a thin black surface soil above bedrock, lots of sunshine, and dry summers.

If you are one of the few gardeners fortunate enough to have one of these meadow remnants on your garden site, there are methods you can use to restore it to a condition close to what it was at an earlier stage in its history.

First, carefully remove anything you don't want remaining on the site. This means anything weedy or invasive. It also means shrubs, because eventually the shrubs—even native species—will crowd out the lower-growing plants. If you want to keep the shrubs, restrict them to the edge of the meadow and keep them back from the wildflowers. Introduced weeds, such as quack grass, sow thistle, groundsel and dock, must be removed. Even native weed species can be damaging in this fragile ecosystem. An example is the native, but very invasive, dandelion-type species, hawkweed (*Hieracium* spp.). If there is broom (*Cytisus scoparius*) anywhere on your site, remove it. Native plants do not necessarily require rich soil and broom enriches the soil, thus inviting invasion by introduced species requiring a high nitrogen content.

You don't want the grasses on the site to overwhelm the flowers. Vigorous clumps of tall-growing grasses, such as the common orchard grass, will grow to heights which will completely obscure your dainty little wildflowers, so you will have to keep them down. A naturalist friend suggests going in with a scythe in mid to late summer, after the wildflowers have set seed. (If you are using a lawnmower, set the blades high enough to clear the base of the plants.) The trick is to try to catch the grasses before they have set seed, but after the flowers have. This may not sound too difficult because, generally speaking, the bulbs will have seeded by late spring and the grasses not until midsummer. However, there are some bulbs, such as harvest brodiaea (*Brodiaea coronaria*), which do not bloom and set seed until July. You will have to be very careful and observant of the growth patterns in your plant community.

Even short grasses can be threatening to wildflowers because of the litter they create and the thatch that builds up around the plants at ground level. The best way to treat this is to rake the grass, just as you would power-rake your lawn (but with a hand-rake), in mid to late summer.

Having removed all the obstructive elements, the best approach is to allow your little meadow community to do what it wants and set the dynamics of the ecosystem in motion. In other words, leave it alone (except for occasional weeding) for at least one or two seasons, and observe what happens. If the ecosystem is healthy and evolving rhythmically, you may be surprised at the interesting new plants that begin to emerge. Unexpected species have frequently been known to appear when a meadow ecosystem is restored to health; spreading camas is often a delightful and astonishing surprise to the gardener who has not planted it.

Once you feel that the community is beginning to restore itself, and your observations have given you new information about the habitat, you can begin to introduce some plants. If, for example, a few shooting stars have timidly shown their beautiful heads among the grasses, try encouraging them with a few more. By observing closely, you will be able to cultivate your meadow sympathetically, and it will respond with vigour and brilliance.

The grasslands section of chapter 4 contains many appropriate species suggestions. Cultivate your plants from seed, or obtain the bulbs or plants from a specialist nursery.

A wildflower mound

If you don't have natural rock outcrops or shallow soils, but do have the enthusiasm and desire to create a native spring-flowering community, here is a suggestion from British Columbia environmentalist Hans Roemer for creating a wildflower mound. Cover a layer of drain gravel, at least 2 feet (60 cm) deep, with permeable landscape fabric, then with 1 foot (30 cm) of black topsoil from a dry site. Now you are ready to go ahead and plant your spring-flowering plants.

Grass meadows

Here are some approaches to consider for developing a meadow that is composed (at least in the initial stages) primarily of grasses, mixed with some flowers.

○ *Working with wild seed*

It is sometimes, though rarely, possible to attain access to some native grasses or seeds. Perhaps there is a wild area near your home with some attractive-looking grasses from which you can collect seed in the summer. If you do so, remember the 10 percent limit to seed-collecting, and be careful not to disturb the clump. If you have an undisturbed area in your own or a friend's garden, collect the seed or try a few small plugs of the grass from that area. The sad thing is that the chances are it won't be a native grass—although it may be a grass that does well in a natural setting. It is sometimes possible to obtain some indigenous bunchgrass or other native grass

seeds through a seed exchange. (Refer to the list of seed exchange suggestions in the Regional Source Guide at the end of the book.)

If you are fortunate enough to obtain such seed, try it in a very small area or even in a container, such as a broad shallow pot or window box. Plant the seed out with a mix of native perennial wildflowers. Give this little experimental section close scrutiny and lots of time before you expand it. Do so piece by piece, nurturing it carefully to allow a complete ecosystem to develop.

○ *Working with an existing lawn*

If you do not have native grasses to work with, which is most often the case, keep in mind that there is a difference between the appearance of a natural meadow and a lawn that has just been let go.

If you want a meadow where you now have lawn, don't rip out your present lawn. Exposed bare soil will be quickly colonized by a whole community of weeds, giving you that major problem to deal with before you even start on your meadow. Start by planting bulbs in small clumps in openings you create in your lawn. On a site that is dry in the summer, some plants to try are camas (*Camassia quamash*), chocolate lily (*Fritillaria lanceolata*), fawn lily (*Erythronium oregonum*) and shooting star (*Dodecatheon hendersonii*). Or start off with just one species, such as camas. If your garden site is sunny but moist, the most appropriate wildflowers for your meadow will be mountain species. For suggestions, refer to the list of mountain wildflowers in "Discovering More Plants" in chapter 4.

A conventional lawn is not the best environment for these wildflowers, but bulbs have a much better chance than seed; in fact your chances of success would probably be even greater if, for the first season, you bought a few fully developed plants from a reputable nursery.

Some lawns create better environments than others. A lawn will work better with the flowers if it is not an extremely tall-growing grass (which could overwhelm the wildflowers). The flowers bloom during April, May and June, so your challenge is to avoid cutting the lawn until mid-summer, after they have flowered and set seed.

This enterprise can be awkward if you are concerned about neighbours' reactions. Your alternatives may be either to confine your meadow-lawn to your backyard, or share your enthusiasm for native plants with your neighbours. You may be surprised at their positive reactions. In an area close to my own home there is a meadow-lawn that literally stops traffic every spring. Its floral display is so dazzling that there is a traffic jam in front of the house on sunny days in April and May. I know the neighbours in that community are proud of their star attraction, and the really encouraging sign is that many of them are now sprouting erythroniums in their own front lawns.

Once you have established your first few flowers in a small corner of the lawn, you can spread out, removing larger pieces of lawn as you progress. If the conditions are right, the flowers will begin to multiply on their own. (Remember: go slowly.) Eventually you will have a beautiful meadow that is more wildflower than grass.

O   *Starting from scratch*

If your present lawn just won't work with wild-flowers, you may have to consider reseeding the grass. To eliminate an area of lawn, one of the most effective methods—if you have the courage —is to cut it very short and cover it with fresh manure, which by rotting, will burn out the grass and at the same time supply rich organic matter to the soil. (It might be wise to consult

with your neighbours before embarking on this enterprise.)

Retailers carry grasses that have been developed especially for particular regions. Be warned, however, that whatever the labels may say, they will not be true native grasses. But there are some locally developed varieties: ask for a short, meadow-like grass, and explain your situation to the dealer. The Parks Department of the municipality of Saanich on Vancouver Island has worked with a botanist to develop this mixture for meadow-type places.

- O   10% Canada blue grass
- O   25% creeping red fescue
- O   15% sheep fescue
- O   20% meadow fescue
- O   15% red top
- O   10% white clover
- O   5% red clover

You should be able to find this mix at retail outlets throughout this region; if you can't, ask your retailer to prepare it for you or to recommend local alternatives. Seed it at 50 to 75 lbs/acre (55 to 85 kg/hectare). The grass is

Lawn literature

For detailed instruction on major lawn reconstruction, these three books include extensive sections on grasslands engineering.

- O   The Wild Lawn Handbook,
     by Stevie Daniels.
- O   Landscaping with Wildflowers,
     by Jim Wilson.
- O   Growing Wildflowers, *by Marie Sperka.*

The wrong way

There is one method for developing a meadow that is strongly advised against: using commercially prepared "wildflower" kits. A true wildflower is a regionally indigenous plant, but many of these packages are assembled elsewhere and the plants are not native to our area. Most gardeners I know who have sown these packaged seeds have been disappointed; the results have ranged from dismal failure to mediocre. Many of the kits are largely composed of annuals—and introduced ones at that—so that if they do grow, it may be a one-time affair. Worse than disappointment is the possible inclusion of such invasive species as purple loosestrife (Lythrum salicaria).

Tempting though they may appear, these all-purpose mixes are full of empty promise, so avoid the disappointment of poor results and stick to regionally indigenous plants for your flowering meadow.

low-growing (no taller than 18 to 20 inches/46 to 50 cm). This is a low-maintenance grass mixture, requiring no weeding. It is quite tough and drought-resistant, and spreads rapidly.

Meadow maintenance

Gardeners who have meadows, or flowering lawns, know how truly maintenance-free this kind of garden really is. Other than a few mid to late summer mowings, the meadow takes care of itself. No weeding, no mulching, no fertilizing and no summer watering!

From the *Vancouver Island Rock and Alpine Garden Society Newsletter*, here is environmentalist Hans Roemer's prescription for appropriate meadow maintenance.

Once all the flowering species have concluded flowering, the last moisture will have disappeared from the soil. It will now take only another week or two until your wildflower meadow is tinder-dry and most of the seeds have been shed. This is the point where the unsightly dry stalks and grass may be cut down with a lawn mower and removed. (Under natural conditions in the past this removal of dry plant matter occurred periodically through grass fires.) By early winter there will be some re-growth of annual grasses which should be clipped again to free the early foliage of the wildflowers as much as possible from any competition.

There is one extra bit of attention this special environment should get: rope it off in the spring, to protect the meadow from foot traffic. It is difficult to overemphasize the need to respect the system's fragility, as the following story illustrates.

The owners of the beautiful traffic-stopping meadow-lawn described earlier have lived in their home for well over twenty years. About eighteen years ago, at a time when they describe themselves as "naive," they found it necessary to clear a small area of their lawn for some sewer-line repair work. In the resultant bare patch in the middle of their meadow they threw some grass seed. This spring, for the first time, the wildflowers have started to come back, but for eighteen years no flowers grew in that place.

Meadow preservation societies

The idea of a meadow has an aesthetic and spiritual appeal that most of us find difficult to resist. Not too many of us have our own wild meadows, and the few surviving meadow systems in our region are very much at risk. You may be intrigued by the idea of joining a group that is dedicated to maintaining and/or restoring a meadow community. Belonging to such a group also provides an opportunity to spend time in idyllic surroundings. If you are interested, there is probably a group in or near your community. For information, contact the Federation of British Columbia Naturalists, (604) 737-3057; in the State of Washington, call the Department of Wildlife, (206) 775-1311; in Oregon, contact the World Forestry Center, (503) 228-1367.

Native plants for the rock garden

A rock garden is a marvellous garden feature. It seems to have the ability to fit appropriately into any type of garden landscape. Victorian gardens often prominently featured elaborate rock gardens, and romantic landscapes often contained a grotto style of rockery. Today it has a new function in the garden: because of the shelter it offers, the rockery is an important component of a wildlife habitat garden.

If your garden contains an established rock garden, if you have a sunny rock wall or a natural rocky outcrop, or if you are considering installing a rock garden, you will be interested in these plant suggestions for specific locations. Be warned, however: some of the plants may be horticulturally challenging and difficult to establish, especially for the novice gardener, and some may be difficult to obtain—a good reason to become associated with a seed exchange program.

Hans Roemer, an environmentalist with the government of British Columbia and a member of the Vancouver Island Rock and Alpine Garden Society, has kindly allowed the use of the following information, originally published in an article which he contributed to a 1994 issue of the Society's newsletter.

Plant suggestions
Plants for the warm sunny slope or rock wall

This is a combined list of plants, from various habitats in our region, which would be suitable for a garden location that is subject to intense sun-warming and occasional drying out, such as south-facing rock walls.

- ○ Kinnikinnick (*Arctostaphylos uva-ursi*)
- ○ Shrubby penstemon (*Penstemon fruticosus*)
- ○ Silverback (*Luina hypoleuca*)
- ○ Woolly sunflower (*Eriophyllum lanatum*)

Low-growing species suitable for this garden habitat

Once deeply rooted, the following species are happy crevice dwellers in full exposure to the sun, although spreading phlox will also do well in a cooler, bright place or in a scree.

- ○ Broad-leaved stonecrop (*Sedum spathulifolium*)
- ○ Columbia lewisia (*Lewisia columbiana*)
- ○ Lance-leaved stonecrop (*Sedum lanceolatum*)
- ○ Oregon stonecrop (*Sedum oreganum*)
- ○ Spreading phlox (*Phlox diffusa*)
- ○ Spreading stonecrop (*Sedum divergens*)

Plants for dry scree

Plants for a sunny, dry scree

These are plants of high elevations which require a cooler situation but will still tolerate relatively dry, sunny conditions, as long as the roots can penetrate to deeper levels.

- Alpine lupine (*Lupinus lepidus* var. *lobbii*)
- Cliff douglasia (*Douglasia laevigata*)
- Olympic onion (*Allium crenulatum*)
- White cushion buckwheat
  (*Eriogonum ovalifolium* var. *nivale*)

Plants for dry scree with cooler conditions

- Davidson's penstemon
  (*Penstemon davidsonii*)
- Spotted saxifrage (*Saxifraga bronchialis*)
- White alumroot (*Elmera racemosa*)

Plants for alpine-type screes

These are plants which have adapted to true alpine conditions. They require a garden location with a not-too-coarse scree substrate, in a very cool microclimate. A protected, south-facing situation is not suitable. Like other plants from high places, these species want the coolest possible conditions, combined with the brightest possible place. The best spot is usually a north-facing slope, exposed to an open horizon without houses or tall trees close by.

- Dwarf azalea (*Loiseleuria procumbens*)
- Moss campion (*Silene acaulis*)
- Purple saxifrage (*Saxifraga oppositifolia*)
- Sitka mistmaiden (*Romanzoffia sitchensis*)

Other mountain plants

These plants grow in various stony, meadow-like habitats at medium to high elevations. They require no special substrates (though crushed gravel top-dressing and good drainage are advantageous), but should enjoy a cool microclimate.

For moderately dry conditions

- Alpine aster (*Aster alpigenus*)

- Blue violet (*Viola adunca*)
- Cliff anemone (*Anemone multifida*)
- Drummond's anemone
  (*Anemone drummondii*)
- Mountain wallflower
  (*Erysimum arenicola*)
- Rosy pussytoes (*Antennaria microphylla*)
- Showy fleabane (*Erigeron speciosus*)
- Small-flowered penstemon
  (*Penstemon procerus*)

Species found in moist meadows, requiring moist garden soil

- Fan-leaf cinquefoi
  (*Potentilla flabellifolia*)
- Mountain buttercup
  (*Ranunculus eschscholtzii*)
- Mountain daisy (*Erigeron peregrinus*)
- Western anemone (*Anemone occidentalis*)

Requiring a strictly acid, slightly peaty soil

- Partridgefoot (*Luetkea pectinata*)
- Pink mountain heather
  (*Phyllodoce empetriformis*)
- White moss heather (*Cassiope mertensiana*)

Small ferns

The dwarf ferns are particularly suitable for rock garden cultivation.

Small ferns for sunny, dry conditions
- Goldenback fern
  (*Pityrogramma triangularis*)
- Indian dream (*Cryptogramma densa*)
- Lace lipfern (*Cheilanthes gracillima*)
- Parsley fern (*Cryptogramma crispa*)

Small ferns for shady rock walls
- Fragile fern, or brittle bladderfern
  (*Cystopteris fragilis*)
- Green spleenwort (*Asplenium viride*)
- Licorice ferns (*Polypodium glycirrhiza*)
- Maidenhair spleenwort
  (*Asplenium trichomanes*)

Penstemons for the rock garden

To tempt you further, here is a short note about native penstemons by the eminent northwest authority, Professor Arthur Kruckeberg, from an article in the Spring 1991 edition of Wildflower *magazine*

> *Penstemons of all sizes abound in the Northwest and a generous number are low-growing and eminently suited to the rockery. First place must go to* Penstemon rupicola, *that cliff-hugging gem with glaucous leaves and purplish-red flowers. Others of outstanding quality are* P. davidsonii, P. procera subsp. tolmiei *and* P. cardwellii. *So easy from cuttings, these penstemons are great for the novitiate in rock-gardening.*

For a wider selection of plants for the rock garden, the book *Alpines: The Illustrated Dictionary*, by Clive Innes, is a well-illustrated catalogue of rock garden plants from various regions.

The mountain habitat section of chapter 4 contains more information on mountain and alpine species.

Crossing the border

This is about crossing some traditional lines, but maybe it should be titled "*Not* crossing the border," because it proposes using plants other than crosses, or hybrids, and cultivars and exotics in the perennial border.

Whether you call it a perennial, herbaceous, or mixed border, a garden border probably has more universal appeal than any other garden element. Who is not charmed by the midsummer beauty of a full-blown perennial border? To many gardeners, a vibrant, well-planned border is the quintessential symbol of garden. It can be a wonderful sight: extensive, colourful, traditional, and, in the height of the season, glorious. It is also labour-intensive, space-demanding, seasonally limited—and English.

The herbaceous borders conceived by Gertrude Jekyll were definitively brilliant. Their effectiveness depended upon consciously chosen plants and their arrangement within a garden whose composition was in perfect harmony with its time and setting. The perennial border was the ideal element for a garden of a golden Edwardian afternoon.

For today's west coast gardeners there are, on one hand, several compelling arguments for considering a transition to a new kind of gardening, using indigenous species. On the other hand, the best rationale for the long hours and hard work we put into our gardens is the pleasure they give us; and if we like perennial borders, why shouldn't we have them?

Many of us do enjoy cultivating beautiful border gardens, but have developed mixed borders instead of following the outdated purist version which excludes all plants other than herbaceous perennials. A typical mixed border of today might include rhodos and other shrubs, some bulbs and early spring blossoms, and even annual plantings in seasonally bare spots. If you are a mixed-border gardener, and do not want to forsake your present gardening style to "go native", consider including a few west coast plants in the mix.

Most of the plants suggested here are commercially available, but there are a few species that will be difficult to find. Persist in asking for them at your local nursery and eventually the demand might encourage a supply.

Plant suggestions
Native plants offer many options, either for adding variety to the border or doing something dramatically different. For example—and this is one of those dramatic differences—look at that row of pyramidal cedars backing your herbaceous border: picture instead, a background hedge of oceanspray (*Holodiscus discolor*) whose graceful white plumes sweep down to mingle with the colourful blossoms of other plants. Or consider a mixed hedge that includes natives with spectacular blossoms, such as the beautiful white-flowering mock orange (*Philadelphus lewisii*).

Several evergreen native shrubs are effective on their own or in hedges. Serviceberry (*Amelanchier alnifolia*), which has been used in English gardens for years, does very well in a shrub border in partial or full sun. The Pacific Northwest native bayberry or California wax myrtle (*Myrica californica*) makes a tall, dense, bushy hedge and thrives in sun or full shade, with a particular tolerance for salt spray. Our lovely

Pacific rhododendron (*Rhododendron macrophyllum*) puts on a stunning show and will adapt easily to a border that has a little moisture in its soil. Its beautiful, large pink blossoms appear in June and July.

If you have hostas in your border, try mixing them with the graceful greenery of indigenous ferns, which usually take well to filtered sun or shade. Most of us are familiar with sword fern (*Polystichum munitum*) and deer fern (*Blechnum spicant*). Two more to try are Anderson's sword fern (*Polystichum andersonii*) and the magnificent chain fern (*Woodwardia fimbriata*), which needs quite a damp spot.

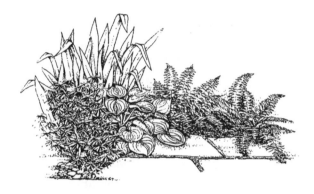

There are many indigenous wildflowers that work beautifully in the border. For the front of the border, try one of the introduced strains of the moss campion of world-wide rock garden fame, *Silene acaulis*, or the pinkish-flowered *Silene douglasii*, which likes a dry, open site. The western pasque-flower (*Anemone occidentalis*), a mountain native, makes an attractive display with its early-flowering, showy white (sometimes blue-tipped) blossoms and conspicuous, feathery fruit. A perfect border plant, if given some moisture, is the mountain sneezeweed (*Helenium autumnale*), a yellow-flowered, daisy-like member of the aster family (Compositae). It is not well-known but is surprisingly easy to find in the wild, although not—despite the common name—at high elevations.

A native monkey flower, *Mimulus lewisii*, with its large, bugle-shaped rose-purple flowers, would be at home toward the back of a border that provided some moisture. A similar location would be appropriate for the showy purplish-blue-flowered coast penstemon (*Penstemon serrulatus*). Other suggestions for the back of the border are tall purple fleabane (*Erigeron peregrinus*) and large-leaved lupine (*Lupinus polyphyllus*), both preferring moist but well-drained soil in sun to semishade.

The border would also be appropriate for some of our more familiar little wildflowers, such as western red columbine (*Aquilegia formosa*), bleeding heart (*Dicentra formosa*), tiger lily (*Lilium columbianum*), white fawn lily (*Erythronium oregonum*) and pink fawn lily (*Erythronium revolutum*). There are also several native species of *Fritillaria*, *Allium*, *Iris*, *Delphinium* and *Penstemon* that adapt well to garden cultivation and would make a splendid show in the border.

For a little border architecture, try the imposing goat's beard (*Aruncus sylvester*) or the attractive false Solomon's seal (*Smilacina racemosa*).

Not a perennial, but a long-blooming annual that makes a splendid cover when bulbs have finished their show, is the pink beauty, sea blush (*Plectritis congesta*). Used in England's Kew Gardens as a carpeting plant for spring beds, this lovely flower requires an open site with good garden soil and some moisture around the roots.

These are just some of the many ways native plants can be incorporated into your border garden.

Site considerations: care and design

When including native plants in an established border, take care to observe the specific soil needs of each plant you introduce and be certain that plants are grouped according to their needs. Many native shrubs and wildflowers do not tolerate excessive summer water and will die if planted among frequently watered exotics. When planting natives among the other plants in your garden, do your best to duplicate the soil and microclimate of their wild communities.

Native plants are well-suited to the naturalistic style of planting in overlapping drifts. If you are concerned about giving visual unity to the border, there are enough native species, from widely diverse habitats, to give you plenty of choice in combining native plants with introduced species of similar—or appropriately contrasting—form, and leaf size, texture and colour. One of the joys of gardening is derived from assembling a group of plants that looks pleasing to the eye, in a combination so appropriate it appears as though the plants belong together.

Shrubs: consider a hedgerow

Once you begin gardening with native plants and visualizing your garden as a home to wildlife, you may notice that you are developing a more nontraditional and innovative gardening style. Perhaps you will find yourself becoming increasingly more adventurous in your approach to landscaping. The new/old idea of a hedgerow, for example, is an imaginative alternative to a boring fence or a rigid stand of conventional hedge plants such as yew or pyramidal cedar. A native-species hedge, or hedgerow, can function as well as any other to define the perimeters of your garden or areas within it, at the same time providing wildlife shelter and an interesting and attractive backdrop to the rest of your garden. This intriguing concept brings together an old-world element with a new-age vision of gardening.

Traditionally, monoculture has been the accepted gardening practice when planting hedges in North America. Hedges have the potential to provide wildlife corridors through our urban and suburban terrains, but a single-species hedge provides very limited use as a wildlife habitat. Far more interesting and richly diverse is a hedgerow of mixed natives, which will attract its own community of animal and plant species.

Our mellow autumn or early spring days are perfect times to look at local examples of this type of hedge and observe its form and structure. The prototype, of course, can be found in rural areas, but in some urban municipalities this type of planting has been put into practice by local parks departments.

Plant suggestions

Include at least one evergreen for winter cover in your hedgerow, and incorporate one or more species of shrubs that offer blossoms, berries and a dense, thorny structure. You may wish to intersperse four or five shrubs that flower and fruit at different times. The following native shrubs are attractive to birds, practical to plant and commercially available. These plants are all described in chapter 4.

- Evergreen huckleberry (*Vaccinium ovatum*)
  —See the forest habitat section.
- Indian-plum (*Oemleria cerasiformis*)
  —See the edgelands habitat section.
- Nootka rose (*Rosa nutkana*)
  —See the edgelands habitat section.
- Oregon grape (*Mahonia* spp.)
  —See the forest habitat section.
- Red-flowering currant (*Ribes sanguineum*)
  —See the edgelands habitat section.
- Salal (*Gaultheria shallon*)
  —See the edgelands habitat section.
- Salmonberry (*Rubus spectabilis*)
  —See the edgelands habitat section.
- Saskatoon or service berry (*Amelanchier alnifolia*)
  —See the edgelands habitat section.

The following are some more shrubs suitable for hedgerow planting.

- Highbush-cranberry, or squashberry (*Viburnum edule*)
- Red elderberry (*Sambucus racemosa*)
- Snowberry (*Symphoricarpos albus*)
- Thimbleberry (*Rubus parviflorus*)
- Twinberry (*Lonicera involucrata*)

Care and maintenance

Hedgerow plants will benefit from a mulch of garden compost, leaf mould, or shredded bark applied each spring. This will discourage weeds (which could strangle a young hedge) and form a host environment for hedgerow plants and other organisms.

Generally speaking, native shrubs are not pruned as rigorously as exotics. In particular, a hedge which is being managed for wildlife habitation requires a very different pruning regimen than a conventional hedge. Wildlife hedges should never be clipped before the nesting period is completely finished, so forego a spring or early summer pruning. In fact, a hedgerow needs to be clipped only to control unruly branches; yearly pruning is not necessary.

The base of a hedgerow offers an opportunity for developing a wildflower colony of native plants that can tolerate dry conditions. Choose plants to suit the position of your hedge: sun-loving species if the hedge is south-facing; shade-tolerant plants for a hedge with a northerly exposure. Use small, healthy plants rather than seedlings. Water regularly for at least the first growing season.

Hedgerow wildlife

A hedgerow is a magnetic wildlife attraction. Native shrubbery is a principal source of food and shelter for birds in the wild and a major attraction for birds in the city. Birds are enticed not only by berries and seeds and the insects feeding on plants, they are also attracted to a sheltered area. The dense growth of a hedge offers an ideal nesting site and the thick shrub and ground litter is a wonderful habitat for many smaller birds.

Hedgerows attract other creatures as well. Frogs, toads and wood mice hide in the shelter of a hedge bottom, and the foliage provides breeding grounds for moths, spiders and crickets. A native hedgerow can become a busy corridor offering shelter, food and an access route to a wide variety of wildlife.

Tip for traditional gardeners

If you still prefer more formal-looking shrubbery, but wish to garden with natives, try evergreen huckleberry (Vaccinium ovatum) *for a clipped, box-like hedge. Or, if you have a naturalistic garden but prefer a single-species hedge, try a showy bank of oceanspray* (Holodiscus discolor) *or Nootka rose* (Rosa nutkana).

A woodland garden

As well as being the most magnificent plants in any landscape, trees are wonderfully useful. Because they are so large, they have a powerful oxygenating effect on the environment. They also have a huge impact on temperature: as well as absorbing solar energy, trees cool by transpiration (the evaporation of water from the leaves), which reduces air temperature. You can cool your house in summer by planting deciduous trees to the south and west, and warm it in winter by siting evergreens on the windward side of the house—but not so close as to block the sunlight. Trees can also be dust interceptors and buffers to traffic and other noises.

Most gardeners recognize the value of tree roots in preventing soil erosion. What many of us do not realize is the harmful impact of rain on the surface of the soil. It is a major cause of soil compaction, and trees lessen the impact by interrupting the fall of rain or snow, causing it to be more gentle.

Considering their beauty and function, trees are highly desirable components of a landscape. Spacious premises are not necessarily required; you can develop your own woodland garden on almost any size of property. Even a garden corner can contain a small thicket—a wonderful home for shade-loving plants. If you already have a hedgerow, you could expand it into a wildlife corridor through your land, and this, in turn, may spread out to become a small woodland. Or your garden may contain a few trees you can use as a nucleus for developing a woodland area, by planting more trees and shrubs around them.

Trees to choose

The existing trees and soil conditions should be your guidelines in selecting plant material. If you already have deciduous trees on the site you may have a dryish soil; conifers or mixed trees would indicate a somewhat acidic, humic soil. Most trees prefer soil that is fairly well drained. The following are some suggestions for trees to try in your woodland garden; *plants marked with an asterisk are described in chapter 4. The list of forest species in "Discovering More Plants," in chapter 4, includes suitable shrubs and other understory plants.

Coniferous
- Douglas-fir (*Pseudotsuga menziesii*)
- Grand fir (*Abies grandis*)
- Pacific silver fir (*Abies amabalis*)
- Shore pine (*Pinus contorta*)
- Sitka spruce (*Picea sitchensis*)
- Western hemlock (*Tsuga heterophylla*)
- Western red cedar (*Thuja plicata*) *

Deciduous
- Bigleaf maple (*acer macrophyllum*) *
- Cascara (*Rhamnus purshiana*)
- Red alder (*Alnus rubra*)

Understory
- Pacific crabapple (*Malus fusca*)
- Red osier dogwood (*Cornus stolonifera*) *
- Vine maple (*Acer circinatum*) *
- Western or Pacific flowering dogwood (*Cornus nuttallii*) *
- Western yew (*Taxus brevifolia*)

Site preparation

If the soil needs improvement, the best form of organic mulch is one that is close to the natural forest elements, such as leaf mould—particularly from trees similar to those on the site. Leaf mulch is also the best antidote to soil compaction, which can be disastrous to trees.

If you are working in an already wooded area, as you prepare your site you may find yourself clearing away undesirable invaders or introduced species. Use the woody debris and brush you accumulate to create a brush pile for wildlife habitation. (For more about creating wildlife habitats, see chapter 5.) Be selective when removing existing vegetation. Every opening you create in the canopy results in increased light to the woodland floor, with a potential to impact drastically on the plants growing there.

There is beauty in a fallen trunk, as well as potential shelter for a diverse population of small animal and plant species. In the forest, when a tree falls, it becomes colonized by various organisms and eventually develops into a nurse log with a large community of species associated with it. In our region over one-half of all forest species are dependent in some way on the beneficial presence of fallen trees.

Garden design

When planning a woodland garden, keep in mind these important design principles: maximize undisturbed areas, preserve existing indigenous trees and plants, particularly the dominant trees, and respect the logic of nature by trying to imitate natural patterns in your plantings. Use trees on the site as indicator plants for developing a more complete plant community around them, thereby encouraging the dynamics of the biosystem and stimulating the growth of affiliated forest floor plants.

To create an environment as close as possible to a natural woodland, pay attention to the edge vegetation. Vegetation at the edge of the forest is usually composed of more shrubs and fewer trees than the forest interior. You can create this effect by planting smaller trees and shrubs. Establish a smooth transition between the woods and the rest of the garden by developing layers of vegetation, with curves and irregular borders, at the edge of the woodland. Enlarge the woodland area to include specimen trees in adjacent lawn.

When planting trees and shrubs, consider their eventual size, and space them accordingly. The site should be large enough to allow each tree to reach its mature height, trunk diameter, and branch and root spread without interfering with the plants around it.

Once you have established a canopy layer of trees, plant the substory shrubs, and finally the ground layer of sedges, mosses, ferns, and wildflowers. This planting pattern follows the designs of nature and is also the design technique used by many landscape architects.

Some garden features

One of the most effective features of a woodland garden is a winding path. As well as being inviting, woodland paths protect ground-layer plants from foot traffic. Landscape designers use paths to create the illusion of space; curves, twists and turns lead the visitor into new and hidden territories, and can add an element of the mysterious unknown to even a small plot. Some appropriate materials for woodland paths are natural wood chips, wood cord, tree rounds, pine needles, flat rocks and gravel.

Rustic benches placed at the side of the path, under a tree or in view of a created or natural vista make a stroll through the woodland garden all the more appealing. Benches, fences, archways and garden ornaments most suitable for a woodland setting are those constructed of natural materials, such as stone or weathered wood.

Some invasive intruders

○ English ivy (*Hedera helix*)
○ Giant knotweed (*Polygonum sachalinense*)
○ Himalayan blackberry (*Rubus discolor*)
○ Holly (*Ilex aquifolium*)
○ Morning glory, or hedge bindweed (*Calystegia sepia*)
○ Purple loosestrife (*Lythrum salicaria*)
○ Scotch broom (*Cytisus scoparius*)
○ Spurge laurel (*Daphne laureola*)

Although weed-like in their behaviour, these plants have long been considered garden ornamentals. They have entered our landscape, sometimes insidiously, but often as garden introductions. They often deceive us with their attractive flowers or foliage, but make no mistake: these are undesirable invaders that can outcompete other garden cultivars as well as native plants. In the wild, some of them, for example broom and loosestrife, have had a disastrous effect on native plant communities. Morning glory has been known to choke out all other species in its neighbourhood, while ivy is capable of killing the trees it entangles. And as Des Kennedy laments, in his book Crazy About Gardening, *the impenetrable, thorny thickets of Himalayan blackberries provide an ominous threat to our garden environments as they "lurk on the perimeter like murderous thugs, waiting to break and enter."*

Maintenance

Once your woodland is established you could conceivably let it go and allow nature to take its course; a natural woodland, after all, was your objective. However, a well-managed habitat has the greatest opportunity to flourish. Be on the alert for invasive plants. Do not disturb native forest-floor species unless weeding becomes necessary, and try to prevent this by occasional mulching. Prune when necessary for the health of a tree or its neighbours, but do not prune excessively, and be careful not to leave long stubs that encourage disease. At the same time, keep in mind that by allowing a dead or decaying tree to remain standing you are providing a valuable resource. In the past few years conservationists and foresters have come to understand the significance of snags in providing habitat in the wild, and you will increase the range of species attracted to your own woodland garden by leaving them standing.

The stewardship of a woodland plot can involve some care and diligence, but as with any native plant gardening, once the woodland is established, the maintenance required is minimum and the rewards are maximum.

4

WHERE?

Identifying Plant Habitats

Any large geographic region contains diverse ecosystems and within each ecosystem are a variety of habitats with their own particular variations of soil, climate, and topography. Associated with each habitat is a community of plants able to grow and reproduce there, within a stable, balanced system which has evolved over time. Despite varying habitat characteristics, plant communities as a rule exist in fairly predictable patterns within geographic regions.

The combination of factors allowing a plant to thrive is different for every species. Some plants are able to adapt to a number of different environments. Others may group together repeatedly in similar habitats, forming an easily recognizable community. Certain plants are found so consistently among particular plant communities that they are known as indicator plants and are studied by scientists to provide clues to the characteristics of their habitats.

As a first step toward native plant gardening, become familiar with plant communities and where they grow. Recognizing the characteristics of native plant habitats leads to an understanding of the plants' needs.

This chapter describes some of the most common of the Pacific coastal region's habitats (wetlands, edgelands, forest, grasslands and mountain). Some of the more prominent and interesting species associated with each habitat are detailed, with cultural requirements and propagation information. Almost all these plants are available at specialist nurseries. Most species included here are perennials; all are suitable for garden cultivation and may be propagated from seed or by other methods which do not involve removal of the parent plant from its setting.

The habitats described here represent only a small segment of this region's lush diversity, and the selection of plants is merely a tempting sample of the multitude of species found in coastal habitats. These plant descriptions are included to help you become familiar with some characteristics of plants associated with various habitats.

Although the plants are grouped here according to habitat, in nature many species do not confine themselves to only one type of location. Red osier dogwood (*Cornus stolonifera*), for example, has been included here with other wetlands species because of its predilection for a damp site, but in nature it is also found in forest settings. Oceanspray (*Holodiscus discolor*) is described as an edgeland plant as it is so often found at the edges of roads, ravines, woods and thickets, but it can also be regarded as a grasslands species because it is frequently associated with an oak meadow system. When you are gardening, remember that some plants possess this adaptability, and remember also that your garden may contain a variety of microhabitats; one damp spot at the bottom of your backyard does not mean that you should necessarily fill your entire garden with wetland plants.

Wetlands

Various types of wetlands habitat are found worldwide. Here in the Pacific coastal region they are extensive and varied in type, some of them unique to our area. Wetlands are rich in plant diversity, and support ferns, mosses and lichens as well as many kinds of flowering shrubs, trees, and herbaceous plants. Some wetland plants have submerged roots that are able to extract minerals from the soil and support and anchor the plant, while the leaves project above the water surface or float on it. There are also many species that do not live directly in the water, but do require a high degree of moisture in the soil.

A wetlands habitat can be the soggy, shallow shore of a lake; a stream bank; a gravel bar; a fen; a marsh; a swamp; a bog; muskeg; damp forest; wet meadow; estuary; or a mucky seepage area or moist roadside ditch. Predominant types of wetland habitat in our region are bogs, swamps and marshes. Swamps are dominated by trees and woody shrubs. Marshes are treeless wetlands where the dominant plants are grasses, sedges and rushes. Subject to flooding, marsh soil is rich and productive. In the spring birdsong fills the air in this protective wildlife habitat. A marsh is commonly a freshwater area. Distinctive to this region is the salt-water marsh, characterized by extensive tidal flats in the coastal plain.

One of the most horticulturally interesting and diverse examples of a wetland habitat is a westcoast lowland bog. Found in cool, moist regions once covered by glaciers, these bogs are similar to others throughout Canada (which has more bog land than any other country). Most bogs are found at low to middle elevations. Our coastal lowland bogs often appear in forest clearings and are characterized by poor drainage, acidic soils, and an ancient, thick buildup of the multicoloured peat moss (*Sphagnum*) which forms the bog surface and the layer of peat below the surface. This moss, which is life-sustaining for many of the plants that thrive in the bog, converts rainwater into an acid which discourages mosquitos from breeding.

The trees that grow in bogs, deprived of adequate nutrition, must struggle to absorb the few nutrients and minerals available in the acidic, waterlogged soil, and as a result may exhibit stunted growth and malformed limbs, which often branch sideways. The most striking example is the shore pine (*Pinus contorta*), which, under completely different conditions in interior British Columbia, grows straight and tall and is known as the lodgepole pine. Another example is the yellow cedar (*Chamaecyparis nootkatensis*), a tree whose growth is so stunted that it looks like a small, distorted shrub.

The bog changes over the millennia, over the years, and over the seasons. Indications of change are the numerous dying trees and old snags at bog margins. Many bogs began when shallow lakes filled in from the edges with *sphagnum* moss. We can see change being created today as we observe layers of *sphagnum* slowly creeping into the surrounding forest, but we do not know what shape the landscape will eventually attain. Easier to observe is the change of seasons. During winter rainstorms the water rises several feet and large areas resemble a shallow stream. When the deep cold sets in, freezing weather conditions rim the bog plants with icy lace. In spring and fall, flowers and berries embellish the bog with brilliant splashes of colour. In summer, it may begin to dry up, but the patterns of the various sedges (*Carex* spp.) indicate continuous growth and change.

What doesn't change is the beauty of the place. Take a walk through a coastal lowland bog. To become really familiar with the Lilliputian scale of the bog landscape it helps to get down to the level of the plants. Here you can observe the interesting forms of the grasslike sedges, the rich texture and various colours of the *sphagnum* moss, and the tiny plants that grow around the moss. What you see will probably delight you with its surprising beauty. Once you recognize the remarkable, though subtle, attraction of bog plants, it does not take long for this kind of landscape to capture the imagination. Awareness of its fragility alerts us to the jeopardy in which we place such a special environment by our mere presence; in this delicate habitat, five minutes of human carelessness can undo twenty-five years of bog development. Knowing this, we can recognize the worth of any endeavour to preserve and replenish the stock of these valuable bog plants.

An inland bog

I live near a rare inland peat bog; it is an area of unique scenic beauty and home to some species that I see nowhere else in the urban area. A wide range of native plants live here, along with some relatively rare insects and birds. (As well as ducks and geese, some of the rare and not-so-rare birds of this bog include Virginia rail, yellowthroat, spotted sandpiper, mourning dove and marsh wren. Unfortunately there have been no recent sightings of the larks that once sang in the surrounding fields.) First Nations elders tell us that this was an important site for the harvesting of bog cranberries. In this richly diverse wetland area, I walk through corridors of bulrushes that reach over my head, listen to the varied bird-songs, inhale the rich peaty fragrance of the place, and feel as though I have left the city far behind. It's easy to forget that a major highway runs past this magic spot, just over the rise of the bog dyke. Knowing this makes me fear for the survival of this fragile ecosystem. Many species that were here only five years ago have disappeared, and even from one year to the next, the balance and composition of the place changes and shifts. In the summer, as my walk takes me past clumps of invasive broom, I can hear, in that peaceful, hushed environment, the insidious snapping of hundreds of bursting seed pods, and I know that in the coming years more

broom plants will spring up and push out even more of the native species. This is just one of the multitude of threats to this fragile habitat. Every time I walk through this special place I am reminded of the importance of preserving these wetland areas of rare biological diversity, historical significance and scenic beauty.

Many bog plants are suitable for cultivation. If you have a damp or even wet spot in your garden, if you have created a bog area, or if your garden just has particularly moist soil, these plants will be appropriate when you observe their cultural requirements. All of the species described below grow throughout most of the Pacific coastal region.

Shrubs

Bog cranberry (*Vaccinium oxycoccus*)
This trailing, ground-covering little evergreen plant is a dwarf, vine-like shrub. A true plant of the bog, it will often be found half-buried in a hummock of peat moss.

The bog cranberry has very slender stems and numerous alternate, widely-spaced leaves which are small, pointed and leathery. The leaves are dark green above and waxy grey beneath, and have rolled-under edges. The small pinkish nodding flowers, which appear between May and July, have protruding stamens and petals which bend sharply backwards, so that they resemble miniature shooting stars. The red berries are small (about 3/8 inch/1 cm wide), but appear oversized on this small plant. Remaining hard and green throughout the summer, the berries then soften and turn red after the first frost. Native people picked the green berries and steamed them until red and soft, or ate them fresh as a thirst-quenching snack.

Propagation and cultivation
Bog cranberry can be propagated by seeds or

by cuttings, rooted suckers or offshoots. It requires a very wet, acidic soil, in a sunny spot. This native plant is just beginning to come on the market for retail availability.

Bog laurel or swamp laurel (*Kalmia polifolia*)
Kalmia polifolia, also known as *Kalmia microphylla* ssp. *occidentalis* is a beautiful, small shrub (about 20 inches/50 cm tall) with a delicate appearance. It has slender branches and dark green, narrow, lance-shaped leaves with inward-rolled edges and a dusty whitish underneath surface. The rose-pink flowers are saucer-shaped, about 1 inch (2 cm) across, with five lobes and ten arched stamens radiating from the centre of the blossom.

The common name *bog laurel* is apparently due to its leaves, which compare in shape to the true laurel, or bay leaves, and are similarly aromatic.

Propagation and cultivation
Kalmia can be propagated from seed, like a rhododendron, but the easier method is to take cuttings in late summer. This plant requires a peaty, acidic soil, in a moist to wet spot in sun to semishade. It's a good idea to pair bog laurel with its companion of the wild, Labrador tea (*Ledum groenlandicum*), to which it has a similar (but not identical) appearance. Take care not to confuse the two, because Labrador tea makes a pleasant drink, but bog laurel contains the poison andromedotoxin.

Hardhack (*Spiraea douglasii*)
Hardhack is a spiraea whose beauty compares favourably with the introduced species of the same genera that have been garden favourites for many years. It is a splendid, showy shrub that can sometimes dominate its bog habitat—in fact, some bogs are referred to as hardhack bogs.

Some wet areas are made almost impenetrable by the dense thickets of this woolly plant.

Hardhack is a tall (up to 6 feet/2 m), rather leggy, deciduous shrub. It has many wiry stems and grey-green, oval leaves, about 1 1/2 to 4 inches (4 to 10 cm) long, with velvety undersides. From June to August its tiny rose-pink flowers appear in large, pyramid-shaped plumes at the tip of the stems. These flowers seem fuzzy because of the numerous long stamens in each blossom. After the leaves of the hardhack have fallen, clusters of several small, pod-like fruit follicles remain on the shrub. These little fruit pods are dry, smooth and shiny.

Propagation and cultivation
Although it can be invasive in a small space, the hardhack is a garden beauty with a pleasing fragrance. It prefers a sunny and open, watery, wild part of the garden or a damp meadow, with a soil very rich in humus.

Hardhack is commercially available. It will grow easily from seed or cuttings taken any time from August to October. It spreads from creeping underground stems whose suckering offshoots can be readily established in the garden. Prune and mulch hardhack in the fall.

Hardhack grows well with sweet gale (*Myrica gale*) and salmonberry bushes (*Rubus spectabilis*), which can also be at home in a wild, wet part of the garden.

Labrador tea (*Ledum groenlandicum*)

Ledum groenlandicum is sometimes mistaken for a small rhododendron, and like the rhododendron, is a member of the heather family. This is not surprising because plants of the heather family, or Ericaceae, make up a large part of the understory of most of the coastal forests and provide much of the shrub cover for wetland bogs.

Labrador tea is a small to medium-sized (about 20 to 60 inches/50 to 150 cm tall), many-stemmed evergreen shrub. Its dull green leaves are long, narrow and leathery, with edges that curl under along the margins and a dense mat of rusty hair on the underside. From May to July the numerous small, bright white flowers appear in showy round-topped umbels, at the ends of the branches. Stamens protrude from the centre of each small bloom.

Labrador tea thrives in our coastal region; you can find dense thickets of it in many damp places. This attractive little shrub is indeed a bog-loving species, a true indicator plant for wet, usually very acid and nutrient-poor soils where peat moss grows. A frequenter of peatlands, swamps and bogs, it also lines damp roadside ditches where it can become quite luxuriant. Labrador tea can be found in moist conifer forests throughout British Columbia. It ranges south to Oregon on the Pacific coast and throughout northern North America and Greenland.

Propagation and cultivation

Labrador tea is a fine shrub for the garden and can take well to cultivation if given a somewhat damp, open spot in the garden. It can be grown from seed or propagated from root-crown division or by layering. After insects pollinate the flower, a dry capsule forms and eventually releases tiny light seeds. The seeds can be planted in the fall or spring, in a moist peaty soil; plant deeply and water in thoroughly. This lovely shrub grows slowly and requires little maintenance other than regular watering. Like its companion plant, bog laurel (*Kalmia polifolia*), Labrador tea prefers a moist, acid site but will thrive as long as the soil is prevented from drying out. Both bog laurel and Labrador tea can be purchased from specialist nurseries.

By the way, the name Labrador tea is legitimate; its aromatic leaves—fresh or dried—do make a flavourful tea. It is said to have relaxing and medicinal qualities—the Haida used it to cure colds and sore throats—but it must be taken only in moderation as excessive doses can cause intestinal disturbances.

Ninebark (*Physocarpus capitatus*)

Often found in dense thickets, this shrub has erect, spreading branches and usually grows to heights of 6 to 12 feet (2 to 4 m). The white, five-petalled flowers appear in early summer, growing in tight, round terminal clusters; in autumn these flowers turn into reddish-brown seed husks. This is a deciduous shrub, with deeply veined, sharply lobed, shiny green leaves. *Physocarpus capitatus* is called *ninebark* because on older stems the grey bark continuously sheds and splits into many layers.

Found in the southern half of our region, ninebark prefers such wet, open places as damp meadows, coastal marshes, streamsides, margins of lakes, and edges and sometimes understories of moist woods.

Propagation and cultivation

With its handsome structure and attractive floral display, this shrub is an appropriate but under-used selection for a dampish garden. It is an excellent choice for an area of disturbed soil, and has been used for rehabilitation projects. Ninebark can be obtained from a specialist nursery. It roots easily from cuttings, or can be grown from seed which should be sown in the fall for spring germination. This is a fine companion for red osier dogwood (*Cornus stolonifera*) or salmonberry (*Rubus spectabilis*).

Red osier dogwood (*Cornus stolonifera*)

Sometimes called the creek dogwood because in nature it is often found in swampy areas or along the shores of creeks, streams and ponds, *Cornus stolonifera* is the perfect tall plant for a wet garden. Although technically a shrub, it reaches tree-like proportions, growing from 3 to 20 feet (1 to 6 m) tall. Freely spreading, with many stems, this deciduous shrub has oval leaves 2 to 4 inches (5 to 10 cm) long. The leaves are heavily veined and dark green in colour, turning brilliant plum-red in the fall. The twigs are usually red (hence the common name). After the leaves have fallen, the bright red stems of this striking plant stand out against the winter landscape, especially in the swampy areas which it often inhabits in dense thickets.

From May to July the small white flowers form dense, flat-topped terminal clusters. In the fall, abundant bunches of small white or bluish berries contrast strikingly with the red stems and foliage. These bitter berries are inedible but apparently not poisonous.

Propagation and cultivation

The red osier dogwood can be propagated from seed. Cold stratification is required at 35° to 41°F (2° to 5°C) for 30 to 60 days. Cuttings also work well: branch tips taken in late summer root easily. This shrub often spreads on its own when the lower prostrate branches root along the ground. *Cornus stolonifera* can be easily obtained from nurseries.

This tall shrub adapts well to many garden settings. It tolerates sun or shade and will be very happy if placed in a moist to wettish part of the garden. (The one in my own garden has proven to be an amazingly fast-growing plant.) *Cornus stolonifera* has been highly successful in habitat reclamation and is a valuable wildlife cover, particularly for moose, elk and deer. It attracts a variety of birds, including thrush, robin, flicker and even pileated woodpecker.

Sweet gale (*Myrica gale*)

Sweet gale sometimes replaces Labrador tea as the dominant shrub in a bog. It is a low (but sometimes up to 5 feet/1.5 m tall), bushy deciduous shrub with long, narrow, leathery leaves. These are covered with fragrant, yellow, waxy glands which release their scent when lightly brushed. The flowers are borne in catkins, in many-clustered terminal spikes. The male and female flowers occur on separate plants, and appear from early April to June, before the leaves.

Propagation and cultivation

Sweet gale, which is obtainable at specialist nurseries, spreads by suckers. It can be propagated from seed, or by layering. As with other bog shrubs, peaty, moist soil is required.

Myrica gale is a desirable plant for your wet garden, perhaps not for its flowers, but for its interesting form, and because it is an important nitrogen-fixing plant. It likes a somewhat sunny site. In the wild it is occasionally found with hardhack (*Spiraea douglasii*); they would probably make good companion plants in the garden.

Herbaceous plants

False lily-of-the-valley
(*Maianthemum dilatatum*)

The leaves of this lovely little plant first appear like twisted spills which unfurl into shiny, green, heart-shaped leaves. Later, from April to June, slender spikes of white waxy flowers form in a clustered tassel at the end of the stems. The stems, which are 4 to 10 inches (10 to 25 cm) long, grow up between the two leaves of each plant. In the summer the flowers are replaced by small round berries which are at first light green and mottled brown, eventually turning transparent red.

False, or wild, lily-of-the-valley is not a true bog plant; it is more likely to be found at the edges of streams, or, if in a bog, perched on a drier hummock. The favourite wild site of this ground cover is a moist forest floor, particularly in a Sitka spruce forest near the ocean.

Propagation and cultivation
False lily-of-the-valley, a true member of the lily family (Liliaceae), grows from rhizomes and spreads easily, allowing it to cover large areas. It is available at specialist nurseries. This plant is a formidable ground cover and care should be taken in introducing it to the garden as it can become quite invasive. (In time, hundreds of plants can be produced from one single plant.) However, where an aggressive ground cover is needed, it is an attractive addition to the garden, forming a beautiful, glossy green carpet.

False lily-of-the-valley likes very moist to wet, nitrogen-rich soil, in a shady to semishady location. Probably the best place for it is a deserted damp corner in a woodsy setting. When planting, mark or remember where you have put it, as the plant withers away after the berries appear and seems to disappear completely over the winter. It is a good idea to cover it with a mulch such as leaf mould when the leaves die away in the fall.

Maianthemum dilatatum is a good candidate for associate planting. It is naturally compatible with deer fern (*Blechnum spicant*), foamflower (*Tiarella trifoliata*) and swamp lantern (*Lysichiton americanum*).

Foamflower (*Tiarella trifoliata*)
Sometimes called *laceflower,* this attractive plant has tiny, foamy-looking white flowers at the ends of thin, wire-like stalks, coarsely toothed maple-like leaves arranged in a basal rosette, and smaller stem leaves. The plant grows to a height of 6 to 24 inches (15 to 60 cm). Preferring a moist soil, *Tiarella trifoliata* is not a bog plant, but a denizen of moist coniferous forests, seepage areas and stream banks throughout our region.

Propagation and cultivation
The foamflower is easily propagated from its rhizomes' leafy offsets, and can be obtained from a specialist nursery. With the bloom often lasting throughout the summer, it is a lovely species for a moist, shady garden, especially when planted in masses. Appropriate companion plants are

vanilla leaf (*Achlys triphylla*), lady fern (*Athyrium filix-femina*), sword fern (*Polystichum munitum*), thimbleberry (*Rubus parviflorus*) and salmonberry (*R. spectabilis*).

Swamp lantern/skunk cabbage/yellow arum (*Lysichiton americanum*)

One of our harbingers of spring, *Lysichiton americanum* is a distinctively attractive herbaceous perennial whose bright colour can dominate a swampy scene. Typical habitats are alder swamps or understories of open canopy stands of Sitka spruce (*Picea sitchensis*), yellow cedar (*Chamaecyparis nootkatensis*) or western red cedar (*Thuja plicata*). This handsome plant does not deserve the unfortunate common name *skunk cabbage*, so I use the less frequently heard, but much more suitably descriptive, term *swamp lantern*.

The flowers of the swamp lantern are actually numerous florets embedded in a thick fleshy spike at the end of a club-like stalk, called a *spadix*. The spadix is partially surrounded by a large, bright yellow, hood-like *spathe*. The

Invasive intruder

Purple loosestrife (*Lythrum salicaria*)
Although it would certainly thrive in a bog garden, purple loosestrife is definitely not a plant to cultivate. Introduced from Europe over a century ago, this marauder has spread relentlessly across North America and has become notorious for invading wetlands and gradually colonizing them completely. This weed ultimately chokes out all native vegetation, creating a dense purple landscape almost totally devoid of wildlife.

Purple loosestrife is not difficult to spot. It has willow-like leaves on square, woody stalks 3 to 6 feet (1 to 2 m) high. From June to September the plants bear long, densely covered spikes of pinkish-purple flowers about 1 inch (2 cm) wide.

Look for examples of purple loosestrife invading low wetland areas throughout our coastal region. If there is such an area near you, offer to participate in an effort to eliminate or at least control the ravages of this destructive intruder. Purple loosestrife is a tough, deep-rooted aggressor which spreads like wildfire. (A single plant is capable of producing over two million seeds per year.)

The only effective method for control is to remove the whole plant. Dig out the root mass, making sure you have removed every piece. It will reroot from the tiniest remnant of root or plant material, so let the plant dry out completely in a container or protected site. Then it can be burned, packaged for disposal, or composted. This should all be done by midsummer, before the flowers begin to go to seed. If digging the plant is not feasible, help retard the spread of the seed by removing the flower: in midsummer before seeds set, cut the flowering head, remove and destroy it.

The widespread havoc wrought by purple loosestrife is an example of the destruction that can occur when inappropriate exotics are imported into our landscape.

spathe, or hood, protects the flowers and conserves warmth which is generated by the plant's protective tissues. The spathe also emits a distinctive odour which attracts pollinating insects. When the leaves are bruised or crushed this odour is released—hence that objectionable common name. The spathes "bloom" from February to March. In late spring the green, berry-like fruit appears, embedded in the spike. The plant is overgrown, in mid or late summer, by the huge, exuberant leaves, which are dark green, quilted, and lanceolate in shape, and can grow up to 5 feet (1.5 m) long and 2 feet (60 cm) wide.

This is a plant favoured by wildlife; squirrel and deer enjoy the ripe, seed-bearing spikes, and bears seek out the thick rootstocks as well as the leaves and fruit.

Propagation and cultivation

Lysichiton americanum is available at specialist nurseries. Although the seeds are reputed to germinate easily, the more sure method would be to use the large underground stem, which can be divided to make transplants.

Plant the swamp lantern in wet to very wet, nitrogen-rich soil. It can tolerate shade or an open site. It is happy growing near false lily-of-the-valley (*Maianthemum dilatatum*) or lady fern (*Athyrium filix-femina*). These are both fairly aggressive plants; of the two, false lily-of-the-valley is probably the more desirable.

Swamp lantern provides a very attractive garden focal point. A plant that is not as appreciated here in its native home as it is on other continents, *Lysichiton americanum* is highly valued in England as an exotic for the wet garden.

Yellow marsh marigold (*Caltha palustris* ssp. *asarifolia*)

A typical coastal wetland plant, the yellow marsh marigold is found in swamps, bogs and shallow pools. It has a deep yellow, buttercup-like flower, about 1 to 2 inches (3 to 5 cm) wide, consisting of six to eight showy sepals, many stamens, and several pistils. The flowers appear in July and August. Each single flower is borne terminally on smooth succulent stems which either arch erectly or creep horizontally. The wide, fleshy leaves, which are attractively round to kidney-shaped, form basal clusters. The plant can grow to a height of 6 to 12 inches (15 to 30 cm).

Propagation and cultivation

The yellow marsh marigold grows from short buried stem-bases or rhizomes. It can be propagated from seed: sow the seeds in a wet peaty medium. It can also be obtained from a specialist nursery. This succulent plant is charmingly appropriate in the bog garden, or at the edge of a pond, where it can be submerged from 4 to 16 inches (10 to 15 cm). Marsh marigolds like some sun.

A compatible plant is deer-cabbage (*Fauria crista-galli*).

Edgelands

Edgelands occur where one habitat type joins another. Edgeland habitats make up a significant portion of our Pacific coastal region and are extremely important because they support a wide diversity of wildlife. The plant community here is often composed of shrubs of varying heights.

The terrain of this habitat is not clearly defined, and can take many forms. It may occupy the roadside border of a woodland area, the edge of a forest trail, a clearing, or sometimes the edge of a coastal bluff. Edgeland habitat is often a sloping field, forming the transition between open grassland and forest cover. Dense thickets of shrubbery, sometimes referred to as brushfields, can be found on mountain slopes facing the ocean, where climate does not permit forest to develop. Similar habitats develop further inland where soil or rock conditions do not favour forest development. Stands of dense brush also spring up temporarily in logged or burned areas of forest before they are slowly replaced by forest trees. Shrubs and young trees gradually invade openings such as grassy meadows, pastures, or partially stabilized dunes. On the coast these stands are often very colourful, being made up of some of North America's most spectacular flowering shrubs.

In the south of the region, forest edge habitats are often brushfields that superficially resemble the chaparral of interior, more southerly regions, but typically consist of different species and are more bounteous. High rainfall and a moderate climate encourage luxuriant growth, and often these brushfields are nearly impossible to walk through. This type of edgeland habitat is a more significant feature of our coastal geography than many of us realize, serving the very important function of providing a dense cover that protects steep slopes from erosion and offers shelter and safe hiding places to various forms of wildlife.

This edgeland habitat is difficult to describe in terms of terrain, soil type and climatic conditions, because of its wide and varied range. The shrub communities, however, offer a broad selection for cultivation. Many of them adapt easily to the garden and most of them are extremely attractive.

Shrubs

Hairy manzanita
(*Arctostaphylos columbiana*)
Hairy manzanita is an intriguing and highly esteemed indigenous plant. A very leafy an

bushy evergreen shrub, it sometimes, but rarely, grows over 10 feet (3 m) tall. The distinctive feature of all manzanitas is the smooth, polished, dark reddish-brown outer bark, which peels in scaly shreds to reveal the new bark beneath. Its grey-green leaves grow only at the ends of the twigs. The young twigs and leaves are very hairy, hence the common name. Charming, tiny (1/4 inch/6 to 7 mm), urn-shaped blossoms, white or pinkish in colour, bloom in May in clusters at the end of the branches, emitting a delightful aroma. The flowers develop into showy bunches of brownish-red berries which are rather mealy, but edible.

The hairy manzanita is found most frequently on rocky slopes or outcrops or in disturbed clearings, or amid stands of Douglas-fir (*Pseudotsuga menziesii*). It ranges from central and southeastern Vancouver Island south through our region.

Propagation and cultivation
Unfortunately, *Arctostaphylos columbiana* is a horticultural challenge not to be tried by the faint-of-heart home gardener, nor is it easily available at nurseries. With much trial and error, it has been propagated from hormone-treated cuttings started in a mixture of sand and peat. If you enjoy a challenge, achieve a distinguished horticultural accomplishment by growing one of these rare and beautiful native shrubs. It prefers a dry, sunny spot and slightly acid soil. Hairy manzanita is a good companion plant for the arbutus tree (*Arbutus menziesii*).

Indian-plum (*Oemleria cerasiformis*, also known as *Osmaronia cerasiformis*)
This many-stemmed shrub can grow to the size of a small tree, sometimes reaching heights of up to 15 feet (5 m). The alternate leaves are broadly lance-shaped and tapering, their colour a pale

green against the shrub's dark purplish-brown bark. The small, greenish-white blossoms hang in nodding terminal clusters; male and female flowers appear on separate plants. The purple, olive-sized, plum-like fruit ripens early and provides a strong attraction to birds and other wildlife. Although the raw fruit tastes slightly bitter, it makes a richly flavoured jelly. The plant has a distinctive odour; the scent of the blossoms has been compared to almonds, the leaves to cucumber or watermelon rind, and the bark, when torn, to wood alcohol.

Oemleria cerasiformis is found in the southern stretches of our region, along the sides of fields and roads and in open woods, particularly alder and maple groves. One of the earliest coastal plants to bloom—usually by early March —it is well known as a harbinger of spring.

Propagation and cultivation
Indian-plum is available at nurseries; to ensure pollination, ask for both male and female plants. Easy to grow from seed or from twig cuttings and preferring a moist, nitrogen-rich soil, this is a lovely shrub for a naturalistic setting or a woodland garden. *Oemleria cerasiformis* does well in association with red elderberry (*Sambucus racemosa*) and snowberry (*Symphoricarpos albus*).

Mock orange (*Philadelphus lewisii*)
Mock orange is a fitting plant to mention here for many reasons: it is a typical resident of forest edges and open, brushy areas; it is outstandingly beautiful; and its inclusion compensates for the unlikely gardening possibilities of *Arctostaphylos columbiana*. *Philadelphus lewisii* is a tried-and-true garden candidate. Indigenous to the lower tip of Vancouver Island and the southern stretches of our region, it is a native that is well known and appreciated abroad, but for some reason is passed over by our own gardeners.

Philadelphus lewisii is an elegant, erect, loosely-branched deciduous shrub which grows to 10 feet (3 m) in height. The light green, three-veined, oval leaves are pointed and slightly sandpapery to the touch. The broad (1- to 1 1/4-inch/2- to 3-cm) snow-white flowers usually have four petals and many golden stamens. These beautiful, fragrant spring-blooming blossoms grow in clusters at the ends of the branches.

Propagation and cultivation
Our mock orange is a highly adaptable, responsive plant and therefore its characteristics are quite variable. For this reason it is particularly well suited to gardens and can be cultivated in a variety of sites. It enjoys sun or shade and would be appropriate in a thicket or shrub border, or as an isolated specimen. As well as being beautiful and showy, it is a hardy, dependable and vigorous-growing plant.

Philadelphus lewisii can be propagated easily from cuttings taken in mid July. It can also be grown from seed scattered in large quantities—or by cold stratification for a higher yield. You will be happy to know that this excellent plant is easily available at nurseries.

Nootka rose or wild rose (*Rosa nutkana*)

Many edgeland plants are medium to low-growing shrubs, and a large number of these are members of the rose family (Rosaceae). The wild rose is an example. All wild roses are prickly shrubs with alternate, pinnately compound leaves. The flowers usually have five petals, and the hips are fleshy and round. Wild roses may be erect, climbing, or trailing on the ground.

A well-known and showy shrub of the Pacific coastal region, the Nootka rose (*Rosa nutkana*) is easily identified by its large pink blossoms (up to 2 inches/5 cm across), which are borne singly on the twigs and bloom in June and July. Another distinguishing feature is its subtle but pervasive scent. A rather spindly plant, it sometimes grows to 10 feet (3 m) in height. Its leaves are deciduous, and at the base of each leaf there is a pair of large prickles.

The Nootka rose and its many hybrids grow in profusion along coastal highways and woodland borders throughout the Pacific coastal region.

Propagation and cultivation

The wild roses can be propagated from seeds sown in the fall; to collect them, pick the hips as soon as they turn red, allow them to dry, then remove the seeds. However, they are very slow to germinate even when helped along by a winter of outside stratification. A much quicker—and quite easy—method is to transplant small offsets from the parent root. Take softwood cuttings in August or hardwood cuttings in late fall.

The Nootka rose does tolerate some shade but blooms best if given a spot in the garden where it will receive five or six hours of sun daily. It can handle dry or moist soil but prefers moist, but well-drained, nitrogen-rich soil. Mulch annually and remove dead stems. Prune in the fall.

The Nootka rose is available at nurseries. It is surprising that we do not see more of this beautiful—and accessible—shrub in our local gardens. It would enhance any landscape, particularly as part of a hedgerow.

Oceanspray (*Holodiscus discolor*)

This tall (to about 13 feet/4 m), many-stemmed shrub is a beautiful sight in midsummer, when it is covered with foamy sprays of creamy white blossoms. The many tiny flowers on close-set interlocking branches form dense, lilac-like clusters, about 4 to 7 inches (10 to 17 cm) long, at the ends of the branches. Later, they turn brown, and remain on the plant over winter. The loose clusters of dried husks give the winter plant a look that some consider bedraggled, but is regarded by others as distinctively attractive. The coarsely toothed leaves of oceanspray have an oval—sometimes triangular—shape. They are dull green in colour, becoming reddish-tinged in autumn. The plant's other common name, *ironwood,* derives from its very strong, hard wood.

Oceanspray grows on Vancouver Island and through the southern areas of our region, where it is possibly the most abundant flowering shrub. It is also found on one strip of land in the Bella Coola area. It grows in meadows, open dry woods, clearings, thickets, logged areas, ravine edges and coastal bluffs, and we cannot fail to notice it along the sides of byroads and highways.

Propagation and cultivation

The seeds of *Holodiscus discolor*, found in the tiny, hairy capsules, require extended periods of cold stratification for germination: 41°F (5°C) for 18 weeks. You would have more success taking semi-hardwood cuttings, or growing from suckers. However, this is one plant that reproduces itself prolifically; if you know of a stand of oceanspray on a friend's property you will find an abundance of seedlings. The plant is also available at nurseries.

Closely related to spiraea, *Holodiscus discolor* is one of the most appropriate native plants for garden cultivation, and is a popular plant with European gardeners. It tolerates sun or shade, but grows taller as the shade increases. Near the ocean it is very tolerant to salt spray. Oceanspray is at home in dry soil and can handle varying soil conditions, dry to moist, and is a good plant for disturbed land. It looks particularly appropriate in an informal garden setting, or as a hedge. Showy and fragrant, oceanspray is a valuable plant for attracting birds and insects to the garden. You may even find the intricately-woven nest of a bushtit hanging from this shrub.

Holodiscus discolor will be happy planted near Oregon grape (*Mahonia nervosa*).

Red-flowering currant (*Ribes sanguineum*)

A brilliant harbinger of spring, the beautiful red-flowering currant blooms from April to June, when it is covered with pendulous clusters of rose-coloured blossoms (with ten to twenty or more blossoms in each cluster). The flowers are followed by the crinkled, five-lobed leaves (like small maple leaves) which are dull green and have a hairy undersurface. The unpalatable, but tempting-looking, berries are round and black and covered with a waxy bluish bloom.

A deciduous shrub which grows from 3 to 10 feet (1 to 3 m) tall, *Ribes sanguineum* is found most commonly in dry, open woods and forest glades, on rocky slopes, logged areas and disturbed sites, or along roadside clearings. Its geographic range is from southern Vancouver Island southward through our region.

Propagation and cultivation
Red-flowering currant can be grown from seeds,

which require cold stratification at 32° to 36°F (0° to 2°C) for three months. It can also be started from hardwood cuttings taken in the fall, and it can be easily layered. *Ribes sanguineum* is quite broadly available at nurseries. There are several commercial cultivars, some with white blossoms.

Introduced to England and Europe in the mid nineteenth century, the red-flowering currant has been a favourite garden cultivar there ever since. It is a beautiful and appropriate plant in many garden sites. Although it can tolerate partial shade, it prefers sun and a dryish soil. This is a lovely plant for attracting the first hummingbirds of spring to your garden.

Salal (*Gaultheria shallon*)

One of the most familiar shrubs to those of us who live near the coast, salal is found in edgeland habitats throughout the Pacific coastal region, except at the northern extremities. It is common along coastal forest borders, where it sometimes forms impenetrable thickets. It also frequents the understory of both dry and wet coniferous forests. Its growth habit can be creeping to erect and of variable height (6 inches to 16 feet/15 cm to 5 m tall). The shiny, leathery green leaves, which are about 1 to 2 inches (2 to 4 cm) long, are roundly oval, sometimes almost heart-shaped. The handsome evergreen foliage is popular in floral arrangements. The plant bears small pinkish-white flowers and abundant blue-black berries.

Propagation and cultivation
The tiny salal seeds germinate well in a moist peat-sand mixture. This is a slow process, taking two to three years for the seedlings to grow to about 4 inches (10 cm). Prick out the seedlings into loam/peat flats for one year, then move to 4-inch (10-cm) pots or a holding bed. Other methods to try are root cuttings or cuttings of new wood taken in late summer. Fortunately, this popular shrub is widely available commercially.

Salal can tolerate open sun or moderate shade and does well in most soil types, although it wants moisture around its roots. A warning: salal is an aggressive plant and once established, spreads rapidly from underground stems.

Salal is attractive in a border or massed around rhododendrons. It is particularly appropriate planted densely as a ground cover in a woodland garden. It enjoys the company of the conifers and is also happy planted near Oregon grape (*Mahonia nervosa*).

Salmonberry (*Rubus spectabilis*)
The salmonberry is a branching, slightly thorny-stemmed shrub which can grow to over 10 feet (3 m) in height and in winter is lent distinction by its golden, satiny bark. This long-blooming bramble bush flowers throughout the spring.

Sometimes partially hidden beneath the leaves, the pretty, reddish-pink nodding blossoms are quite large (over 1 inch/3 cm across). The sharp-toothed, dark green leaves usually grow as three leaflets. Salmonberry has an edible fruit (its tastiness appears to be a question of personal preference), which appears from June to August in the form of a raspberry-like berry, either yellowish-orange or red in colour.

Throughout our region, *Rubus spectabilis* is quite commonly found along roadsides, often forming dense, tangled thickets. It is also found in damp or swampy bottomlands or around the edges of marshes and creeks.

Propagation and cultivation
Salmonberry can be easily planted from rooted runners. It is also available at specialist nurseries. The best garden location for this pretty but brambly shrub is in a wild part of the garden, in a damp to wet site, sunny or shady. It is a good plant for attracting birds to the garden. *Rubus spectabilis* is an excellent companion plant to many other species: red alder (*Alnus rubra*), lady fern (*Athyrium filix-femina*), swamp lantern (*Lysichitum americanum*), devil's club (*Oplopanax horridus*), thimbleberry (*Rubus parviflorus*) and foam flower (*Tiarella trifoliata*).

Saskatoon berry/service berry
(*Amelanchier alnifolia*)

This shrub sometimes grows to the size of a small tree, occasionally reaching heights of over 15 feet (5 m). The smooth bark is brown or grey and the rounded, oval leaves are bluish-green. Bright white flowers appear in short, leafy clusters toward the ends of the branches. The small, globe-shaped, berry-like fruit is purplish-black, covered with a greyish bloom. The fruit quality is quite variable; it can dry out quickly, becoming mealy and flavourless, but before this stage it is juicy and sweet. Here on the coast we usually encounter berries of a poor, mealy quality.

Amelanchier alnifolia thrives throughout our region along rocky shorelines, on bluffs and slopes, in meadows, thickets and dry to moist open forests, and at roadside edges.

Propagation and cultivation

Saskatoons can be grown from seed or self-sown seedlings. Commercially available, the bush is easy to cultivate on a sunny, well-drained soil. Plant it in late winter or early spring in a moderately rich, but not heavily fertilized soil, and give it mulch and water.

As well as a yield of delicious fruit for baking in pies or eating off the tree, the Saskatoon can provide a showy display for your garden. It is a beautiful sight in the spring, when the bloom is at its peak, or in the fall, when the yellow-to-red leaves provide bright autumn colour.

Herbaceous Plants

Fireweed (*Epilobium angustifolium*)

Most of us are familiar with the sight of dense stands of this bright flower in disturbed areas throughout our region, particularly in clearings and recently logged or burned sites (hence the common name). It also appears along roads, railways, and riverbeds, in thickets, and in abandoned fields. *Epilobium angustifolium* is an unusually tall flower, often growing to well over 3 feet (1 m), and has smooth, leafy stems and lance-shaped leaves up to 8 inches (20 cm) long. Fireweed is a colourful, showy plant. The flowers are large (to 1 inch/2 to 4 cm across) plumes of vivid rose-pink with conspicuously long, drooping white pistils. They bloom during the summer, and at the end of the season prolifically disgorge myriad fluffy white seed-parachutes from the burst seed pods.

Propagation and cultivation

Epilobium angustifolium is included here because it plays such a significant role in the wild by indicating increased decomposition of plant materials in disturbed sites. It tolerates various soil conditions but prefers a sunny location. Fireweed transplants easily from pieces of the underground stem, and is easy to establish but extremely invasive. Cut it back to the ground after flowering, just before it goes to seed.

Not every gardener will readily consider this plant for the flower garden, but you may give it some thought if you have some disturbed land to which you would like to lend some cheerful colour. A white-flowered cultivar is also available.

One of the rewards of growing fireweed is the excellent honey it produces.

Pearly everlasting (*Anaphalis margaritacea*)

This vigorous and robust flowering perennial is widely used in dry flower arrangements. The stiff, erect stems reach 8 to 24 inches (20 to 60 cm) in height. Dense woolly hairs cover the stem surface and the undersides of the alternate, narrow leaves. Near the top of each stem several short branches each bear four to eight small heads of flowers, which have the typical composition of the aster (Compositae) family, to which this plant belongs. Each yellowish floral disk is densely packed with individual male and female florets, forming dense, flat-topped structures. On each head, many pearly white dry bracts crowd around the main structure of the blossom.

Except in the northernmost reaches, pearly everlasting can be found throughout this region in open forests, clearings, meadows, rocky slopes, and particularly along roadsides. In fact, it grows across Canada as far east as Newfoundland, ranging from southern Alaska far south into the United States.

Propagation and cultivation
Grown from rhizomes, *Anaphalis margaritacea* is very easy to propagate, and is available from garden centres. To start a new plant, simply remove pieces of rhizome and replant in a moist, sunny site. Or you can sow seeds in fall or early spring and transplant the seedlings the following autumn. To harvest the flower for dry bouquets, pick the stalks just before the blooms open and hang them upside down to dry.

A suitable plant for disturbed sites, pearly everlasting can tolerate almost any soil, as long as the site is well-drained. It is interesting to note that, in a reversal from the common pattern, this plant has been introduced into Europe from North America.

Anaphalis margaritacea has been used as a companion to tansy (*Tanacetum douglasii*), which inhabits coastal sand dunes, and mugwort (*Artemisia ludoviciana*), a species more common to regions drier than ours.

Tiger lily/Columbia lily
(*Lilium columbianum*)
Lilium columbianum, the wild tiger lily, is the coastal region's most familiar, true native lily. The common name is probably derived from the colours of the flowers, but our tiger lily is quite different from the large Asian exotic of the same name. Our vibrant orange beauty is highly decorative amid the wild thickets of its native home.

From a deep-seated true bulb that is white, oval and thickly-scaled grows a stiff, narrow, greenish stalk up to 4 feet (1.25 m) in height. At the top of this tall leafy stem the showy, nodding flowers hang, bell-like, in open clusters, with the petals curving backward in a graceful Turks' cap. The bright orange flowers are about 2 inches (5 cm) across, with deep red or purple spots near the centre. The dark green leaves are narrowly lance-shaped, arranged in several whorls which circle the stem at intervals.

The typical native habitat of the tiger lily includes roadsides, open forest, thickets, clearings, meadows and well-drained mountain slopes. It ranges from northern Vancouver Island and the Powell River area southward through the region.

Propagation and cultivation
Tiger lilies can be grown from seed, but the process is slow. Sow in pots in humus-rich sandy soil in late fall or early winter to undergo a cold season. They should germinate the following spring, or maybe not for another year. After a year or two in the pot, transplant the bulb during the fall dormant season to its permanent garden location. A total of three to five years must pass before the plant will be large enough for flowers to appear. This will occur from late May to early July, depending on the local climate.

An easier option is to obtain the plants or bulbs from a specialist nursery. Plant bulbs in the fall or early spring. Garden-grown bulbs can be divided in the fall, or their bulb scales can be used for propagation. When planting, select a partly shaded site with shrub or perennial cover that will keep the soil cool and moist but allow the lily stalk—leaves and all—to emerge into the sunlight. The soil must be very well drained, sandy and rich in organic matter such as compost. Lily bulbs suffer from slug attacks, so if you have a slug problem try a very coarse sand.

Tiger lilies do not like being disturbed during the growing season and may dwindle away under the wrong conditions. Once established, however, the lily should flower for many years.

Western red columbine (*Aquilegia formosa*)

The columbine is a well-known and beloved wildflower common throughout our region from the lowlands to the timberline. This charming, eye-catching little plant blooms from May to August along roads, streams, forest fringes, and mountain meadows. Columbines grow in almost every area of our region.

Growing from a taproot, *Aquilegia formosa* has a stem about 39" (1 m) high and divided basal leaves. The nodding crimson and yellow flowers are composed of five long petals which are turned backward and upward to form tubular spurs.

Propagation and cultivation

Columbines grow very easily from seed, but do not use seed taken from garden plants; wild columbines hybridize with cultivated species. Collect the black, wrinkled *Aquilegia formosa* seeds in late summer and plant before winter; the seed has a life span of about three months. They will germinate the first spring and send up their flowering stems the second summer. Western red columbine is available at specialist nurseries.

Aquilegia formosa is a superb garden species. Plant it in a moist, sunny or semishaded site and it will provide colour for your flower garden for many years, and hummingbirds and swallowtail butterflies will flock to it for its nectar.

Forest

Much of the forest and woodland of our Pacific coastal region receives a rainfall of well over 100 inches (250 cm) yearly, which is the determining criteria for the definition of *rainforest*. While only a fragment of our present wooded areas are original old-growth forests (which have existed since the retreat of the last ice age, about 10,000 years ago), it is nonetheless accurate to refer to most of the forested area in this region as *temperate rainforest*.

These forests extend along the Pacific coast from Alaska to northern California—a distance of almost 1,700 miles (2,800 km). They are the most extensive and productive temperate rainforests in the world. They are also among the most massive ecosystems on earth, and support the greatest amount of biological diversity found anywhere in North America. By nature's design, within the forest all forms of organic matter are recycled back into the living elements. A vast array of interdependent life-forms are supported by the environment within this complex, intricately balanced ecosystem.

Our forests do not experience the steamy temperatures of the jungles of the southern hemisphere or the frigid extremes of the tundra. The climate here is moderate: mild temperatures are common year-round, with generally cool summers and winters that are not unduly harsh. This cool, wet, but moderate climate explains the richness and diversity of the rainforest. The wide medley of vegetation that thrives within the forest includes shrubs, wildflowers, grasses, sedges, ferns, mosses, lichens, and fungi. Along with the birds that roost and nest in the sheltering canopy of the trees, a multitude of varied wildlife inhabit and feed from live trees as well as decaying trees and logs, the shrubby foliage, and the litter of the forest floor. Insects, bats, amphibians, reptiles, and small mammals forage and seek shelter here. Salmon spawn in the forest streams. Large mammals, such as deer, elk and bear, feed on the forest's abundant vegetation and find protective cover within its shelter.

Unlike other coastal regions of the world, where the forests are usually mixed or deciduous, the dominant trees of our temperate forests are conifers, which have the special property of being able to use sunlight and grow almost year-round. Some of the largest and oldest trees on earth are found here. (A few individuals are well over 1,000 years old.)

The intricacies of the plant relationships within the forest ecosystem cannot be described simply. In very basic terms, the vegetative layers of the forest can be broken down into canopy, substory, and ground layer, or, even more simply, canopy and understory. The tall trees, which often reach a height of over 300 feet (92 m), form the canopy layer of the forest. The substory is made up of a variety of shrubs and smaller trees. A dense screen is formed by the crowns of trees touching overhead in the canopy layer and the shrubs massing thickly in the substory. This screen filters out most light from the forest floor. The shade-tolerant plants that grow on the cool forest floor, often producing a continuous mat, make up the forest's ground layer of vegetation.

A matter of consideration is the age of the forest, which has a huge effect on its composition. With large-scale forestry has come a shift in the landscape from older forests to a predominance of younger forests. Within the more mature forest there are varying degrees of shade. The canopy is somewhat patchy and irregular because it is multi-layered and because trees and limbs fall, leaving gaps where young shrubs and saplings spring up to fill the space. When we walk through these older forests we observe the shifting patterns of light as we move from sun-touched openings to the interior gloom of the forest's depths.

The predominant trees and forest plants vary within the region, dependent largely upon the amount of rainfall and moisture available. Near the coast, in the moister sites, Sitka spruce (*Picea sitchensis*) is dominant. Farther inland, western red cedar (*Thuja plicata*) and western hemlock (*Tsuga heterophylla*) prevail. On the driest coastal forest sites the dominant species is Douglas-fir (*Pseudotsuga menziesii*). In southern sections of the region (southeastern Vancouver Island, the Gulf and San Juan Islands, the east side of the Olympic Peninsula, and in the Willamette Valley), the most extensive type of forest is the rainshadow forest. The most diverse forest type in the region in terms of total numbers of plant species, this is dry, open forest typified by stands of Douglas-fir, Garry oak (*Quercus garryana*) and sometimes *Arbutus menziesii*.

The hardwood stands are less widespread than the conifers in the Pacific coastal region, and are frequently interspersed among them. Hardwood forests usually contain such deciduous, broadleaf trees as bigleaf maple (*Acer macrophyllum*) and red alder (*Alnus rubra*). They often form groves, particularly in moister sites. They provide a source of food for species of wildlife that are not well adapted to coniferous groves. Because the overhead canopy is somewhat less dense, ground-layer plants of deciduous forest receive a little more sun than those in coniferous areas and therefore will be somewhat less shade tolerant when cultivated.

West coast rainforests are important, biologically diverse systems; they support a wide variety of plant and animal species found nowhere else in North America. In addition, they store vast amounts of carbon (organic material) to help offset the greenhouse effect, they are a valuable source of oxygen to the atmosphere, and they act as natural filtering systems for our water. Our rainforest estuaries are among the most productive in the world.

As well as their practical purposes, our forests have unparalleled value as wilderness. When we enter an old-growth rainforest, most of us sense a special quality, an almost spiritual atmosphere, due possibly to the cathedral-like grandeur of the trees, the muted tone of the light, the hushed silence, and the vastness.

Today, the last few remnants of old-growth coastal rainforest are in serious jeopardy. We owe it to ourselves and to future generations to act wisely as the stewards of these forests.

If you have an appropriate garden site, you may be able to contribute to the restoration of the forest habitat. Many forest plants are beautifully ornamental and suitable for cultivation. They will feel at home in your garden if you provide the conditions of their forest homes, such as a cool-moderate microclimate and the overhead shade of some large trees. The optimum soil condition is somewhat acidic and rich in humus, with a texture that is loam to sandy loam with gravelly stones. Your soil should be deeper than 3 feet (1 m) over bedrock and able to retain some moisture year-round, with some seepage areas.

Trees

Bigleaf maple (*Acer macrophyllum*)

This noble deciduous tree can grow as tall as 100 feet (30 m) and has a uniquely distinctive form. Huge vertical limbs emerge from soaring lateral branches arising from the squat, massive trunk. Smooth and green when young, the bark becomes grey-brown and ridged in an old specimen. The bark and branches are often covered with mosses, lichens and ferns; in fact, there are more mosses and other plants associated with *Acer macrophyllum* than with any other tree species in our region.

The leaves of this majestically spreading shade tree are the largest of any in the province of British Columbia. Typically shaped maple leaves, they are often more than 12 inches (30 cm) across, with three to five lobes, dark green turning yellow before they fall in the autumn. In winter, fat green buds develop at the ends of the branches. In the spring the long cylindrical clusters of numerous bowl-shaped, greenish-yellow flowers burst into bloom. The fruit is the golden-brown V-shaped wing, or samara, typical of the maple.

Acer macrophyllum ranges from Vancouver Island and the adjacent mainland, south along the coast to California. It inhabits dry to moist sites, often alongside Douglas-fir (*Pseudotsuga menziesii*). In the forest it is frequently found in stands interspersed among the conifers. It enjoys the moist rich soils along rivers, streams and floodplains and can be found on moist rocky slopes.

Propagation and cultivation

The seedlings of the bigleaf maple, which are often found in profusion beneath the parent tree, can be easily transplanted in winter or spring, or the plant can be raised from seed and planted in ordinary soil. Also called *broadleaf maple,* this tree is available from nurseries.

This is another one of our natives that, inexplicably, has not widely caught on as a garden plant in spite of its outstanding value as a shade tree. It is a wonderful specimen for street planting or for a large yard or park, its airy canopy casting a soft, filtered shade on the ground below. Because it voraciously absorbs the moisture at its roots, the bigleaf maple may present difficulties in growing some plants around its base. Appropriate companion plants that thrive in its shade are salal (*Gaultheria shallon*), Oregon grape (*Mahonia* spp.), and sword fern (*Polystichum munitum*).

Vine maple (*Acer circinatum*)

In the open, this is a small, upright tree sometimes growing to a height of 21 feet (6.4 m), but in the forest understory it is more often a broadly spreading shrub. It usually has several trunks with sprawling branches, pale green when young and turning brown with age. Showy upright clusters of small white flowers with wine-coloured sepals appear in April, before the tree is in full leaf. The large, palmately veined leaves, which grow in a distinctive tiered pattern, are shallowly lobed, with toothed margins. In the fall they become golden in the shade, or bright red in full sun, providing the most vivid autumn colouring of any coastal tree or shrub. The seeds are the typical samara, or keys, of the maple, with two wings that stretch in an almost straight line.

Found in southern sections of the region, vine maples flourish in moist places, often in forest understory, but also at edges of forests, meadows and brush fields. Basket-like nests of the tiny vireo can sometimes be found hanging in the forks of its branches.

Propagation and cultivation

Acer circinatum can be grown from seeds sown shortly after harvesting in the fall, in rich sandy loam. It can also be propagated from well-rooted, layered branches. An increasingly favourite plant of landscape designers, vine maple is commercially available. Outstanding as a garden attraction, it is very shade-tolerant, preferring moisture at its roots. A vine maple can be planted as a single ornamental in the garden, but is particularly showy when massed in drifts. It does well in the shade of conifers, and also

in association with sword fern (*Polystichum munitum*).

Western or Pacific flowering dogwood (*Cornus nuttallii*)

This beautiful flowering tree often appears as a small cluster because it is common for many trunks to branch outward from a single base. It is relatively small by forest standards; although known to reach a height of 65 feet (20 m), it quite often appears as a bushy shrub less than 10 feet (3 m) tall. It grows with scattered frequency in woodland and edgeland habitats of the coastal region ranging from southern British Columbia to southern California.

This is a tree to enjoy throughout the year. The abundant blossoms appear before the leaves from April to June and often again in the early fall, when the tree is in full foliage. The beautiful creamy blossoms that we see are actually four, five or six large bracts (1 to 3 inches/2 to 7 cm long) surrounding a small, tight cluster of the true flowers, which are tiny (about 1/4 inch/ 5 mm wide), greenish-white, and inconspicuous.

The deciduous leaves usually cluster toward the ends of the branches. They are oval with sharply pointed tips and grow to about 4 inches (10 cm) long, with the distinctive dogwood characteristic veins, curving parallel to the leaf edges. These dark green, waxy-edged leaves turn pinkish-purple in the fall. Once the petals have fallen, the tiny flower heads are replaced by clusters of brilliant scarlet berries. In winter, the symmetrical branches of this tree present a stark, eye-catching beauty of their own.

Propagation and cultivation

If you wish to grow this tree yourself, the best method of propagation is from seed. Harvest the seeds in the fall, remove the fleshy coat, and plant as soon as possible in well-mulched outdoor seed flats. To plant from cuttings, take them in the early summer and use a rooting hormone. Layering is another alternative.

Attractive in all seasons, the western flowering dogwood is a desirable garden ornamental. The floral emblem of British Columbia (and the only tree legally protected by this province), it is considered to be among the world's finest flowering trees.

Cornus nuttallii tolerates partial shade and, once established, does not require much watering. Unfortunately, it is quite vulnerable to disease and is particularly sensitive to any damage to the trunk. It is at its best when planted alongside coniferous evergreen trees, or with red alder (*Alnus rubra*).

Western red cedar (*Thuja plicata*)

One of the most beautiful giants of the coastal forest, the western red cedar can grow to 195 feet (60 m) tall and live for over a thousand years. This is a conifer which does not have needles: the foliage is tiny scaled leaves. The overlapping shingled arrangement looks like a flattened braid, giving a feathery, frond-like appearance to the long, irregular, downward-pointing branches. The leaves are a glossy yellowish-green which, on a mature tree, turn brown and are shed in the fall. When the foliage is crushed it has an unusual, sweet fragrance. The small, elongated seed cones are about 1/2 inch (1 cm) long. They grow in loose clusters and remain on the tree over winter.

Propagation and cultivation
Cold stratification is recommended for propagating the seeds. Soak them in water for about 24 hours and then gently towel dry. Place the seeds in a plastic bag in the refrigerator for approximately 21 to 28 days. Shake the bag gently once a week to help keep the air circu-

lating. Following this stage, place the seeds in a watered peat pocket in a warm location. The seeds should germinate in about 21 days.

Be careful not to overwater the peat pocket or let it dry out. In the spring, when the threat of frost has passed, if the seedlings have grown to about 2 inches (5 cm) tall, they can be planted outside.

A much simpler but less certain method is to plant the seeds in a pot directly outside in the fall, hoping they will germinate in the spring. *Thuja plicata* can also be grown from cuttings.

Large as it is in its mature form, this tree makes a beautiful and versatile garden ornamental. Western red cedar is much appreciated in Britain, where it is frequently used as garden architecture, forming a beautiful screen. Here, we often use it for tall hedges or clump plantings, or as perimeter trees in large gardens and parks. It can tolerate shade and grow in a wide variety of soil and moisture conditions. The drawback to gardening with cedar trees is that very few understory plants are able to flourish around their roots.

In nature, *Thuja plicata* sometimes grows in pure stands, but more often is found in mixed groves throughout our region with such other trees as sitka spruce (*Picea sitchensis*), western hemlock, (*Tsuga heterophylla*), bigleaf maple (*Acer macrophyllum*), red alder (*Alnus rubra*), Pacific yew (*Taxus brevifolia*) and grand fir (*Abies grandis*). Although a grouping of any of these large trees could be overpowering for the average-sized garden, if you have the room you might consider planting one or two of these species near your western red cedar. Many of them are available at nurseries.

Shrubs

Devil's club (*Oplopanax horridus*)

Found in extensive dense clumps in moist woods throughout our coastal region, this prickly shrub has menacing spines on its stems and on the undersides of its enormous (up to 16 inches/40 cm wide), maple-shaped leaves. Its small, whitish flowers grow in terminal clusters and are relatively nondescript in appearance. The fruit, however, is showy and handsome: large clusters of shiny red berries that are deliciously attractive to bears (but not humans).

Propagation and cultivation

An easy plant to propagate from cuttings, devil's club is just beginning to be available commercially. It can also be started from seed, but the seeds seem to need scarification in order to germinate, and the plant will be slow to establish. With its almost tropical-looking foliage it is highly decorative in a variety of garden settings, as long as it is kept in full shade. Try it in a woodland garden, a shrub border, or on its own as a garden ornamental—it has even been used as a container plant. It is useful, as well, for privacy screening—its prickliness discourages unwelcome visitors. Be careful when working with this shrub; the spines are poisonous and inflict nasty scratches which become sore and inflamed.

In the wild *Oplopanax horridus* is associated with such ferns as sword fern (*Polystichum munitum*), oak fern (*Gymnocarpium dryopteris*) and lady fern (*Athyrium filix-femina*), as well as baneberry (*Actaea rubra*) and foam-flowers (*Tiarella* spp.). These would be interesting combinations to try in the garden.

Dull Oregon grape (*Mahonia nervosa*)

Found in a dry woodland more commonly than in a damp forest, Oregon grape is a stiff-branched evergreen understory shrub which does not grow much taller than 2 feet (60 cm). The oblong leaves are green and leathery, with prominent spiny teeth, like a holly tree. The clusters of yellow flowers appear in April, May and June, followed by numerous grapelike (and edible—they make delicious jelly) blue berries which have a dull grey bloom. *Mahonia nervosa* is also known botanically as *Berberis nervosa*.

Propagation and cultivation

Oregon grape can be propagated from seed. Collect the mature seeds and sow immediately in damp peat moss in a cool spot outdoors in flats, or in their permanent location, and cover them with a thin layer of mulch. Germination usually occurs the following spring but sometimes the process is slow, making it necessary to maintain the flats for two years, with germination occurring after the second winter. Transplant the seedlings to pots after the first growing season and move to the garden after the second. *Mahonia nervosa* is rather slow to establish, but it is quite widely available in nurseries. It is also easily propagated by root divisions made in the spring, or cuttings of green twigs made in the early summer. Plant divisions or rooted cuttings 1 foot (30 cm) apart and keep them moist, but not wet, until reestablished.

Oregon grape is common in the southern areas of our region. It is very attractive in the garden, either in a woodland setting, or as a low evergreen for the border. It prefers shade but it is a good drought-tolerant plant, tolerating dry to moist soil conditions. The other *Mahonia*, tall Oregon grape (*M. aquifolium*), is even more suited to dry conditions, and is often found on rather rocky sites.

Mahonia nervosa will enjoy being planted near salal (*Gaultheria shallon*) and sword fern (*Polystichum munitum*).

Evergreen huckleberry (*Vaccinium ovatum*)

Among the many huckleberries in our region, this shrub is the tallest, growing from 3 to 12 feet (1 to 4 m). It branches profusely and has shiny, dark green leaves which are sharp-toothed and leathery. From April to July the small, pinkish-white, bell-shaped blossoms appear in clusters along the slightly hairy stems.

The colour of the small (1/4-inch/2 mm-wide), globe-shaped berry of the evergreen huckleberry matures from reddish-brown to glossy black. The taste of the fruit also alters, from slightly bitter in the young berry to the sweeter blueberry flavour of the mature fruit, which sometimes remains on the plant until December.

The evergreen huckleberry is found growing in clumps in moist coniferous forests at low elevations, often on the beach fringe, in the southern half of our region.

Propagation and cultivation

Vaccinium ovatum can be propagated from winter hardwood cuttings: dip the cutting in rooting hormone and place in sandy peat. You can sow the tiny seeds in the fall in peaty soil and keep them moist in a shady spot, but don't expect a shrub for about three years from seeding. Evergreen huckleberry is available at specialist nurseries and, as with any native plant, should not be dug in the wild for ethical reasons. In this case there are also practical reasons for not transplanting from the wild, as the plants invariably fail to survive in the garden setting.

Evergreen huckleberry is a lovely plant for a moist part of the garden, in shade or semishade. The soil should be sandy, acid, and rich in humus or peat. This is a plant that benefits from an organic mulch to conserve moisture at all times of the year. Plant it as a companion to sword fern (*Polystichum munitum*), near conifers if possible.

Pacific rhododendron (*Rhododendron macrophyllum*)

This glorious shrub forms an extensive understory in coniferous and mixed forests throughout the southern part of our region, lending them delightful late-spring colour. It is very similar to the cultivated varieties of rhododendron which are so much more familiar to us, and as beautiful as many. In its tallest form it can grow to 24 feet (8 m) in height; those plants that grow shorter are thicker and more spreading. This evergreen species has the typical thick, leathery rhododendron leaves which are oblong-elliptic in shape and can grow from 3 to 8 inches (8 to 20 cm) long. The large, rose-purple flowers are borne in round clusters which are sometimes 6 inches (15 cm) across, producing a spectacular floral display in late spring.

Propagation and cultivation

Although it is a slow process, *Rhododendron macrophyllum* can be grown from seed. Collect the seeds after the bloom is over, as soon as the capsules turn brown. Sprinkle the seeds into flats, over a germinating mix of sand and peat moss, cover with some fine gravel for protection, then place a plastic cover over the flats. The seeds need humidity, so mist regularly. They will germinate in about three weeks, but it will take a whole growing season (four to six months) before you can put the seedlings outside. This shrub can also be propagated from cuttings, or by layering. The good news is that Pacific rhododendron is now available at nurseries (and not just specialists).

Rhododendron macrophyllum can tolerate moist to dry soil and varying degrees of sun and shade. Its profuse blooms make a glorious display in a woodland garden. This lovely shrub grows well near Douglas-fir (*Pseudotsuga menziesii*) or western hemlock (*Tsuga heterophylla*). It can be successfully underplanted with the annual Siberian miner's lettuce (*Claytonia sibirica*).

Herbaceous plants

Bunchberry (*Cornus unalaschkensis*)

Sometimes thought of as a shrub, this low-trailing perennial grows from 2 to 10 inches (5 to 25 cm) tall. In moist coastal forests and openings it sometimes forms a beautiful carpet on the forest floor, or often grows on tree trunks, logs and stumps. The broad leaves form a circle which supports a single bloom; this is not a flower, but a set of four white bracts which surround the actual blossoms—small florets forming a tiny central cushion. These blossom in May, then mature into bunches of showy red berries, making a spectacular display in late summer and early fall.

Propagation and cultivation

Cornus unalaschkensis is now available at some specialist nurseries. It roots easily from dormant cuttings, or it can be planted from seed. Cold stratification can be used, but there is an easier method: plant the seeds in a peat and sand mixture. Keeping them moist, leave the seeds outdoors for the winter and wait for germination in the spring. Some of the seeds will germinate in the first year; some will wait until the following spring.

Bunchberry is a spectacular plant that spreads to form a lush, low ground cover, a beautiful addition to the garden. It wants a shady spot with acid, gritty soil that retains some moisture for most of the year. This is a good plant to grow on a fallen log or some decaying wood placed on the ground, or try it under azaleas or vine maple (*Acer circinatum*). A secluded part of the garden is the best place for bunchberry, as it is extremely sensitive to root disturbance.

A similar species, found a little to the east of our region in more interior areas, is *Cornus canadensis*.

False Solomon's seal (*Smilacina racemosa*)

This boldly attractive plant can grow up to 3 feet (1 m) tall. Its small creamy-white flowers grow in abundant plume-like clusters at the tips of profuse unbranched stems. The flowers bloom from April to June, then give way to reddish-coloured berries. The parallel-veined leaves are long (up to 8 inches/20 cm), broad and elliptical, alternating along the stem in two rows.

Propagation and cultivation

Smilacina racemosa can be propagated from seed, but the process requires cold stratification, and even then the seeds often take two years to germinate. The far easier and more satisfactory method is to plant from rhizome divisions, taken in the fall or early spring. Make sure there is at least one bud on each rhizome piece. Spacing them at 12-inch (30-cm) intervals, place the divisions horizontally at a depth of 1 1/2 inches (4 cm), covering with a thin layer of mulch. You can expect the plants to flower in the second year. This handsome plant is now available at some specialist nurseries.

False Solomon's seal is found throughout our region except on the Queen Charlottes and in the most northern reaches. It is best grown in an open woodland setting (partial to full shade), in moist, humus-rich, somewhat acidic soil. Its frequent companions in the wild are sword fern (*Polystichum munitum*), small-flowered fairybells (*Disporum hookeri*), wood sorrel (*Oxalis oregana*), and western bleeding heart (*Dicentra formosa*).

Vanilla leaf (*Achlys triphylla*)

One of the most common woodland ground covers on Vancouver Island and southward through the region is the vanilla leaf, which in spring lights up the forest floor with its tiny white flowers. These flowers are actually many florets, which in June arise in a showy spike from a stiff stalk that sticks up above the leaves. Each leaf has three fan-shaped leaflets. In some areas of the forest, these leaves will form a dense, solid, light green carpet about 12 inches (30 cm) high, covering the forest floor. When dried or wilting, the leaves emit a sweet, vanilla-like fragrance. The leaves die back in the fall until about March.

Propagation and cultivation

Vanilla leaf is available at specialist nurseries. It can be propagated from seed or rhizomes; divide the rhizomes in the spring. It makes a beautiful, dense ground cover in a very shady woodland garden under shrubs and trees. *Achlys triphylla* is particularly at home planted with sword fern (*Polystichum munitum*).

Western bleeding heart (*Dicentra formosa*)

Our wild bleeding heart is much like the introduced plant we commonly grow in our gardens, except somewhat smaller and with a longer flowering season—from spring to late summer. Its height varies from 6 to 20 inches (15 to 50 cm), and its basal leaves are almost as high as the stem of the plant. The leaves are much divided into many narrow segments, delicately fringed and fern-like, and so numerous that they almost hide the drooping row of heart-shaped pink flowers.

Propagation and cultivation

The easiest propagation method is root division. Divide the rhizomes during the fall or in early spring before leaves appear. Plant large divisions about 1 1/4 inches (3 cm) deep and smaller ones about 1/2 inch (1.5 cm) deep, and then mulch. Bleeding heart can also be propagated from seed; the process is fairly simple, but it takes several years to grow from seed to flowering plants. Collect fresh seeds in the summer, remove the oily, starchy appendages known as *elaiosomes*, and plant the seeds outdoors 1/4 inch (1 cm) deep and mulch lightly. The plant is available at nurseries.

Dicentra formosa ranges from Bella Coola south through our region. In the wild, it is most frequently found in the understory of deciduous, broadleaf forests, so it will enjoy the company of those trees in your garden. It is also a good companion plant to false Solomon's seal (*Smilacina racemosa*).

Wood sorrel (*Oxalis oregana*)

Thriving in woodland shade, wood sorrel will sometimes be found completely carpeting the forest floor. This lovely little plant grows from 2 to 6 inches (5 to 15 cm) high. The leaves are described as *obcordate,* which means reverse heart-shaped, or clover-shaped. They are also all basal, growing on stalks from the base of the plant. The leaves fold together at night and on cloudy days, and droop when exposed to strong sunlight. The flowers grow singly on each slender stem. Blooming from February to July, depending upon the site, they are white or pink and only about 1/2 to 3/4 inch (12 to 20 mm) long. The flowers are tucked down between the leaves, so that the overall effect of a mass of these plants is of a dense carpet of leaves, which are often more noticeable than the flowers.

Wood sorrel is found sparsely in the southern Queen Charlotte Islands and southwest Vancouver Island; it is more common from the Olympic Peninsula south along the coast to California.

Propagation and cultivation
Oxalis oregana is available at specialist nurseries. It grows from scaly underground rhizomes and is easily propagated from rhizome pieces buried just below the soil surface, with attached buds and leaves just emerging at the surface of the ground.

Wood sorrel will flourish in a shady spot with a rich, humic soil. Under these conditions it spreads quite rapidly, and makes a wonderful ground cover for a large garden. It also does well in dry shade, where its spread is less rampant.

Oxalis oregana enjoys the company of bleeding heart (*Dicentra formosa*), and is one of the few plants I know that thrives around the roots of a western red cedar (*Thuja plicata*). Because of its low light requirement, it can perform well as a house plant.

Invasive intruder
Spurge laurel (*Daphne laureola*)
Although not a menace to the same degree as broom or purple loosestrife, spurge laurel can be an aggravating nuisance in a woodland garden, popping up unbidden in random spots, especially in areas of heavy shade. This evergreen deciduous plant grows about 3 to 4 feet (1 to 1.5 m) tall, with stalkless clusters of yellow, scented flowers nestled among glossy, dark green leaves. If this strange plant appears unexpectedly in your garden, unless you enjoy its presence you may want to remove it immediately; when it appears in one spot, you can be certain that before long it will crop up in some other spot close by.

Although we know that the seeds of this unwelcome exotic are randomly deposited by birds, there is something rather sinister about the way it mysteriously pops up in shady gardens.

Because the roots are so tenacious, a mature plant is almost impossible to pull out; an easier way to eradicate it is to cut the stem just below ground level, letting the roots decay.

Grasslands

Grasslands, or meadow systems, occur particularly in the south of our Pacific coastal region. Some of these are natural, reflecting soil and environmental conditions. Others were created by the burning of tree and shrub cover, usually by early aboriginal peoples. At one time, before the coming of European settlers, these meadow systems occupied vast tracts of land throughout some sections of this region; now they have been greatly reduced. According to some botanical authorities, these few remaining communities are in decline, which means survival of some of our most beautiful and rare native plants is threatened. Severely invading broom has been among the many hazards to this plant community.

Grassland communities usually consist of stands of Garry oak (*Quercus garryana*)—sometimes in association with other trees such as Douglas-fir (*Pseudotsuga menziesii*) or arbutus (*Arbutus menziesii*)—and a variety of understory plants, including many native wildflowers, grasses and shrubs. The oak stands vary from dense, closed-canopy forests to open savanna with scattered trees in a predominantly grassland area, sometimes extending to shallow-soil rocky slopes. This rare system forms one of the richest, most diverse plant communities in the Pacific coastal region and beyond.

In the Pacific coastal region, the distribution of this system extends from southern and eastern Vancouver Island to the Gulf islands and the lower Fraser Valley, through the Puget Sound lowlands and the Willamette Valley, and into the lower reaches of the Siskiyou and Klamath ranges.

A Garry oak plant community is a beautiful sight to behold, particularly in the spring: a meadow of grasses and wildflowers spread out under an open canopy of oak trees. In the north-ern Pacific coastal region, most of the landscapes associated with Garry oak are this type of parkland with meadow-like openings; dry deciduous woodlands; or rocky slopes, headlands, outcrops, or crevices. To the south, the habitat is likely to be a savanna landscape, with a dense stratum of herbs and woody plants.

The extensive animal population associated with this ecosystem is impressive. The list of over fifty native species of birds found in grasslands areas includes turkey vulture, bald eagle, red-winged blackbird, western meadowlark, and various hawks, woodpeckers, hummingbirds, owls, swallows, thrushes, sparrows and finches. Among the native grassland mammals are bear, deer, elk, wolves, cougars, otters, mink, racoon, beavers, squirrels, shrews and bats. This habitat is also home to salamanders, newts, tree frogs, lizards and snakes.

Many developed areas in our region were once oak meadows. For example, only 150 years ago, much of the municipality of Oak Bay, in the city of Victoria, was a vast Garry oak system. If you live in an area that was once one of these meadows, you may have an open, sunny site and a mild, dry microclimate. These are perfect conditions in which to establish or restore a meadow in your own garden.

Trees

Arbutus (*Arbutus menziesii*)

This bold and massive, yet elegant, broadleaf tree is an evergreen. Its large, oval, shiny green, rhododendron-like leaves are shed sporadically throughout the year. The most distinctive feature of the arbutus, however, is its bark, which peels off in large, raggedly curly scales. The bark below is smooth and chartreuse green when young; the older bark is an equally attractive cinnamon colour. Drooping clusters of small, white, bell-shaped flowers appear in the spring, followed by masses of small, dull red berries which attract many birds. The arbutus is a medium-sized tree that rarely achieves 100 feet (30 m) in height.

Stands of *Arbutus menziesii* can be seen on rocky promontories and sunlit slopes, primarily in the southern limits of the region. Very often the arbutus is part of the Garry oak system, frequently in association with Douglas-fir (*Pseudotsuga menziesii*).

Propagation and cultivation

It is not difficult to grow arbutus from seed: plant the seeds—obtained from the berries—in the fall, in a mixture of half peat and half loam. Cold stratification for three months will help germination. The much easier and more dependable method is to grow from seedlings, which are not difficult to obtain as birds distribute the seeds so freely. Look for them in waste areas or friends' gardens. Be careful when handling the seedlings; they have long roots which are easily damaged. Arbutus is available at nurseries and garden centres.

A dry, exposed, sunny part of your garden is the best location for an arbutus, and it prefers a coarse-textured soil or even a rocky site. It wants to keep its feet dry so it requires a location with good, fast drainage.

Commonly known in the United States as madrone, *Arbutus menziesii* is another of our native plants that is treasured in the gardens of England and Europe. This highly distinctive tree looks splendidly ornamental in the garden. It would be happy planted near—but not in the shade of—its natural companion, a Douglas-fir. For shrubbery underplanting, try tall Oregon grape (*Mahonia aquifolium*), salal (*Gaultheria shallon*) or snowberry (*Symphoricarpos albus*). Arbutus creates a fair amount of litter beneath its branches: discarded bark, fallen leaves, twigs, flowers and berries; although this vegetative material is slow to decompose, it will eventually add to the enrichment of the soil.

Garry oak (*Quercus garryana*)

The noble Garry oak, with its great reaching crowns and gnarled branches, plays an important ecological role, and often dominates its landscape. It is an indicator plant for its own habitat, and has a distinct set of plant species associated with it. The only Canadian native oak west of Manitoba, *Quercus garryana* is a broadleaf, deciduous hardwood tree (sometimes a shrub) with heavy limbs that stretch out at odd angles, and a brownish-grey bark with thick, scaly furrows and ridges. The foliage is the typical leathery, round-lobed oak leaf and the fruit is a smooth brown acorn. Tiny, deep-red female flowers appear with the emerging leaves in late winter to midspring while male flowers, which are yellowish catkins, hang in clusters.

In its rocky habitats the Garry oak is often short and crooked, but in open meadow settings it has been known to grow as tall as 117 feet (36 m). It is a long-lived tree; some specimens indicate a lifespan of over 300 years.

In the United States, *Quercus garryana* is commonly known as *Oregon white oak*.

Propagation and cultivation

Urban development in our region has decimated much of the habitat of the venerable and enduring Garry oak, and what is left is seriously threatened. In its most preferred natural setting —an open, gentle meadow—it is a magnificent tree. Gardeners are encouraged to cultivate it in order to compensate for its decline in the natural landscape, and there is no doubt that it makes a valuable ornamental.

Although it prefers an open site and a mild,

dry climate, this tree tolerates a variety of conditions. Garry oak and the plant community associated with it are particularly adapted to conditions of winter and spring moisture followed by summer drought, and gardeners should take care to avoid overwatering in the summer months. *Quercus garryana* is remarkably resilient to damage and disturbance, although rather slow-growing. It will be at home in your garden in association with most of the plants described in this section.

Acorns can easily be gathered and planted; healthy ones germinate freely. (Acorns require thirty days of refrigeration before planting.)

The acorn bathtub test

When selecting acorns for planting, here is a quick tip for choosing those which will develop into the healthiest oak trees. Put all your acorns into the bottom of the bathtub and fill the tub three-quarters full of water. Discard any acorns that surface. Remove and discard any acorns left on the bottom that emit bubbles. If the water has not become too murky, examine the remaining acorns for any flaws or blemishes.

The best, healthiest acorns are the meatiest: those that have the densest volume. These are the acorns that will sink to the bottom; those that float will be less substantial.

A strong, solid plastic garbage can, because it is deeper than a bathtub, makes an even better receptacle for this test.

Probably the best way to establish oak trees in your garden is from young seedlings. Because its survival is threatened, some communities offer programs that encourage reproduction of Garry oaks and make seedlings available to gardeners, so check with your local parks department for information on plant sources.

Wildflowers

Broad-leaved shooting star (*Dodecatheon hendersonii*)

One of the most common wildflowers to frequent a Garry oak meadow is the tiny (never much more than 12 inches/30 cm tall) but dazzling shooting star, so called because its nodding, cyclamen-like flowers really do resemble a shooting star. (Its other common name, peacock, is due to its brilliant colour.) This little plant has thick succulent stems with a group of thin, smooth, broad basal leaves held flat at the ground. The colours of *Dodecatheon hendersonii* are stunning: pinkish rose flowers with a ring of clear yellow at the base and a floral tube (formed from the joined bases of the stamens) which is deep purple.

Propagation and cultivation

Although it grows from small bulblets, *Dodecatheon hendersonii* is easily grown from seed; many small seeds are contained within each capsule. Sprinkle the seeds on top of a good sterile potting mix pressed into a 4-inch (10-cm) plant pot with drainage holes. Cover the seeds with a little sand, water it and put it outside. Keep the soil damp, and by spring you may have germination.

Related to the primula, the small but showy shooting star is a perfect plant for the garden, in a summer-dry place in sun to semishade. It does very nicely in the rock garden. Another suggestion for a garden site is a flowering lawn.

Because the shooting star blooms early—from March to May—and its leaves sit flat on the ground, the basal rosettes are not damaged by an early mowing.

Removing bulbs from the wild is not an ethical gardening practice. The easiest method for growing wild bulbs, and probably the surest guarantee of success in your garden, is to obtain the plants from a specialist nursery; all the meadow bulbs described here are available.

Chocolate lily (*Fritillaria lanceolata*)

Fritillaries are admired the world over and some of the best species, of superior garden quality, are right here in our own backyard. *Fritillaria lanceolata*, the charming chocolate lily (sometimes known as *checker lily* or *mission bells*), is one of these.

The chocolate lily grows from a deep-seated scaly bulb with numerous rice-like bulblets. The tallish stalk bears whorls of lance-shaped leaves and nodding, bell-shaped, terminal flowers. These are dark purple, mottled with greenish-yellow in a checkered pattern.

The chocolate lily is found in open woodlands (particularly oak), grassy meadows and bluffs. It is a matter of concern that this rare beauty is rapidly disappearing from its native habitat.

Propagation and cultivation

The chocolate lily is amenable to garden culture. It is best suited for dryish bulb beds, rock gardens or sunny borders. To grow from seed, a patient approach is needed with fritillary, as with other bulbous plants. Seed pans may show no seedlings for up to six months. On emerging, the seedlings send their tiny bulblets rapidly down to the bottom of the pot. Hold young plants until the dormant period (fall) of the second year before replanting.

Common camas (*Camassia quamash*)

Scarcely any other perennial is so closely tied to the culture of the aboriginal peoples as the camas. To coastal peoples it was a mainstay food, the most important vegetable plant.

Camassia quamash grows in grassy slopes and meadows. A blue drift of camas is a common sight in a Garry oak meadow. From a deep, egg-shaped bulb it grows to about 1 to 2 feet (30 to 60 cm) tall. It has numerous, basal, grass-like leaves and five or more lovely blue-violet flowers on a terminal spike.

Propagation and cultivation

Camassia quamash is far less fastidious than some other species of the lily family (Liliaceae) to which it belongs, and does best in heavy soils. It comes easily from seed and will flower in four to six years. To sow, use a good sterile potting mix pressed into a 4-inch (10-cm) pot with drainage holes. Sprinkle the seeds on top and cover with a small amount of clean, sharp sand. Water, label, and place outside. Check during the early fall to ensure the soil is damp and by spring you may have germination.

This delightful native is well-suited to the sunny perennial border or bulb garden, or can be left to naturalize in an open meadow. Though camas likes its feet wet in winter and early spring, it needs to dry out after flowering, like most other native bulbs.

Less common and slightly later blooming, but occupying a similar range, is the somewhat larger species, great camas (*C. leichtlinii*). Also occurring in similar habitats is the creamy-blossomed death camas (*Zygadenus venenosus*), whose toxic bulbs, although similar in appearance to those of *Camassia quamash*, are potentially fatal.

Hooker's onion (*Allium acuminatum*)

Hooker's onion is a species of the *Allium* genus of the lily family (Liliaceae).

It develops from a small, grey-brown, egg-shaped bulb. The blossoms, which flower in late spring, are generally pinkish but vary from intense rosy purple to nearly white. They are stiff and parchment-like, born in upright clusters of many flowers, on a firm rounded stalk from 4 to 12 inches (10 to 30 cm) tall. The entire plant has a characteristic onion odour and taste.

Often associated with a Garry oak meadow system, *Allium acuminatum* can be found in a variety of sites: open forest, dry hills and flats, dry rocky knolls and coastal headlands. Unlike the other plants associated with these meadow systems, its geographical range does not extend to the full southern limits of our region.

Propagation and cultivation

The site should be dry, in full sun, sharply drained and with a sandy soil. Hooker's onions are best suited for rock gardens, pots, or the front of dry perennial beds. Avoid summer watering.

Plant bulbs about 2 inches (5 cm) deep and about 2 to 5 inches (5 to 12 cm) apart. Divide the clusters every five to ten years in late summer. You can also grow wild onions from the seeds, which are easy to harvest. After the capsules split in July, shake the black seed heads into a bag. Sow the seeds in the fall; they are easy to germinate using a gritty mixture of sand and loam. After germination it is best to plunge the deep seed pans in a protected site. The plants develop from seed to flowering bulb in two years.

Satin flower (*Sisyrinchium douglasii*)

Small but showy, this delightful little spring wildflower grows in low clumps (4 to 12 inches/ 10 to 30 cm high) from a small mass of matted rhizomes. The delicate flower stalks rise up between a pair of sheath-like bracts amid a spray of thin, grass-like, silvery-green, prominently veined leaves. The flowers, about 1 1/2 inches (4 cm) wide, are delicate bells of a stunning reddish-purple colour with a satiny sheen.

One of our earliest wildflowers, the satin flower comes into bloom as early as February, with the leaves sometimes emerging in January. The plant can be found in association with a Garry oak system or on a dry rocky cliff, on the southern tip of Vancouver Island through the lower ranges of our region, south to California. It also occurs in sagebrush country in the American interior.

Propagation and cultivation
Sisyrinchium douglasii, sometimes referred to botanically as *Sisyrinchium grandiflorum*, is a rare and fragile species and should be purchased from a nursery or started from seed. You can sow mature seeds in the summer, to be left over the winter. Germination, however, cannot be expected from more than 20 percent of the seeds.

Related to the blue-eyed grasses, satin flower is a beautiful addition to the spring garden, particularly when planted in masses. You will find that it adapts quickly but spreads slowly. In our region it thrives most successfully in the wild in open settings, on shallow mossy soil, in sun to semishade. Like so many other meadow wildflowers, it can tolerate an extremely dry summer site, but requires a wet spring soil. Satin flower will be at home wherever you have planted other meadow flowers, or in a sunny rock garden.

Western buttercup (*Ranunculus occidentalis*)
There are over thirty buttercup species in our region, all identifiable by their varnished gold petals, each with a little nectar scale at the base. The western, or field buttercup, is differentiated from the other species by its tufted roots, deeply cleft basal leaves, larger flowers, and globe-like clustered head of the fruit, or achenes, hooked at the top. Most of us are familiar with this pretty little plant; it is a common field flower throughout our region, found in meadows, woodlands, thickets, glades, and along beaches and streams.

Propagation and cultivation
This is a native plant that does not seem to be available commercially, even from specialist nurseries. Perhaps because it is such a common little wildflower, it has not yet come to be widely regarded as an appropriate garden species. For gardeners establishing a flowering meadow or a wild garden, the western buttercup is a lovely companion to camas, creating the delightful carpet of blue and gold which we often see in a natural setting. The buttercup prefers a very sunny site but is adaptable to a variety of soils, from moist to dry, and has the added advantage of blooming over a long period, from March until July.

A perennial with fibrous roots, *Ranunculus occidentalis* seeds prolifically. For anyone wishing to establish some buttercups in the garden, probably the most practical way is to collect seed from the wild plant, carefully observing the 10 percent guideline. To establish plants for transplanting by the next growing season, harvest the seeds when ripe, which can be as early as July, and sow immediately. Put them outdoors in a pot and by midwinter you may see tiny rosettes beginning to form. By spring your buttercups should be sending up new shoots.

Ask for this and other native plants at your local nursery or garden centre. Enough gardeners' interest in a plant will stimulate response from the nursery industry.

White fawn lily, or Easter lily (*Erythronium oregonum*)
Erythronium oregonum, the white fawn lily, is an outstandingly beautiful native plant. You may have seen it massed gracefully in moist meadows or woodland glades where it self-sows to form enchanting, snowy drifts.

Erythronium oregonum can vary from 4 to 18 inches (10 to 46 cm) in height. The basal, paired leaves are lance-shaped to oblong, pale green with chocolate mottling, forming a base for the white, orange-based flowers. These nodding

Invasive intruder

Scotch broom (*Cytisus scoparius*)

The most popular story of how Scotch broom was introduced to this region tells of a Scotsman who obtained it in 1850 from the British consul in the Sandwich Islands (now Hawaii). There are several versions of the story, and interestingly enough they all involve a homesick Scot. Whatever the means of its arrival, it was an unfortunate event for our native plant species. We are all familiar with broom; we have seen it in prolific abundance alongside highways and over meadows. It is so aggressively invasive that it has endangered much of the native flora. Broom is a deciduous shrub that can grow to 10 feet (3 m) in height, with strongly angled branches and sparse, small leaves. Its most distinctive feature is the bright yellow—almost phosphorescent—colour of its many pea-type flowers. Its pungent scent is another distinctive characteristic. It is a tough plant that requires little care and can thrive on poor soil, particularly in a sunny site. Broom colonizes not only roadsides and meadows, it can be seen everywhere: disturbed sites, thickets, open forests. Not only are they prolific seed producers, broom plants are invidious propagators; their seeds can remain in the soil for years until conditions become suitable for germination. And you must be vigilant even when you do succeed in removing broom, as its presence on a site enriches soil, encouraging invasion by some introduced species that require a higher nitrogen content than natives.

There are various types of broom in different genera. Cytisus scoparius is the plant that has done the most damage in our part of the world, but there is evidence that every species has invasive tendencies.

The destructive effect of this invasive plant cannot be overemphasized. It has decimated entire communities of some of our most beautiful and rare wild flowers, and frequently invades valuable farm pastures. Broom is a threat to more than our native vegetation; the seeds have been used as a coffee substitute, the flowers have been used in wine-making, and the pods and seeds suggest culinary qualities in their resemblance to small peas, but broom is a dangerous plant to consume as it contains several toxic alkaloids.

Broom is extremely difficult to remove effectively. One method is to cut and burn it, then till the soil to turn up the old roots and plant the ground with a densely rooted crop. Another strategy, best suited for younger plants, is pulling the broom—not an easy task. In the spring, many communities send out volunteers to parks and other broom-infested public areas for broom pulls. For such a program to be effective, participants must be willing to return to the site for repeated labour. If you are interested in participating in an effort to remove broom from a site near your own home, horticultural societies, nature sanctuaries, and native plant groups should be able to give you information about such programs.

blossoms have upturned tips and hang from a long slender stem, with their necks turned down.

The name *Easter lily* is really a misnomer for *Erythronium oregonum*; other than its white colour, it is really nothing like the true Easter lily, a large exotic. *Erythronium oregonum* has been given various common names, but the most appropriate seems to be *fawn lily,* which probably alludes to the mottled leaf colouring.

Propagation and cultivation
This erythronium takes fairly well to garden culture. A spring display of white fawn lilies in a semishaded woodland garden or grassy meadow is a rewarding sight. It does well in either of these situations as long as it gets some moisture.

Like these other meadow bulbs, fawn lily may be purchased from specialist native plant suppliers. It can also be propagated from seed; from seed to bloom takes from three to six years. Sown in flats or pots in the fall, seeds usually germinate well. The containers should then be plunged into the soil in a semishaded to shady place and patiently kept there for four or five seasons—remember to keep them watered

—until the bulbs grow large enough to support a flowering. Don't move or repot the seedlings in the early stages, and don't mistake them for tiny blades of grass, which they resemble. After transplanting to a permanent location, the bulbs reach deeper and deeper into the ground as the plant matures.

The pink fawn lily (*Erythronium revolutum*) is similar to the white fawn lily in most respects, other than its rose-pink colour. Another graceful beauty, its pink drifts will strikingly enhance a garden. Unlike the white fawn lily, the pink fawn lily is not a frequenter of meadows, but prefers damper spots under alder trees or along stream courses.

Mountain

Many plants that grow in the mountain ranges of the Pacific coastal region are species that are also found at various other elevations, but a few are limited to the higher mountain reaches. Plants of the alpine-tundra community are found above the timberline, which is the uppermost limit of tree cover. Species of the subalpine zone grow in the region below the upper limit of tree growth.

Above the timberline, the environment is so harsh that trees are unable to survive. Here, the mountain landscape lies under the cold snow of winter for most of the year and frost is possible any month, but the searing solar radiation is nearly twice as intense as that at sea level. The wind is ceaseless, and the soil, often a very thin layer, tends to dry out during the brief summer; the growing season is sometimes no longer than one month. The habitat can be a wet, peaty meadow dominated by sedges, rushes and alpine grasses; or it can be a dry, rocky field or slope supporting tufted mats of heath shrubs, small woody plants, and tough little wildflowers. These flowering plants are particularly adapted for survival in this harsh and demanding environment. They often have short stems and large flowers and can thrive in a dry, rocky soil: in other words, perfect specimens for the rock garden.

Lower down the mountain slopes, in the subalpine zone below the upper limit of tree-growth, there is a longer snow-free period, possibly as much as three or four months, but snowfall is heavy. Here, isolated specimens or clumps of stunted mountain hemlock and alpine fir grow amid early summer meadows of brilliant wildflowers.

Wildlife found in these mountains includes grizzly and black bear, deer, hare, squirrel, elk and mountain goat; among the many birds we can see here are grouse, ptarmigan, owl, raven, and pileated woodpecker.

You don't have to live in the mountains to garden with these intriguing mountain plants, but for most of them a sunny site is required. A rockery, a warm patio or the side of a rock wall are ideal places for many of these species; others are happy in a sunny border.

Most of these plants are available at nurseries, but if you have a problem obtaining any of them, the best source is probably a garden club plant exchange or sale.

Shrubs

Sitka mountain-ash (*Sorbus sitchensis*)

Unlike the well-known European mountain-ash (*S. aucuparia*), the Sitka mountain-ash is not a tree but a shrubby bush of the higher mountains, where it frequently grows in abundant thickets. The shrub has several thin stems which spread from a common base, growing to about 3 to 12 feet (1 to 4 m) in height. The alternate leaves of this deciduous shrub are dull bluish-green, turning red in the autumn. In June, small white flowers form dense, flat-topped clusters. The fruit of this species are large, orange-red berries, differing from the small crimson fruit of the tree species. A favourite meal of birds such as waxwings and grosbeaks, the berries appear in the fall, beautifully set off against the blazing bronze-red of the foliage, and will often stay on over the winter.

Sorbus sitchensis is frequently found in association with subalpine fir (*Abies lasiocarpa*) and mountain hemlock (*Tsuga mertensiana*), in upper mountain to subalpine areas throughout our region. It grows on avalanche slopes, in open forests, on stream banks, and at meadow edges.

Propagation and cultivation

Because the Sitka mountain-ash is a difficult plant to start from cuttings, it is usually propagated by seed. Try cold stratification at 32°F (0°C) for two to four months, or plant fresh seeds outdoors in fall or winter. The plant is available at specialist nurseries, where it is sometimes classified as a tree.

Although *Sorbus sitchensis* will take well to a sunny garden at lower elevations, it usually produces fewer flowers and fruit under these conditions. (The berries are not very appetizing, although they are fine for making jelly.) This shrub is attractive when grouped with rhododendrons and azaleas in a mixed shrub border.

Mountain wildflowers

Columbia lewisia (*Lewisia columbiana*)

In a feature titled "The Impact of American Plants on British Gardens," the Summer 1987 issue of the distinguished British garden magazine *Hortus* states that "no collection of alpine plants would be considered complete if it did not contain some members of the genus *Lewisia*, a family of plants confined in its natural distribution to North West America." Named after

Captain Meriwether Lewis of the Lewis and Clark expeditions, many species from this group have acquired universal popularity as rock garden plants.

Found on dry gravel slopes, rock crevices and outcrops up to the timberline throughout the southern parts of our region, Columbia lewisia (*Lewisia columbiana*) is probably the easiest of the lewisias to cultivate. It is a succulent perennial that develops from a deep-seated, fleshy taproot. The tongue-shaped basal leaves give rise to several slender, branching stems, about 2 to 12 inches (5 to 30 cm) tall. From May to August these stems bear open, branched clusters of smallish (1/8 to 3/8 inch/5 to 13 mm) flowers. These vary in colour from white with subtle pink veins to lavender or magenta-rose.

Propagation and cultivation
Lewisia columbiana can be grown from seed, and is also obtainable from nurseries. It is a fairly easy garden plant, undemanding if given a sunny site, particularly in a rock garden, and is especially attractive when grown in drifts.

Its suitability as a rock garden plant has lent *Lewisia columbiana* so much popularity that its survival in the wild has become dangerously jeopardized by unscrupulous collectors of native plants.

Harebell (*Campanula rotundifolia*)
Several species of the campanulas known as *harebells* are found in the mountains of our region; the common harebell (*Campanula rotundifolia*) is also found at lower elevations. In fact, it is common throughout the northern hemisphere and is the same plant known in Scotland as bluebells of Scotland.

The common harebell grows in abundant flowering mats on grassy subalpine slopes and open rocky sites. Several leafy stems grow from a branched stem base with oval or heart-shaped basal leaves; the alternate stem leaves are narrowly lance-shaped. The flowers are 1/2 to 1 1/4 inch (1.5 to 3 cm) long, very occasionally white but usually lavender or purplish-blue. Nodding and bell-shaped (like thimbles), they grow in thin wiry stalks in loose clusters at the tip of the stem, from June to September. Alpine harebells flower more abundantly than the sea-level plants.

Propagation and cultivation
Campanula rotundifolia is another appropriate and popular rock garden perennial that can be grown from seed, and reseeds itself. The capsules of each plant contain numerous seeds. Harebell can also be obtained from nurseries. It grows in spreading mats and prefers a sunny site, but can tolerate light shade.

Moss campion (*Silene acaulis*)
A plant of such beauty that it has gained a world-wide reputation, moss campion (*Silene acaulis*) looks like a moss but is actually a herbaceous perennial from the same family as pinks,

or carnations (Caryophyllaceae). These tight little moss-like cushions grow in ground-hugging clumps about 1 inch (2.5 cm) high, forming mats over rocky slopes, cliffs and crevices at high elevations.

The many-branched stems of moss campion carry tiny, leathery, bright green leaves. Amid the mats of tough little leaves, the pink-rose flowers appear in great profusion from June to September, creating a splendid show against the rocky surfaces and turfy tundra barrens.

Propagation and cultivation
Moss campion can be propagated from stem cuttings, but it also grows easily from seed. When the rosettes reach 1 1/4 to 1 1/2 inches (3 to 4 cm) across, transplant the little clumps to their permanent garden spot. If you wanted to obtain a mature plant, the best place would probably be through a rock and alpine plant society plant exchange.

Silene acaulis requires full sun and some moisture and is an excellent plant for rock gardens, its long woody tap-roots anchoring deeply into rock crevices. In the garden you will find it a trouble-free plant that spreads easily but not invasively.

Our native *Silene acaulis* flowers sparsely in contrast to strains from other parts of the globe; the most favoured moss campion among rock garden enthusiasts is the Icelandic plant.

Tall purple fleabane (*Erigeron peregrinus*)
Erigerons are our wild daisies. *Erigeron peregrinus*, the tall purple fleabane, is sometimes called *subalpine daisy* because it is found most frequently at subalpine levels, where it has a widespread range. In fact, this herbaceous perennial is probably our most common daisy.

Each erect stem of tall purple fleabane can grow from 4 to 28 inches (10 to 70 cm) tall. The many flower petals—30 to 80—are white-to-lavender rays arranged around disk-like centres of tiny yellow flowers. Leaves are usually lance-like and fairly large.

Propagation and cultivation
Erigerons are easy to grow from seed or from rhizome segments. They want a rich, damp soil in sun to semishade. *Erigeron peregrinus* is available at specialist nurseries.

Tall purple fleabane is very similar in appearance to leafy aster (*Aster foliaceus*), another plant of high elevations.

Western anemone (*Anemone occidentalis*)
As soon as the snow melts, flocks of these showy little wildflowers cover high mountain meadows in the southern part of our region. Western anemone is a hairy little herbaceous perennial, with a short (4 to 12 inches/10 to 30 cm), thick stem and grey-green, feathery, deeply dissected leaves. The cup-shaped flowers are proportionately large (1 1/2 to 3 inches/4 to 7 cm wide) and creamy-white, often with a blueish tinge. The flowers are followed by conspicuous, hairy, long-stalked mops of wavy, drooping seeds. Anemones are also called windflowers, pasque-flowers, and sometimes tow-headed babies.

Propagation and cultivation
Western anemone is grown from seed, sown soon after it is collected in the fall. Showy both in flower and fruit, it is a highly appropriate candidate for a rock garden environment.

Anemone occidentalis is a member of the buttercup family (Ranunculaceae), many of which are to some degree poisonous when fresh. The leaves contain chemicals that can sometimes cause skin irritation and blistering, or if part of the plant is swallowed, internal tissues will become inflamed. So take precautions: wear gloves when handling this plant, and plant it away from a children's play area; *Anemone occidentalis* is a poisonous plant.

Yellow mountain avens (*Dryas drummondii*)

A wide-ranging species, this low-growing, mat-forming mountain plant grows on roadsides, gravelly river bars and rocky slopes from the lowlands up into the alpine tundra, southwards from Alaska. Its distinctive feature is the evergreen foliage: small (about 1 inch/2 cm long), oblong-oval leaves, leathery and wrinkly with scalloped edges; intense, glossy dark green above and almost startling white below. In June and July the yellow flowers appear singly at the top of each stem, 6 to 10 inches (15 to 25 cm) in length, demure, nodding blossoms that never fully open their petals. The fruit follows each flower with a golden-yellow, feathery plume, later opening up to a fluffy mass that is eventually carried off in the wind.

Propagation and cultivation

Although we think of it as a mountain wildflower, the yellow mountain avens is really a prostrate evergreen shrub. Its trailing, woody stems root freely: establish the rooted cuttings in a pot, then set them out in rocky scree. This method is preferable to planting from seed, which is slow and uncertain. *Dryas drummondii* can be obtained at nurseries, where it is usually categorized as a perennial flower.

Yellow mountain avens is a popular and much-cultivated rock garden plant. Give it a well-drained sunny site, preferably in a rockery or stone pavement. Here, instead of burning out as some plants do in the reflected heat of the stone, it will demonstrate its exceptional ability to flourish in intense sun.

Plant associations

Here is a summary of the various plant combinations suggested in this chapter, plus a few more. Use these companion planting ideas—or try a little creative experimenting with various combinations —wherever your garden conditions are similar to the plants' natural habitats.

Wetlands or damp forest areas

○ False lily-of-the-valley (*Maianthemum dilatatum*) with deer fern (*Blechnum spicant*).

○ Foamflower (*Tiarella trifoliata*) with vanilla-leaf (*Achlys triphylla*), lady fern (*Athyrium filix-femina*), sword fern (*Polystichum munitum*), thimbleberry (*Rubus parviflorus*), salmonberry (*R. spectabilis*), or swamp lantern (*Lysichitum americanum*).

○ Hardhack (*Spiraea douglasii*) with sweet gale (*Myrica gale*) and salmonberry (*Rubus spectabilis*).

○ Labrador tea (*Ledum groenlandicum*) with bog laurel (*Kalmia polifolia*).

○ Marsh marigold (*Caltha palustris*) with deer cabbage (*Fauria crista-galli*) and yellow-eyed grass (*Sisyrinchium californicum*).

○ Ninebark (*Physocarpus capitatus*) with red osier dogwood (*Cornus stolonifera*) or salmonberry (*Rubus spectabilis*).

○ Swamp lantern (*Lysichitum americanum*) with false lily-of-the-valley (*Maianthemum dilatatum*) and lady fern (*Athyrium filix-femina*).

Edgelands areas

O Arbutus (*Arbutus menziesii*) with hairy manzanita (*Arctostaphylos columbiana*) or kinnikinnick (*Arctostaphylos uva-ursi*).

O Indian-plum (*Oemleria cerasiformis*) with red elderberry (*Sambucus racemosa*) or snowberry (*Symphoricarpos albus*).

O Oceanspray (*Holodiscus discolor*) with Oregon grape (*Mahonia nervosa*).

O Pearly everlasting (*Anaphalis margaritacea*) with tansy (*Tanacetum douglasii*).

O Red-flowering currant (*Ribes sanguineum*) with Douglas-fir (*Pseudotsuga menzeisii*) and hairy manzanita (*Arctostaphylos columbiana*).

O Salmonberry (*Rubus spectabilis*) with red alder (*Alnus rubra*), lady fern (*Athyrium filix-femina*), swamp lantern (*Lysichitum americanum*), devil's club (*Oplopanax horridus*), thimbleberry (*Rubus parviflorus*) and foamflower (*Tiarella trifoliata*).

Forest or woodland garden

O Bigleaf maple (*Acer macrophyllum*) with salal (*Gaultheria shallon*), Oregon grape (*Mahonia* spp.), sword fern (*Polystichum munitum*), or licorice fern (*Polypodium glycyrrhiza*).

O Bunchberry (*Cornus unalaschkensis*) with vine maple (*Acer circinatum*).

O Copper bush (*Cladothamnus pyroliflorus*) with evergreen huckleberry (*Vaccinium ovatum*), oval-leaved blueberry (*V. ovalifolium*) and red huckleberry (*V. parvifolium*), or with false azalea (*Menziesia ferruginea*) or mountain hemlock (*Tsuga heterophylla*).

O Devil's club (*Oplopanax horridus*) with sword fern (*Polystichum munitum*), oak fern (*Gymnocarpium dryopteris*), lady fern (*Athyrium filix-femina*) and foamflower (*Tiarella trifoliata*).

O Evergreen huckleberry (*Vaccinium ovatum*) with sword fern (*Polystichum munitum*).

O False Solomon's seal (*Smilacina racemosa*) with sword fern (*Polystichum munitum*), small-flowered fairybells (*Disporum hookeri*), western bleeding heart (*Dicentra formosa*), wood sorrel (*Oxalis oregana*), or vanilla leaf (*Achlys triphylla*).

O Low Oregon grape (*Mahonia nervosa*) with salal (*Gaultheria shallon*) and sword fern (*Polystichum munitum*).

O Pacific dogwood (*Cornus nuttallii*) with fringecup (*Tellima grandiflora*), red alder (*Alnus rubra*) and various conifers.

O Vine maple (*Acer circinatum*) with sword fern (*Polystichum munitum*) and native conifers.

O Western red cedar (*Thuja plicata*) with sitka spruce (*Picea sitchensis*), western hemlock (*Tsuga heterophylla*), bigleaf maple (*Acer macrophyllum*), red alder (*Alnus rubra*), Pacific yew (*Taxus brevifolia*) and grand fir (*Abies grandis*), or with large fringecup (*Tellima grandiflora*), or wood sorrel (*Oxalis oregana*).

O Western rhododendron (*Rhododendron macrophyllum*) with Douglas-fir (*Pseudotsuga menziesii*) and grand fir (*Abies grandis*). Underplant with Siberian miner's lettuce (*Claytonia sibirica*).

Meadow or grassland

O Arbutus (*Arbutus menziesii*) with Douglas-fir (*Pseudotsuga menziesii*), tall Oregon grape (*Mahonia aquifolium*), salal (*Gaultheria shallon*) and snowberry (*Symphoricarpos albus*).

O Garry oak (*Quercus garryana*) with the above associations, and also with satin flower (*Sisyrinchium douglasii*), spring gold (*Lomatium utriculatum*), fawn lily (*Erythronium oreganum*), chocolate lily (*Fritillaria lanceolata*), shooting star (*Dodecatheon hendersonii*); common camas (*Camassia quamash*), broad-leaved stone-crop (*Sedum spathulifolium*), harvest brodiaea (*Brodiaea coronaria*), Hooker's onion (*Allium acuminatum*) and western buttercup (*Ranunculus occidentalis*).

Discovering More Plants

A surprising number of plant species native to this region have been known to adapt to garden settings. The following plants, listed according to their preferred habitats, are appropriate for garden cultivation.

Plants excluded from these lists are considered unsuitable for cultivation for various reasons. Some species are too fragile and/or rare to be brought into the garden. Most of our wild orchids fall into this category; examples are fairyslipper (*Calypso bulbosa*), which is rapidly being exterminated, and ladyslippers (*Cypripedium* spp.), also being threatened by overcollecting (and usually not successful in cultivation; mountain ladyslipper, for example, takes fifteen years to flower). Some plants are difficult to establish for no discernable reason; the white rhododendron (*Rhododendron albiflorum*), for example, provides no known specimens in local garden cultivation.

There are particular plants with unique survival requirements we do not yet fully understand. Some natives will not succeed when removed from their home environment because of dependency on mycorrhizal fungi which sup-

ply water and other essential nutritional components required by the plant. One example of this phenomenon is the red huckleberry (*Vaccinium parvifolium*), which thrives in its own environment amid the rich, humic soil of the forest floor. In any other setting the roots of this plant appear to require the mycorrhizal fungi in a rotten log or some other base of decaying wood.

Some plants are dangerous in garden situations because of their exceptionally poisonous properties; examples are false hellebore (*Veratrum viride*) and some members of the buttercup family (Ranunculaceae), which includes some delphiniums.

A few plants are excluded because they are considered to be to some degree parasitic: for example, wood betony (*Pedicularis bracteosa*) and some other louseworts.

Unfortunately, not all of the plants included here are commercially available. Be persistent in asking for them at your local garden centre.

(* A species which has been described in a habitat section above is marked with an asterisk.)

Wetland plants

A number of these natives are found in low coastal bogs, others inhabit such wetland areas as stream banks, marshes, damp forests or wet meadows. Many can tolerate cool shade to semi-shade; plants that are known to prefer sun are indicated. All will be at home in an appropriately cultivated damp-to-wet part of the garden.

Trees
bitter cherry (*Prunus emarginata*)
cascara (*Rhamnus purshiana*)
Oregon ash (*Fraxinus latifolius*)
red alder (*Alnus rubra*)
shore pine (*Pinus contorta*)
Sitka willow (*Salix sitchensis*)
yellow cedar (*Chamaecyparis nootkatensis*)

Learning from field guides

To become adept at wild plant identification, start exploring local—and not-so-local—wilderness areas. On such expeditions a good regional field guide is an essential companion. Field guides are also useful when gardening with native plants because of the full plant descriptions they provide; every native plant gardener should possess at least one of these valuable handbooks.

The following field guides are some of the best.

○ Coastal Wildflowers of British Columbia and the Pacific Northwest, by Elizabeth Horn.

○ Field Guide to Wild Flowers in the Pacific Northwest (series), by Lewis Clark (Adapted by John Trelawny).

○ Plants of Coastal British Columbia, by Jim Pojar and Andy MacKinnon.

○ Trees, Shrubs and Flowers to Know in British Columbia, by C.P. Lyons.

○ Wayside Wildflowers of the Pacific Northwest, by Dr. Dee Strickler.

Not a field guide, but traditionally the definitive source of information for native plant gardening in this part of the world, Gardening with Native Plants of the Pacific Northwest by Arthur R. Kruckeberg, is full of information about the plants and their cultivation. Once you become a seasoned native plant gardener you will probably find it indispensable.

Trees specific to the inland bog
dwarf birch (*Betula pumila* ssp. *glandulifera*)
paper birch (*Betula papyrifera*)
trembling aspen (*Populus tremuloides*)
western white birch (*Betula papyrifera* var. *commutata*)

Deciduous shrubs

bog cranberry (*Vaccinium oxycoccus*) *
bog laurel, or swamp laurel (*Kalmia polifolia*) *
hardhack (*Spiraea douglasii*) *
high-bush cranberry, or squashberry (*Viburnum edule*)
Labrador tea (*Ledum groenlandicum*) *
ninebark (*Physocarpus capitatus*) *
red osier dogwood (*Cornus stolonifera*) *
salmonberry (*Rubus spectabilis*) *
swamp gooseberry (*Ribes lacustre*)
sweet gale (*Myrica gale*) *
twinberry honeysuckle (*Lonicera involucrata*)

Herbaceous plants

Small herbaceous plants (up to 1 foot/30 cm)
false lily-of-the-valley (*Maianthemum dilatatum*) *
gold thread (*Coptis asplenifolia*)
Jeffrey's shooting star (*Dodecatheon jeffreyi*)
Merten's saxifrage (*Saxifraga mertensiana*)
white shooting star (*Dodecatheon dentatum*)
yellow willow-herb (*Epilobium luteum*)
○ preferring sun
Douglas gentian (*Gentiana douglasiana*)
fringed grass-of-parnassus (*Parnassia fimbriata*)
leatherleaf saxifrage (*Leptarrhena pyrolaefolia*)
marsh violet (*Viola palustris*)
northern starflower (*Trientalis arctica*)
swamp gentian (*Gentiana sceptrum*)
white marsh marigold (*Caltha biflora*)

Medium-sized herbaceous plants (1 to 3 feet/ 30 cm to 1 m)
false bugbane (*Trautvetteria caroliniensis*)
foamflower (*Tiarella trifoliata*) *

marsh hollyhock (*Sidalcea hendersonii*)

small-flowered forget-me-not (*Myosotis laxa*)

smooth heuchera alumroot (*Heuchera glabra*)

swamp lantern/skunk cabbage/yellow arum
    (*Lysichiton americanum*) *

water plantain (*Alisma plantago-aquatica*)

yellow-eyed grass (*Sisyrinchium californicum*)

yellow marsh marigold (*Caltha palustris* ssp.
    asarifolia) *

O preferring sun

bog buckbean (*Menyanthes trifoliata*)

common monkey flower (*Mimulus guttatus*)

deer cabbage (*Fauria crista-galli*)

tall lungwort (*Mertensia paniculata*)

Tall herbaceous plants (3 to 10 feet/1 to 3 m)

broad-leaved cattail (*Typha latifolia*)

goat's beard (*Aruncus sylvester*)

O preferring sun

figwort (*Scrophularia californica*)

Ferns

lady fern (*Athyrium filix-femina*)

maidenhair fern (*Adiantum pedatum*)

Edgeland plants

These are species found in a variety of edge habitats: edges of forests, roads and streams; on disturbed lands; in clearings.

Shrubs

baldhip rose (*Rosa gymnocarpa*)

evergreen huckleberry (*Vaccinium ovatum*)

gummy gooseberry (*Ribes lobbii*)

hairy manzanita (*Arctostaphylos columbiana*) *

Indian-plum (*Oemleria cerasiformis*, also known
    as *Osmaronia cerasiformis*) *

kinnikinnick (*Arctostaphylos uva-ursi*)

mock orange (*Philadelphus lewisii*) *

Nootka rose or wild rose (*Rosa nutkana*) *

oceanspray (*Holodiscus discolor*) *

red-flowering currant (*Ribes sanguineum*) *

red huckleberry (*Vaccinium parvifolium*)

redstem ceanothus (*Ceanothus sanguineus*)

salal (*Gaultheria shallon*) *

salmonberry (*Rubus spectabilis*) *

saskatoon berry/service berry
    (*Amelanchier alnifolia*) *

silk-tassel (*Garry elliptica*)

snowbrush (*Ceanothus velutinus*)

tall Oregon grape (*Mahonia aquifolium*)

thimbleberry (*Rubus parviflorus*)

western azalea (*Rhododendron occidentale*)

Wildflowers/herbaceous plants

blue violet (*Viola adunca*)

blue-eyed grass (*Sisyrinchium Idahoense* var.
    macounii)

California poppy (*Eschscholzia Californica*)

common red paintbrush (*Castilleja miniata*)

cow parsnip (*Heracleum lanatum*)

farewell-to-spring (*Clarkia amoena*)

fireweed (*Epilobium angustifolium*) *

goat's beard (*Aruncus sylvester*)

harsh paintbrush (*Castilleja hispida*)

large-leaved lupine (*Lupinus polyphyllus*)

Nootka lupine (*Lupinus nootkatensis*)

Oregon stonecrop (*Sedum oreganum*)

pearly everlasting (*Anaphalis margaritacea*) *

Sitka valerian (*Valeriana sitchensis*)

sweet coltsfoot (*Petasites frigidus*)

tiger lily/Columbia lily (*Lilium columbianum*) *

western buttercup (*Ranunculus occidentalis*)

western red columbine (*Aquilegia formosa*) *

woodland strawberry (*Fragaria vesca*)

Forest plants

The majority of these plants are indigenous to the coniferous forest and will require a location in your garden that offers some shade and a fairly moist, humus-rich soil. (Plants from deciduous woodlands will require somewhat more sun.)

Some of the lesser-known selections from the long list of woodland herbaceous perennials will appeal to the more adventurous gardener. This list includes many species that hug the forest floor as ground covers as well as a few herbaceous perennials that reach up to about 3 feet (1 m) in height.

Trees
Canopy
○ coniferous
Douglas-fir (*Pseudotsuga menziesii*)
grand fir (*Abies grandis*)
Pacific silver fir (*Abies amabalis*)
shore pine (*Pinus contorta*)
Sitka spruce (*Picea sitchensis*)
western hemlock (*Tsuga heterophylla*)
western red cedar (*Thuja plicata*) *
○ deciduous
bigleaf maple (*Acer macrophyllum*) *
bitter cherry (*Prunus emarginata*)
cascara (*Rhamnus purshiana*)
paper birch (*Betula papyrifera*)
red alder (*Alnus rubra*)

Understory
Pacific crabapple (*Malus fusca*)
vine maple (*Acer circinatum*) *
western or Pacific flowering dogwood
    (*Cornus nuttallii*) *
western yew (*Taxus brevifolia*)

Shrubs
baldhip rose (*Rosa gymnocarpa*)
black huckleberry (*Vaccinium membranaceum*)
devil's club (*Oplopanax horridus*) *
dull Oregon grape (*Mahonia nervosa*) *
evergreen huckleberry (*Vaccinium ovatum*) *
false box (*Pachystima myrsinites*)
false azalea (*Menziesia ferruginea*)
hazelnut (*Corylus cornuta*)

ninebark (*Physocarpus capitatus*)
oceanspray (*Holodiscus discolor*)
osoberry (*Osmaronia cerasiformis*)
oval-leaved blueberry (*Vaccinium ovalifolium*)
Pacific rhododendron
    (*Rhododendron macrophyllum*) *
red huckleberry (*Vaccinium parvifolium*)
red elderberry (*Sambucus racemosa*)
salal (*Gaultheria shallon*)
salmonberry (*Rubus spectabilis*) *
snowberry (*Symphoricarpos albus*)
thimbleberry (*Rubus parviflorus*)
western tea-berry (*Gaultheria ovatifolia*)

Trailing and climbing shrubs
creeping raspberry (*Rubus pedatus*)
creeping snowberry (*Symphoricarpos mollis*)
orange honeysuckle (*Lonicera ciliosa*)
purple honeysuckle (*Lonicera hispidula*)

Herbaceous/forest floor
bunchberry (*Cornus unalaschkensis*) *
Canada violet (*Viola canadensis*)
clasping twisted stalk (*Streptopus amplexifolius*)
evergreen violet (*Viola sempervirens*)
false lily-of-the-valley (*Maianthemum dilatatum*)
false bugbane (*Trautvetteria caroliniensis*)
false Solomon's seal (*Smilacina racemosa*) *
feathery mitrewort (*Mitella breweri*)
foamflower (*Tiarella trifoliata*)
fringecup (*Tellima grandiflora*)
goat's beard (*Aruncus sylvester*)
large-flowered fairy bell (*Disporum smithii*)
large-leaved sandwort (*Arenaria macrophylla*)
leafy lousewort (*Pedicularis racemosa*)
Lyall's anemone (*Anemone lyallii*)
miner's lettuce (*Montia perfoliata*)
pathfinder plant (*Adenocaulon bicolour*)
pink fawn lily (*Erythronium revolutum*)
rosy twisted stalk (*Streptopus roseus*)
Scouler's harebell (*Campanula scouleri*)

Siberian miner's lettuce (*Claytonia sibirica*)
slender boykinia (*Boykinia elata*)
small twisted stalk (*Streptopus streptopoides*
star-flowered Solomon's seal (*Smilacina stellata*)
starflower (*Trientalis latifolia*)
toothwort (*Cardamine pulcherrima*)
twin flower (*Linnaea borealis*)
vanilla leaf (*Achlys triphylla*) *
western bleeding heart (*Dicentra formosa*) *
western trillium (*Trillium ovatum*)
western meadow rue (*Thalictrum occidentalis*)
wild asparagus or sarsaparilla (*Aralia nudicaulis*)
wild ginger (*Asarum caudatum*)
wood sorrel (*Oxalis oregana*) *
yellow wood violet (*Viola glabella*)
yerba buena (*Satureja douglasii*)
youth-on-age (*Tolmiea menziesii*)

Ferns
deer fern (*Blechnum spicant*)
fragile fern (*Cystopteris fragilis*)
licorice fern (*Polypodium glycyrrhiza*)
maidenhair fern (*Adiantum pedatum*)
narrow beech fern (*Thelypteris phegopteris*)
oak fern (*Gymnocarpium dryopteris*)
shield fern (*Dryopteris expansa*)
sword fern (*Polystichum munitum*)

Meadows

Trees
arbutus (*Arbutus menziesii*) *
Douglas-fir (*Pseudotsuga menziesii*)
Garry oak (*Quercus garryana*) *

Shrubs
Rocky mountain juniper (*Juniperus scopulorum*)
snowberry (*Symphoricarpos albus*)

Meadow wildflowers
blue-eyed Mary (*Collinsia parviflora*)

bluefield gilia (*Gilia capitata*)
broad-leaved shooting star (*Dodecatheon hendersonii*) *
chocolate lily (*Fritillaria lanceolata*) *
common camas (*Camassia quamash*) *
death camus (*Zygadenus venenosus*)
early blue violet (*Viola adunca*)
field larkspur (*Delphinium menziesii*)
harvest brodiaea (*Brodiaea coronaria*)
Hooker's onion (*Allium acuminatum*) *
satin flower (*Sisyrinchium douglasii*) *
thrift (*Armeria maritima*)
western buttercup (*Ranunculus occidentalis*) *
white fawn lily, or easter lily (*Erythronium oregonum*) *
yarrow (*Achillea millefolium*)

Species found on rocky slopes and outcrops
big-leaved sandwort (*Moehringia macrophylla*)
broad-leaved stone-crop (*Sedum spathulifolium*)
goldenback fern (*Pentagramma triangularis*)
goldenrod (*Solidago canadensis*)
hyacinth brodiaea, or fool's onion (*Brodiaea hyacinthina*, also known as *Triteleia hyacinthina*)
little monkey flower (*Mimulus alsinoides*)
small-flowered alumroot (*Heuchera micrantha*)
smooth alumroot (*Heuchera glabra*)
spreading phlox (*Phlox diffusa*)
spreading stonecrop (*Sedum divergens*)
spring gold (*Lomatium utriculatum*)
turtle-head (*Penstemon nemorosus*)
western saxifrage (*Saxifraga occidentalis*)
woolly sunflower (*Eriophyllum lanatum*)

Grasses
Agrostis exarata
Bromus carinatus
Elymus glaucus
Poa canbyi

These are some of the few truly native grasses that can be found in our meadows. Native grasses are not available at nurseries. They are not recommended for cultivation, as seed must be collected and does not always germinate readily, and native grass populations are plant communities under stress. Probably the best way to start a local grass in your garden is to obtain a clump from a fellow native plant gardener.

For more information about grasses, refer to the meadows section of chapter 3.

Mountain Plants

Mountain shrubs and trees

Alaskan blueberry (*Vaccinium alaskaense*)
alpine fir (*Abies lasiocarpa*)
arctic willow (*Salix arctica*)
black huckleberry (*Vaccinium membranaceum*)
cascade huckleberry (*Vaccinium deliciosum*)
Douglas maple (*Acer glabrum*)
dwarf blueberry (*Vaccinium caespitosum*)
dwarf nagoonberry (*Rubus acaulis*)
mountain hemlock (*Tsuga mertensiana*)
oval-leaved blueberry (*Vaccinium ovalifolium*)
pink mountain heather (*Phyllodoce empetriformis*)
red twin-berry (*Lonicera utahensis*)
Sitka mountain-ash (*Sorbus sitchensis*) *
snow willow (*Salix reticulata*)
white moss heath (*Cassiope mertensiana*)
yellow mountain heather (*Phyllodoce glanduliflora*)

Wildflowers

Alaska harebell (*Campanula lasiocarpa*)
alpine anemone (*Anemone drummondii*)
alpine speedwell (*Veronica wormskjoldii*)
alpine saxifrage (*Saxifraga tolmei*)
arctic lupine (*Lupinus arcticus*)
Brewer's mitrewort (*Mitella breweri*)
broad-leaved fireweed (*Epilobium latifolium*)
broad-petalled gentian (*Gentiana platypetala*)
chocolate tips (*Lomatium dissectum*)

coast penstemon (*Penstemon serrulatus*)
Columbia lewisia (*Lewisia columbiana*) *
crowberry (*Empetrum nigrum*)
cut-leaf fleabane (*Erigeron compositus*)
Davidson's penstemon (*Penstemon davidsonii*)
douglasia (*Douglasia laevigata*)
Fendler's waterleaf (*Hydrophyllum fendler*)
globeflower (*Trollius laxus*)
harebell (*Campanula rotundifolia*) *
heart-leaved arnica (*Arnica cordifolia*)
lance-leaved stonecrop (*Sedum lanceolatum*)
low mountain lupine (*Lupinus lyallii*, also known as *L. lepidus* var. *lobbii*)
moss campion (*Silene acaulis*) *
mountain arnica (*Arnica latifolia*)
mountain goldenrod (*Solidaga multiradiata*)
mountain sorrel (*Oxyria digyna*)
northern gentian (*Gentiana amarella*, also known as *Gentianella amarella*)
northern geranium (*Geranium erianthum*)
Olympic onion (*Allium crenulatum*)
partridgefoot (*Luetkea pectinata*)
pink monkey flower (*Mimulus lewisii*)
purple saxifrage (*Saxifraga oppositifolia*)
queen's cup (*Clintonia uniflora*)
showy Jacob's ladder (*Polemonium pulcherrimum*)
sibbaldia (*Sibbaldia procumbens*)
silky phacelia (*Phacelia sericea*)
silver-back (*Luina hypoleuca*)
Sitka mistmaiden (*Romanzoffia sitchensis*)
Sitka valerian (*Valeriana sitchensis*)
spring beauty (*Claytonia lanceolata*)
tall purple fleabane (*Erigeron peregrinus*) *
villous cinquefoil (*Potentilla villosa*)
western anemone (*Anemone occidentalis*) *
white dryas (*Dryas octopetala*)
white avalanche lily (*Erythronium montanum*)
woolly pussy-toes (*Antennaria lanata*)
yellow avalanche lily (*Erythronium grandiflorum*)
yellow mountain avens (*Dryas drummondii*) *

5

WHEN?

A Year-round Wildlife Garden

Across North America the idea of wildlife habitat gardening is spreading with surprising rapidity—surprising because the idea of wild creatures in the backyard does not appeal to everyone. Even those who are intrigued by the idea may have a preference for some forms of wildlife and feel dubious, at the very least, about others. (There can be no doubt about the favourites: we all love to hear the songs of birds in our own backyards.)

Native plants are a principal provider of food and shelter for wildlife creatures, especially those who are indigenous and thrive in the same ecological conditions as the plants. A healthy native plant garden which has been thoughtfully planned for consideration of wildlife is a delightful landscape for all animals (including humans) all year round.

Through the Seasons

Wildlife in our gardens varies throughout the year. We can increase the numbers and diversity of wild visitors to our gardens by supplying their needs in each season: in spring, nesting sites are important; in summer, water; and in winter the requirement is for food and shelter.

Spring

Here on the Pacific coast, spring arrives early. Throughout this season of renewal and discovery, activity heightens in the animal kingdom as many species begin their breeding season. Intervals of sun may be interspersed with sudden showers, unexpected frosts, and possibly even snow flurries, but once spring has arrived, the swell of new life and growth cannot be halted.

On a warm spring day, shrews, moles and tiny wood mice may emerge from hibernation, vulnerable targets for birds of prey. If your garden has a warm microclimate and you are fortunate enough to have a pond that is home to frogs, you will hear the repetitive mating call of the males until spawning time.

Throughout most of our region, blossoms of the red-flowering currant (*Ribes sanguineum*) vie with the arrival of swallows as harbingers of spring. This is a time to watch for new birds visiting your garden or passing by overhead. As well as swallows you may see red-winged blackbirds and perhaps a common nighthawk. One of the most exciting events of spring is the arrival of rufous hummingbirds looking for nectar-producing flowers and shrubs.

As the busy migration period subsides and the breeding season commences, every available nest box, hedge and dense tree will be appropriated by birds busily building nests. In the close quarters of an urban garden, much bird chatter

can be heard as various species claim and protect their own territories. Among the birds looking for nesting sites in March, April and May are cedar waxwings, house finches, juncos and sparrows. If you have a snag in your wild garden it may attract woodpeckers, chickadees or nuthatches.

Our own endeavours—providing birdhouses, food, and nesting materials—can assist the frenetic activity of the birds. Even the condition of the garden can make a difference; an overly tidy garden will not provide the same abundance of nesting materials as one which offers such items for salvage as moss, lichen, straw, twigs, cedar bark, mud and dead leaves.

In rural areas, hillside meadows bloom with such spring wildflowers as satin flower (*Sisyrinchium douglasii*), camas (*Camassia quamash*) and broad-leaved shooting star (*Dodecatheon hendersonii*); pink fawn lilies (*Erythronium revolutum*), trilliums (*Trillium ovatum*) and yellow wood violet (*Viola glabella*) are scattered through the woods and forests. The edges of woodland paths, coastal bogs and stream banks burst with displays of new growth which, year after year, never cease to be a source of wonder and inspiration to the wildlife gardener.

Summer

There is more to a summer garden than intense heat, lush abundance and lazy days. Early summer is a period of wildlife parenting, and with the good weather the wildlife garden is a centre of busy enterprise. As summer advances we become accustomed to the dawn chorus—a welcome sound when it does not include the cacophony of crows. The birds have timed this stage of family responsibility to coincide with the most favourable weather and abundant food resources.

Following the interval of nest-building and egg-laying, the garden sounds slowly subside, and by July and August there is almost a hush over the garden. Many adult birds are taking refuge in the undergrowth. For a number of species, this is the rather stressful period of summer moult, when mature birds lose feathers. During this interval flight becomes difficult and most species prefer to rest in a secluded spot. There is less birdsong and activity, although a few fledgings are about, and you may see some adults around the pond. The thoughtful wildlife gardener will attempt to provide a quiet, protected place where adults can seek respite and the young can acquire necessary survival skills.

The rufous hummingbirds, cedar waxwings, house finches, sparrows, juncos, woodpeckers, chickadees and nuthatches of spring are joined by the birds of summer: wrens, robins, warblers and goldfinches, among others. Although early summer brings an abundance of natural foods, the salmonberries favoured by robins and thrushes are not in season until June or July. Squirrels will then get into the act, collecting berries, nuts and seeds.

Dragonflies, who earlier in the season dazzled us with acrobatic mating displays, are now

concentrated around the garden pond. Here they lay their eggs just under the water, or on the stems and foliage of aquatic plants. Later, the surface of the pond will come alive with their progeny, and with a multitude of other summertime insects. The dragonflies feed on the tinier specimens, which are also devoured voraciously by swallows. Many salamanders forage at night and spend the daylight hours under litter, logs or rocks, but occasionally it is possible to see one of these interesting creatures sunbathing on a flat rock.

As summer moves toward its zenith, food is plentiful throughout the garden. In the flower borders bees and butterflies forage from blossom to blossom in search of nectar and pollen while caterpillars feed on the lush foliage. In the air, birds and bats devour flies, mosquitos and other flying insects. The warmer temperatures bring in greater numbers of ladybugs who help keep the aphid population in check. On the ground, slugs provide quick meals for garter snakes.

By midsummer, a hedge that is planted with salal (*Gaultheria shallon*) will be attracting grouse and band-tailed pigeons, who enjoy the purplish-black berries. In more rural areas, black-tailed deer may visit the garden to gorge on the foliage as well as the fruit. Deer are also attracted to the summer-ripening fruit of red osier dogwood (*Cornus stolonifera*).

Wildlife habitat or traditional landscape, roses belong in the summer garden. The native *Rosa nutkana* and *Rosa gymnocarpa* now come into full flower, requiring less cosseting than the hybrids, while providing an abundance of food for insects and birds with their hips and nectar. A wildlife garden should not need constant summer attention; natives planted in the appropriate site tend to be quite resilient to dry spells.

On summer evenings, moths and butterflies are lured by plants of the night, such as summer-flowering species with pale luminous colours, and night-scented plants, like honeysuckle (*Lonicera* spp.) and evening primrose (*Oenothera biennis*), which is indigenous not to the west coast, but to eastern North America. [Our native species is contorted-pod evening primrose (*Oenethera contorta*, also known as *Camissonia contorta*).] Adult bats leave their roosts at night to hunt for insects for their newborn, and can be seen at dusk swooping around the house and garden.

Although food is plentiful, at the height of summer garden wildlife can suffer from lack of water. Mammals such as raccoons may become irresistibly attracted to the garden pool and, worn out with thirst, may behave with less than their usual caution and emerge into a clearing to drink at the pond in the heat of the day. In prolonged dry spells, pool levels drop and some wetland areas may dry up completely. The need for water can be easily satisfied in a garden environment. During the summer months we can do a great service to our garden creatures by setting out extra birdbaths and dishes of water.

Fall

As summer melds into autumn, the days remain warm enough for gardeners to stay outside until dusk and enjoy this pleasant and productive season. The birds have recovered from their late summer moult, some resident species who have been feeding farther afield will return to the garden, and during the daytime the air once again reverberates with birdsong. Over the garden pond, dragonflies can still be seen dancing in the air and at night the shadowy shapes of bats flit through the darkening skies.

As fall progresses, we awaken to chilly mornings, but the afternoons are warm with the lingering sun. In years when we enjoy mellow autumn weather, the flowering plants continue to supply nectar for insects and seedheads for birds. In a mixed border, crowds of butterflies flock to imbibe for the last time on buddleia, Michaelmas daisies, yarrow, goldenrod and other exotics and natives. Myriad little creatures scrounge amid native shrubs which are still generously laden with hips and berries. Shrubbery foliage continues to protect birds, and many native shrubs are still abundant with fruit. One of the best food sources at this time of year is the long-lasting berry of the tall Oregon grape (*Mahonia aquifolium*).

Shorter days and cooler nights indicate the approach of winter and the start of the southward migration period for some of the bird population. Garden hedges may still be visited by robins, thrushes, nuthatches, western tanagers, chickadees, evening grosbeaks, sapsuckers, juncos or siskins, and many of them will remain, but soon the swallows' aerial antics will foretell their imminent departure, while other flocks huddle in nervous bunches preparing for their southward flight. Soon after the summer birds depart, the northern migrants begin to arrive. With new visitors to the garden reinforcing the ranks of the remaining birds, there is a greater need for supplemental food sources.

With winter drawing near, the wildlife gardener may forsake the usual garden houseclean-

ing tasks of autumn for jobs that help provide for the well-being of garden animals over the winter. Fallen leaves, rotting matter and dying plants provide vital warmth, nourishment and protective cover for a wide range of living creatures. By clearing, cutting back, and removing the debris, we limit their chances of survival. The considerate wildlife gardener will leave the garden to die back naturally.

Winter

Winter is welcome in the wildlife garden. Here, the season is not a dull and uneventful time: rich in its diversity of seasonal plants, birds and animals, the winter landscape of the wildlife garden teems with life beneath the frost, or, here on the west coast, behind the mist. In some years our winters are damp and mild, in other years a long chill settles over the winter garden. At those times the garden is quieter than usual, but the quiet is the serenity that visits the garden after a light snowfall, or the perfect stillness of a winter morning after a hard frost.

When that first frost does hit, a surprising number of foraging birds appear, seeking shelter in the sanctuary of the wildlife garden. Joining the flocks hardy enough to remain during the cold weather—the familiar sparrows, chickadees and Steller's jays—we may see finches, thrushes, pine siskins, juncos, bushtits, wrens, and possibly some woodpeckers, quail, a northern flicker or an Anna's hummingbird. As many as 130 species of birds have been sighted in our coastal region during a Christmas season.

Feeding winter birds is a favourite cold-weather activity, possibly because we can enjoy it from within our homes; watching the busy feeding tables from the kitchen window is a splendid way to while away the winter.

When setting up feeding stations, place different foods in separate locations in order to segregate the larger birds from the smaller, as well as to attract a broader range of species. Water should also be supplied. You may want to supplement the shelter provided by plants for roosting, refuge and cover from prevailing winds.

Some native trees and shrubs produce fruit that hangs on through autumn and into the winter. Examples are black hawthorn (*Crataegus douglasii*), Pacific crabapple (*Malus fusca*), orange honeysuckle (*Lonicera ciliosa*), salal (*Gaultheria shallon*), vine maple (*Acer circinatum*) and bigleaf maple (*Acer macrophyllum*).

Squirrels do not hibernate in winter but may become dormant in their nests or dens during extreme cold spells. As the winter cold intensifies, voles, shrews and moles spend increasingly greater portions of time underground, but during a rare mild break the occasional field mouse may venture out from the bottom of a brush pile on a quick scavenging excursion. Some mammals remain active in the woods and hedges throughout winter. A pair of black-tailed deer, or in some areas a snowshow hare, may wander into the garden in search of green foliage.

Toward winter's end the weather may still be cold, but wildlife will begin to prepare for the mating season. Female birds are developing

their strength for breeding, and supplemental food is more important than ever. It is still a bit too cold for the frogs, but they will soon begin to emerge from hibernation. A spell of weak sunshine will arouse some of the insects overwintering amid emerging greenery. It is still winter, but spring is stirring in the wildlife garden.

Attracting Wildlife to the Garden

It is almost inherent in the nature of a native plant garden to be a wildlife habitat garden as well, for it is a certainty that the plants will attract at least some members of the animal kingdom. The principles of native plant gardening can be applied to planning for wildlife: know your site and know the forms of wildlife native to the habitats found in your type of ecosystem and the area where you live. This is how you will know which species you can expect in your garden. For example, butterflies are usually associated with sunny open spaces, so if you have a dense woodland garden you may think that you cannot have butterflies. However, the western tiger swallowtail is a summertime frequenter of mixed and deciduous forests, so you may be able to attract it to your garden.

Creating a backyard nature sanctuary is an achievable goal, even in a small urban space. In establishing a wildlife garden there are a few points to consider.

○ It is possible for humans and wildlife to coexist harmoniously if we respect certain natural boundaries.

○ Native plants are optimal providers of food and shelter for wildlife.

○ On a restricted scale, a wildlife garden has the potential to expand naturally to attract an ever-increasing variety of wildlife species—even

within the physical limitations of a typical residential lot.

○ Converting your garden into a wildlife habitat is not an enterprise you can accomplish overnight; the best strategy is to proceed in stages, starting with a small corner of your garden.

Cover

Providing appropriate areas for potential wildlife visitors to your garden is a much more complex undertaking than putting up a few nesting boxes (although they are certainly important). Plants—even dead ones—are the best providers of shelter. Leaving a pile of leaves or a stack of decaying logs in a secluded part of the garden is an encouraging gesture to insects, birds and small mammals. Tall grasses and dense plantings of herbaceous plants help provide low cover. Thick shrubby hedges offer safe shelter to ground-foraging birds while others seek refuge in trees of various heights.

Your objective is a variety of safe, sheltered, undisturbed places which offer warm shelter, escape from danger, places to rest, and nesting areas for raising young. To be truly safe, these areas should offer protection not only from other wildlife but also from human traffic, household pets, and noise and air pollution. Such places should not be too difficult to find in a native plant garden where the plantings duplicate the vegetative layers found in the wild. Certain areas of your garden may be more appropriate than others, and you may want to designate these spots exclusively for wildlife use. The more undisturbed by humans the better, so consider placing buffers of dense vegetation between these designated areas and the busier and more cultivated parts of your garden.

Avoid disturbing your wildlife area. Vegetative litter, such as leaves, bark and small branches that accumulate and decompose on the ground provides a loose, moist, organic cover for diverse forms of life including spiders, earthworms, salamanders, and some birds of the underbrush, such as towhees and winter wrens. Allow patches of moss, fungus and lichen to remain undisturbed, grasses to go to seed, and shade-providing trees and shrubs to flourish unhindered by pruning shears. The only amendment to consider is the addition of a brush heap or a rock pile to help start things off and provide some extra cover. Do not allow the area to become a repository for garden and household odds and ends; garbage dumps and junk piles, as well as being unsightly, can contain objects and materials dangerous to wildlife. A thoughtfully maintained wild area can be as much a beauty spot as any other part of the garden.

Brush, logs and trees

If your garden does not contain many dense hedges or thickets of shrubs, a good alternative is a brush pile. Start with a foundation of rocks or logs to help prevent decomposition, then build a pile up to about 6 feet (2 m) high, piling the branches on top of each other in a loose criss-cross pattern. Although you may want to add to the pile as it dwindles, avoid disturbing it at nesting time. You may be rewarded by some very welcome occupants, such as ground-nesting bird families.

Logs and heavy branches can also be piled up to create a home for some wild creatures. Use varying lengths of logs and arrange them randomly—on end and lengthwise. You can create hiding places among the logs with rocks, bricks, clay drain tiles, or flower pots. Cover the pile with leaves and small twigs. Once it is in place, disturb it as little as possible. As the logs decay, you will find that they become damp and spongy, encouraging the growth of mosses, lichen and fungi, and the occupancy of beetles, centipedes, sowbugs, ants and spiders. In time, this insect population will invite toads, shrews, salamanders, and probably several more surprising visitors to this fertile haven. You may be fortunate enough, for example, to attract a pair of ruffed grouse, who must have a log for courtship purposes. If you do not wish to build a log pile, even a single log will do; one fallen log can develop into a nurse log with the potential to become colonized by a wide spectrum of wildlife species.

It may come as a surprise to learn that standing trees are most valuable to wildlife when they are in a state of decay. Mammals, birds, amphibians and insects use them for feeding, hunting, roosting, nesting and hibernating. If your garden contains a dead or decaying tree, you can trim it down a bit, leaving a few branches, and use it as a snag for wildlife habitation. It becomes even more attractive as shelter if you plant some native vines—honeysuckles (*Lonicera* spp.), for example—at the base.

Rocks

Rocks assembled in any form in the landscape offer crevices, crannies and cavities that provide shelter to small wildlife. The beauty of rock, from the animal's point of view, is that it is rarely disturbed. A pile of rocks near the edge of a pond is cover that offers amphibians insect-hunting grounds as well as safety from predators and shelter from the sun.

If your garden landscape has no natural rock outcrop, you can create one. In its simplest form this merely entails piling up rocks and stones of various sizes and shapes (include some flat ones for sunbathing) and arranging them to form openings for shelter. If you want to be a little more creative, you can construct tunnels in the base with lengths of clay drainpipe.

Stone walls and rockeries provide more

options for safe cover. Suitable rock garden plants are suggested in chapter 3.

Reading about rock structures

A number of books provide detailed information on building rock structures. The following books contain sections on rock construction.

- Attracting Backyard Wildlife, *by Bill Merilees.*
- The John Brookes' Garden Design Book, *by John Brookes.*
- Landscaping with Nature, *by Jeff Cox.*
- Northwest Landscaping, *by Michael Monro.*

Nesting boxes

At mating and nesting time a wide assortment of bird species are on the lookout for tree cavities in which to build homes for their broods. Because an urban garden can rarely offer enough trees to supply the demand, nest boxes are most welcome. Each box should be designed appropriately for the native species your environment will attract. In our Pacific coastal region some of the possibilities include chickadees, wrens, bluebirds, swallows, purple martins, and maybe flickers, owls, kestrels and woodpeckers. Choose boxes that are inconspicuous in colour and place them in low-traffic areas; swallows prefer open locations and chickadees, wrens and woodpeckers prefer shaded seclusion. Hang them with a slight forward tilt to keep rain from blowing in, and face the entrance hole away from the prevailing wind. Maintain the boxes annually by making any necessary repairs. Remove old nests before winter and pour in boiling water to destroy parasites. Although these are nesting boxes, designed for springtime use, if you rehang them for the winter they might be used for cold-weather roosting places.

You can sometimes help the birds in your vicinity by providing some natural nesting materials that can often be difficult for birds to find. These could include string or yarn in very short lengths (no more than 2 inches/6 cm for safety's sake); fleece; dried grass; small feathers; bulrushes; twigs, bark, moss, lichen and rootlets (from your own garden only); hair, spider webs, and other suitable natural materials. Place your offerings in a basket or mesh bag and hang it in a conspicuous spot in the garden.

Building nest boxes

Wildlife and nature shops carry nesting boxes specifically designed for various local bird species; if you wish to build your own, there are several good books that provide instruction. Two books that contain instructions as well as just about anything else you want to know about our local land birds, including feeding, are: Attracting Backyard Wildlife, *by Bill Merilees, and* A Guide to Feeding Winter Birds in British Columbia, *by Bob Waldon. The State of Washington Backyard Wildlife Sanctuary Program (see address at the end of this chapter) publishes an informative leaflet called* Nest Boxes for Birds, *as well as a* Winter Bird Feeding *guide.*

Bats and their shelters

Hallowe'en imagery and stories of vampire bats have given these creatures a bad reputation, but the bat is an innocuous, highly endangered mammal species. The smaller bats of this region are the most important predators of night-flying insects. They are not blind; a bat has an amazingly accurate sonar navigation system which enables it to manoeuvre adroitly in the dark.

Most of our local bat species roost and nest in loose bark, hollow trees, tree foliage, or remote caves. They can also be found in attics, under eaves, under shingles, or in outbuildings. To augment their nesting sites around your garden, try creating a bat shelter by placing a side-enclosed, open-bottomed box about 10 to 15 feet (3 to 5 m) above the ground on a tree or the side of a house, in a warm, sunny location. The inside should have a rough surface for bats to cling to when roosting.

Squirrels

Most squirrels are ingenious little creatures who need little help from us in locating appropriate tree holes or high shrubby branches in which to build their nests of leaves and twigs. In fact, squirrels often manage to have several nests in different places, a ruse to avoid detection by predators. Squirrels can derive the same benefits as other wildlife from dense, protected areas where there is ground litter and natural cover. They are herbivorous; their diets include nuts, seed, berries, bark, mushrooms and—to the gardener's chagrin—bulbs, buds and the shoots of young plants. They enjoy the produce of many of the shrubs suggested in the food-source list.

The squirrel is one mammal who has had no difficulty adapting to urban life. There is no doubt that squirrels—recently introduced species in particular—can be viewed as pests, but from another perspective they are amusing to observe in the garden as they nimbly run up trees, along branches, and from tree to tree, scolding and chattering, in search of food or a suitable hiding place for booty in the form of nuts or seeds.

Deer in the garden

Deer are sometimes regarded as adorable visitors to a garden, but more often they are seen as plant-devouring nuisances, particularly in rural areas. In some parts of the country deer present a serious environmental threat. The list of down-home solutions to the deer problem is prodigious—a watchdog for the garden, green soap hung on a tree or post, various forms of scarecrow—but in most cases these have not been highly successful. Wildlife gardeners often prefer not to resort to fences (and even they do not necessarily keep out the deer).

A wildlife corridor planted with tempting berry bushes may deflect interest from the garden vegetation. Another suggestion is the simple expedient of cultivating so many plants that there is enough for both deer and gardener. Or try planting some natives that are reputed to discourage deer from browsing. It's not a guarantee, but here are some suggestions: monkshood (*Aconitum* spp.), pearly everlasting (*Anaphalis margaritacea*) and Western red columbine (*Aquilegia formosa*).

Food

Feeding stations thoughtfully distributed throughout the garden help supplement nature's offerings when weather is harsh or if you wish to attract less common species. However, nothing can match the resources of nature for feeding wildlife. Native plants provide leaves, twigs, roots, seeds, nuts, berries, nectar and associated insects. A rich diversity of plants will feed a greater number of species. Some forms of wildlife eat a variety of vegetation, others feed exclusively from specific plants, and different creatures feed at different levels of the landscape.

In the wild, all forms of plant life provide food for wildlife. In our own gardens we can plant grasses, herbaceous plants, and trees that will offer some form of food to wildlife, but of all the plants we grow, very few will have greater potential than shrubs for providing meals—and other services—to a variety of animal life.

Food-providing shrubs

These are some of our native shrubs and the animals they feed and shelter. (* A species marked with an asterisk is described in chapter 4.)

○ Blue elderberry (*Sambucus caerulea*). One of nature's most abundant food storehouses, this plant feeds rabbits, squirrels, mice, chipmunks, and many species of birds, which consume the fruit; and deer and elk, which browse on the young twigs and foliage.

○ Bog, or swamp laurel (*Kalmia polifolia*).* Although this bog-loving little plant has the reputation of being poisonous to livestock and humans, wildlife seems immune to the toxic properties.

O Crowberry (*Empetrum nigrum*). The abundant fruit ripens in August and is important to the diet of the black bear. When midwinter snows make other foods scarce, grouse and ptarmigan eat the shiny black crowberries.

O Evergreen huckleberry (*Vaccinium ovatum*).* Birds and mammals are irresistibly drawn to the sweet, juicy fruit.

O Hairy manzanita (*Arctostaphylos columbiana*).* As soon as the fruit ripens it is devoured by grouse, jays, sparrows, chipmunks and ground squirrels. Birds and small mammals shelter in the dense foliage during all seasons. In some areas browsing deer keep the shrubs low and compact.

O Hazelnut (*Corylus cornuta*). Squirrels and jays harvest the brown nuts before they are ripe.

O Highbush-cranberry, or squashberry (*Viburnum edule*). Many birds enjoy the bright berries, and deer browse on the foliage.

O Kinnikinnick (*Arctostaphylos uva-ursi*). Grouse, band-tailed pigeons and bears feed on the brilliant red berries; deer browse on the twigs and leaves.

O Labrador tea (*Ledum groenlandicum*).* Animals do not tend to browse on this attractive evergreen shrub, perhaps because of its spicy odour, but the lovely white blossoms do attract bees.

O Red elderberry (*Sambucus racemosa*). Birds eat the fruit that ripens in July, and build their nests in the dense, closely-spaced branches. Bees and butterflies are attracted to the fragrance of the blossoms. Although the seeds do contain some properties that are toxic to humans, this is one of the most valuable plants for wildlife. (The fruits apparently are not harmful to other mammals or birds.)

O Red huckleberry (*Vaccinium parvifolium*). Grouse and birds snatch the edible, slightly tart berries as soon as they ripen—and later on inadvertently plant them. Deer and mountain goats browse on the twigs and leaves.

O Red osier dogwood (*Cornus stolonifera*).* The summer-ripening fruits feed many bird species. Moose, elk, deer, and small mammals browse on the twigs and foliage. Beaver and muskrat use the twigs to repair dams and build dens.

O Salal (*Gaultheria shallon*).* By midsummer, the seedy, purplish-black berries become a source of food that is relished by grouse and band-tailed pigeons. The fruit attracts bears, elk and black-tailed deer, which eat the foliage as well.

O Saskatoon, or serviceberry (*Amelanchier alnifolia*).* An important and nutritious food source to moose, deer and elk, which browse on the leaves and twigs. Birds and mammals feed on the berries.

O Shrubby cinquefoil (*Potentilla fruticosa*). Birds and small mammals eat the seeds and foliage.

O Slender wintergreen (*Gaultheria ovatifolia*). The bright red, summer-ripening berries attract many birds.

O Snowberry (*Symphoricarpos albus*). The nesting cover and protection that its many branches provide for birds and small mammals makes this an important and useful plant for wildlife. Pheasant and grouse consume the fruit in winter when wild foods become scarce (although humans find the taste unpleasantly bitter), and deer eat the foliage.

O Trailing raspberry (*Rubus pedatus*). The fruit is highly desirable to many bird species: wood thrushes, cedar waxwings, western tanagers, pine grosbeaks and grouse are among the multitude of birds that throng to this plant for its juicy berries.

❍ Wax myrtle (*Myrica californica*). Small mammals eat the wax-coated berries and deer browse the twigs and foliage.

❍ Western rhododendron (*Rhododendron macrophyllum*).* This beautiful native plant is unusual because it is not a good food source for wildlife: although mountain beaver nibble on the twigs, both leaves and flowers contain poisonous toxins, so the shrub has limited value as a food source for most animals.

Feeding the Birds

If birds are the wildlife creatures you are most interested in attracting, here is a list of plants that offer food to a variety of feathered species. (* An asterisk indicates that the species is described in chapter 4.)

Arbutus (*Arbutus menziesii*) *
Bitter cherry (*Prunus emarginata*)
Black gooseberry (*Ribes lacustre*)
Black hawthorn (*Crataegus douglasii*)
Black twinberry (*Lonicera involucrata*)
Blue elderberry (*Sambucus caerulea*)
Bunchberry (*Cornus unalaschkensis*) *
Coastal strawberry (*Fragaria chiloensis*)
Common juniper (*Juniperus communis*)
Creeping raspberry (*Rubus pedatus*)
Devil's club (*Oplopanax horridus*) *
Dull Oregon grape (*Mahonia nervosa*) *
Dwarf nagoon berry (*Rubus acaulis*)
False lily-of-the-valley (*Maianthemum
    dilatatum*) *
Garry oak (*Quercus garryana*) *
Gummy gooseberry (*Ribes lobbii*)
Hairy manzanita (*Arctostaphylos columbiana*) *
Highbush-cranberry or squashberry
    (*Viburnum edule*)
Indian-plum (*Oemleria cerasiformis*) *
Kinnikinnick (*Arctostaphylos uva-ursi*)
Mountain cranberry, or lingonberry
    (*Vaccinium vitis-idaea*)

Nootka rose (*Rosa nutkana*) *
Orange honeysuckle (*Lonicera ciliosa*)
Purple honeysuckle (*Lonicera hispidula*)
Red elderberry (*Sambucus racemosa*)
Red-flowering currant (*Ribes sanguineum*) *
Red huckleberry (*Vaccinium parvifolium*)
Red osier dogwood (*Cornus stolonifera*) *
Rocky Mountain juniper (*Juniperus scopulorum*)
Salal (*Gaultheria shallon*) *
Salmonberry (*Rubus spectabilis*) *
Saskatoon (*Amelanchier alnifolia*) *
Sitka mountain-ash (*Sorbus sitchensis*) *
Snowberry (*Symphoricarpos albus*)
Soap berry (*Shepherdia canadensis*)
Stink currant (*Ribes bracteosum*)
Tall Oregon grape (*Mahonia aquifolium*)
Thimbleberry (*Rubus parviflorus*)
Trailing snowberry (*Symphoricarpos mollis*)
Western yew (*Taxus brevifolia*)
Western tea-berry (*Gaultheria ovatifolia*)
Western flowering dogwood (*Cornus nuttallii*) *
Woodland strawberry (*Fragaria vesca*)

Hummingbird flowers

Hummingbird nests are difficult to spot because they are so tiny, delicate and well camouflaged. Whether or not you are able to find the nests, your native plant garden may be home to some hummingbirds, particularly if it contains some red and pink tubular flowers, or some of the native flowering plants listed below.

A red-coloured feeder placed in a shady location is a good supplementary food source, and will help attract even more of these tiny beauties. The recommended feeding solution is one part sugar to three or four parts water, boiled for about four minutes, then cooled. Honey, too much sugar, or artificial sweeteners can all have disastrous effects if substituted in the hummingbird diet.

The following plants are attractive to hummingbirds (*An asterisk indicates that the species is described in chapter 4; ❤ denotes a hummingbird favourite.)

Arbutus (*Arbutus menziesii*) *
Black twinberry (*Lonicera involucrata*)
Bog rosemary (*Andromeda polifolia*)
Bog laurel (*Kalmia polifolia*) *
Coast penstemon (*Penstemon serrulata*)
Davidson's penstemon (*Penstemon davidsonii*)
Dwarf raspberry (*Rubus acaulis*)
Evergreen huckleberry (*Vaccinium ovatum*) *
False azalea (*Menziesia ferruginea*)
Fireweed (*Epilobium angustifolium*) *
Gummy gooseberry (*Ribes lobbii*)
Hairy manzanita (*Arctostaphylos columbiana*) *
Kinnikinnick (*Arctostaphylos uva-ursi*)
Lingonberry (*Vaccinium vitis-idaea*)
Nodding onion (*Allium cernuum*)
Nootka rose(*Rosa nutkana*) *
❤ Orange honeysuckle (*Lonicera ciliosa*)
Purple honeysuckle (*Lonicera hispidula*)
Red huckleberry (*Vaccinium parvifolium*)
❤ Red-flowering currant (*Ribes sanguineum*) *
Salal (*Gaultheria shallon*) *
❤ Salmonberry (*Rubus spectabilis*) *
Shrubby penstemon (*Penstemon fruticosus*)
Slender blue penstemon (*Penstemon procerus*)
Snowberry (*Symphoricarpos albus*)

Trailing snowberry (*Symphoricarpos mollis*)
Twinflower (*Linnaea borealis*)
❤ Western red columbine (*Aquilegia formosa*) *

Water

"A garden without water is not a garden at all."

Those words were written over thirty years ago by the English writer Beverley Nichols in his popular book *Garden Open Today*. Mr. Nichols was not a wildlife habitat gardener, nor was he North American; in fact, he was a conventional English gardener (with a not-so-conventional personality). But water as a necessary garden ingredient is a universal and enduring concept among gardeners, and in a wildlife habitat garden, it becomes almost a natural extension of planting.

Birdbaths

When we see birds happily splashing away in a birdbath, most of us probably do not realize that they are engaged in an activity of far greater importance than getting clean and feeling fresh; they are dampening their feathers to make them waterproof and more efficient for flight. They also use the birdbath for relieving the discomfort of feather growth during moulting. After their baths the birds groom themselves, removing parasites and performing the critical task of oiling their feathers for insulation during cold, wet weather. They do this by running their bills through their feathers to spread oil from a gland located at the base of the tail.

Water is also important, of course, for regular drinking and bathing; not only for birds but also for many insects and amphibians. If you add a pond or birdbath to your premises, you will be amazed at the way it brings your garden to life. Without water, the range of wildlife attracted to the garden is limited.

Water can take many forms; almost any container will do, as long as it is clean. You can use an old pot (or a new one) or a half-barrel sunk into the ground. When you recycle an old container, scour it thoroughly to destroy damaging toxins before use by wildlife. A rock with a shallow depression makes an excellent birdbath, or you can go to the other extreme and develop a complex water garden with pools, water channels, waterfalls and fountains.

If you are going to have only one watering-place in your garden, you will probably want birds to be able to make use of it, so it should conform to the following criteria for birdbaths.

O At least part of the birdbath should be shallow (1 to 2 inches/3 to 5 cm), but a varied depth (up to 3 inches/8 cm) is optimal for satisfying different species. Rocks can be used to create different levels.

O The birdbath should be positioned for protection from predators. Try to locate it away from ground cover where a hunter (such as the household cat) can lie in wait. The reason so many birdbaths have pedestals is for protection. However, a shallow dish placed at ground level can provide water for insects and small mammals, as well as for birds. Some birdbaths are now designed to be hung from branches.

O Birdbath water should be changed at least every other day (a refill from the garden hose will do), and the birdbath should be kept clean with regular scouring to prevent a build-up of mosquito larvae and pond scum. Try to locate the bath far enough away from bird boxes and feeders to keep the water free from pollution by shells, seeds and bird droppings.

O Chemicals should never be added to water being used by wildlife. If fertilizers are added to the soil or to lawn close to the edge of a pond, run-off into the water may alter its chemical structure and encourage algae. To prevent this, consider incorporating thick plantings or other barrier materials around the perimeter.

However, all forms of wildlife suffer to some degree from exposure to chemicals, so the best solution is to avoid chemical fertilizers; they are really not appropriate in a wildlife garden.

O The birdbath should not be constructed of metal, since wet birds may freeze to metal in very cold weather. During cold spells it is a good idea to set a plastic saucer into the birdbath so that ice can be popped out and replaced with fresh water.

O Feathered creatures seem to be happiest in natural (meaning muddy) ponds, so if you have such an area in your garden consider how to make it most accessible to your birds. A mud puddle not only seems to give the birds great pleasure, the mud is useful at nest-building time. (Butterflies also visit patches of moist soil to drink up the minerals.)

O The sound of running water is very alluring to birds. Whether from the splash of a fountain or the slow drip of a water spout or hose nozzle, the presence of moving water can help attract birds to your garden.

Amphibian ponds

Installing a small pond can multiply your garden's biodiversity and attract wildlife other than birds. Many amphibian habitats have been sacrificed to urban development, and few of us have the pleasure of hearing the once-familiar sound of a spring frog chorus. Toads, too, can be lured by a pond, as most species prefer to stay close to a body of water, particularly at breeding time when the eggs are deposited in shallow water or submerged vegetation.

Providing a home to small amphibians can be advantageous in terms of controlling the insect population. Although the frog population is rapidly diminishing on a global scale, in the Pacific coastal region we can still find some tailed frogs, Pacific treefrogs, red-legged frogs, and spotted frogs as well as western toads. Toads can be identified by the singing of the adult males; they make a sound like the peeping of baby chicks! Other native creatures who would be happy in or around a pond are painted turtles, rough-skinned newts and a variety of salamanders.

Toads are night-hunters, feeding on a diet that includes slugs, sowbugs, earwigs and cutworms. Although they like to be near a source of water, the adults actually live in dryer areas of the landscape, preferring cool, dark, out-of-the-way places, sometimes near rocks. You can provide homes for these beneficial, insect-eating little creatures by placing rocks or chunks of wood over depressions in the ground, or cutting a small round entrance hole in the rim of an old clay pot—the best size is 4 inches deep by 8 inches in diameter (10 cm by 20 cm). Place the pot upside down in a secluded, shady spot amid vegetation.

If you are thinking about building a pond for amphibians, take these factors into consideration.

○ Pool sides should slope gently. The steep sides of some constructed ponds are hazardous for amphibians, who often cannot climb out. Using logs and rocks to build up the bottom is one means of offering an escape route. Extending some rocks and logs above the pond's surface provides a stand for birds to drink from and an island where dragonflies may lay their eggs. A log or a rock pile near the pool will offer further escape routes.

○ Plants and grasses in and around the pond provide cover and forage for amphibians.

○ Do not put goldfish in the pond because fish eat amphibian eggs.

○ To keep the water temperature desirably warm, locate the pond in full sunlight.

○ Keep the water level constant.

○ If you are fortunate enough to be close to a natural wilderness area, try, if possible, to plan your garden so that the pond location is linked to this area by your own natural plantings.

○ When there are amphibians in a pond, water algae is not a problem, as tadpoles feed on it.

○ If you despair of being able to naturally attract amphibians to your garden, it is possible to collect tadpoles from the wild. Do this only if there is a tadpole population within 5/8 mile (1 km) of your home, and talk to a professional environmentalist before taking this step, as it could be environmentally threatening.

Pond construction

Select the pond location carefully. Choose a site that does not disturb existing natural habitat or wildlife communities. Locate the pond where it will receive at least five hours of sunlight each day during the growing season. Also consider the kind of wildlife you want in your pond. Goldfish are beneficial in a small pond because, as well as being interesting and attractive, they eat mosquito larvae. But they also eat amphibian eggs, so you will have to make a choice between fish and frogs. As for birds, we know that they require clean, shallow baths, and the habits of some amphibians may create a pond that is too messy for the birds. Each creature has its own requirements and they cannot all be housed together.

To construct a pond, first dig a hollow to the desired shape and size of your pool. Generally speaking, a wildlife pond should be at least 7 feet (2.5 m) wide by 30 inches (75 cm) deep. Line it with a pool liner material. Flexible synthetic rubber is the common choice and PVC is a preference because it comes in large seamless sheets. Cover the bottom, fitting the liner well up and over the sides. Bury the edges with soil and rocks. Slowly fill the pond with water, then wait about a week (for any chlorine to dissipate) before adding plants. Plants can be plunged container and all into the pool, or you can add a 1-foot (30-cm) layer of soil to the bottom and install your water plants directly into the soil. (The latter method requires a deeper pool because of the added soil.)

Pond publications

If you are considering constructing a pond yourself, books about general garden design often contain instructions. These are some publications you may find helpful.

O Attracting Backyard Wildlife, *by Bill Merilees.*
O The John Brookes' Garden Design Book, *by John Brookes.*
O Landscaping with Nature, *by Jeff Cox.*
O Sunset Water Gardening, *edited by Sunset Books.*
O The Water Garden, *by Peter Robinson.*
O Water Gardens: A Harrowsmith Gardener's Guide, *edited by David Archibald and Mary Patton.*
O Water Gardens, *by Philip Swindells.*

Native plants for the pond

Bladderwort (*Utricularia vulgaris*) is a yellow-flowering plant that floats on the surface of the water. As well as being attractive it is interesting and useful, as it is carnivorous. The plant's bladders, borne on the leaves, trap and absorb any tiny, crustacean-like aquatic creatures floating nearby. Look for bladderwort in a friend's pond or at a plant exchange; it is difficult to obtain. The other plants mentioned here are all available at specialist nurseries.

An overabundance of algae in the water indicates an unhealthy pond. More oxygen is required, and this can be added with a water pump or by adding oxygenating plants to your pond. One example of a useful oxygenator is the creeping underwater coontail (*Ceratophyllum demersum*).

When selecting most of the plants for your pond, water depth is a consideration. Here are some appropriate natives in descending order of the water depth to which they may be submerged.

O Wild calla lily (*Calla palustris*)—Submerge up to 14 inches (35 cm) deep; very ornamental with a dazzling white flower spathe.
O Common cattail (*Typha latifolia*)—Submerge to 12 inches (30 cm); grows up to 10 feet (3 m) tall.
O Water plantain (*Alisma plantago-aquatica*)—Submerge to 10 inches (25 cm); small white flowers.
O Broad-leaved arrowhead (*Sagittaria latifolia*)—Submerge to 8 inches (20 cm).
O Marsh marigold (*Caltha palustris*)—Submerge to 4 to 6 inches (10 to 15 cm).

A garden wetland

A wetland area is a desirable element in a native plant garden. If you have such a spot in your garden, instead of trying to solve the problem by draining the water, why not encourage the site's natural dynamic by planting some wetland natives? (Refer to the list in the wetlands section of chapter 4.)

Lacking a natural wetland area, you can create one by using a liner to retain moisture. If you are interested in constructing such a bog garden, *Garden Pool Design*, by Helmut Jantra, provides instruction.

Insects in the wildlife garden

The wildlife gardener, unlike some conventional gardeners, is in a position to welcome insects into the garden, regarding them as an integral part of a biodiverse ecosystem. Insects are fascinating creatures, and most of us—not just wildlife gardeners—find some of them very attractive. Almost everyone recognizes the beauty of butterflies, and a realistic gardener will accept the sacrifice of a few leaves to caterpillars in order to enjoy the later butterflies. Dragonflies, too, are usually appreciated, especially when they skim over a quiet pond on a lazy summer afternoon. But what about all the other insect forms that so many of us find repellent and damaging to our garden plants?

Ladybugs have come to be valued in the garden for their usefulness as predators of plant-damaging insects, particularly aphids, and there are many other insects we can welcome into the garden as beneficial predators. In a biodiverse garden with a healthy, balanced ecosystem the beneficial predators and parasites maintain a natural control of the garden's insect population. In a well-established native plant garden, no other methods of pest control should be necessary. In fact, pesticides will debilitate the beneficial insect population, destroying the garden's natural control system.

Predators are those insects that prey upon other insects. As well as ladybugs and their lar-vae, some garden predators are lacewings and their larvae, syrphid fly larvae, ground beetles and their larvae, yellowjacket wasps and some mites. The much-maligned spider clan feeds almost entirely on insects.

Parasites are such insects as braconid and icheumonid wasps and tachnid flies, which destroy other insects by living on or in them. These parasites can inhabit the egg, the larva, or sometimes the adult insect.

Two sure methods of attracting beneficial insects are growing a seasonal succession of flowering plants, particularly small flowers rich in nectar, and encouraging biodiversity by planting a wide variety of species in a mix of habitats. This offers insects the necessary nectar sources, alternate hosts, shelter, overwintering areas and pupation sites.

Insects are critically important creatures in the natural food chain. In a healthy garden an active insect population adds to wildlife diversity by providing food for birds, reptiles and amphibians and some mammals. We must also consider their valuable contribution to plant life and garden cultivation. Insects pollinate flowers, break down decaying vegetation and aerate the soil.

Butterflies

A butterfly garden has much popular appeal. Planning a garden expressly to attract these beautiful insects is not difficult, because each butterfly species has surprisingly specific association with certain plants. You have probably noticed that butterflies tend to frequent only certain areas of your garden; they are concentrating on particular plants (although sometimes it is a patch of wet soil—or manure—that lures them). To attract more butterflies to your garden, learn the food preference of each species—both the food source for the larvae and the nectar source for the adults.

A butterfly garden can be a beautiful show-case for some of your more spectacular introduced species. Butterflies are attracted to bold, bright colours and sometimes exotics are the most showy and vibrant plants in the garden.

Here is a list of some of the butterflies of our region and their preferred food-source plants, native and exotic.

O Species: Anise swallowtail
Caterpillar food: cow-parsnip, fennel, carrot, dill, *Lomatium* spp.
Nectar source: penstemons, zinnia, lantana butterfly bush, *Lomatium* spp.

O Species: Brown elfin
Caterpillar food: apple, arbutus, kinnikinnick (*Arctostaphylos uva-ursi*), salal (*Gaultheria shallon*)
Nectar source: bitter cherry

O Species: Leto fritillary
Caterpillar food: violets (*Viola* spp.)
Nectar source: flowers in the composite family (Compositae), mint, dogbane

O Species: Lorquin's admiral
Caterpillar food: spiraea, poplar, cottonwood, birch, pacific crabapple (*Malus fusca*), willow, oceanspray
Nectar source: thistles, dogbane, many others

O Species: Milbert's tortoiseshell
Caterpillar food: willow, stinging nettle
Nectar source: Compositae

O Species: Mourning cloak
Caterpillar food: willows (*salix* spp.), poplars, elms
Nectar source: Compositae, buddleia, sap, fruit

O Species: Mylitta crescent spot
Caterpillar food: thistle
Nectar source: Compositae

O Species: Ochre ringlet
Caterpillar food: grasses
Nectar source: dandelion, sweet clovers, many others

O Species: Pale tiger swallowtail
Caterpillar food: red alder (*Alnus rubra*), poplar, chokecherry, hawthorn, Saskatoon (*Amelanchier alnifoia*), *Ceanothus* spp.
Nectar source: cascara (*Rhamnus purshiana*), *Penstemon* spp., many others

O Species: Purplish copper
Caterpillar food: potentilla, docks, sorrel, cinquefoil
Nectar source: docks, baby's breath, fennel

O Species: Red admiral
Caterpillar food: stinging nettle
Nectar source: fireweed (*Epilobium angustifolium*), asters, chrysanthemum

O Species: Sara orange-tip
Caterpillar food: mustard family plants, especially *Arabis* spp.
Nectar source: bitter cherry, strawberry, *Mimulus* spp.

O Species: Satyr anglewing
Caterpillar food: stinging nettle
Nectar source: blackberries, rotting fruit

O Species: Silver-bordered fritillary
Caterpillar food: Canada violet (*Viola canadensis*)
Nectar source: Compositae

O Species: Silvery blue
Caterpillar food: legumes, including lupines, purple peavine (*Lathyrus nevadensis*)
Nectar source: lupines, Compositae, bitter cherry, *Lomatium* spp.

○ Species: Snowberry checkerspot
Caterpillar food: snowberry (*Symphoricarpos albus*)
Nectar source: Compositae

○ Species: Spring azure
Caterpillar food: oceanspray (*Holodiscus discolor*),
dogwood (*Cornus* spp.), *Spiraea* (pink forms),
Vaccinium spp., *Ceanothus* spp.
Nectar source: violets (*Viola* spp.), *Ceanothus* spp.

○ Species: Western meadow fritillary
Caterpillar food: violets (*Viola* spp.)
Nectar source: Compositae, buckwheats

○ Species: Western sulphur
Caterpillar food: legumes
Nectar source: Compositae

○ Species: Western tiger swallowtail
Caterpillar food: willow, poplar, aspen, maples
Nectar source: blackberry, phlox, lilac, hibiscus,
buddleia

○ Species: Woodland skipper
Caterpillar food: grasses
Nectar source: pearly everlasting (*Anaphalis margaritacea*), Compositae

Backyard Habitat Programs

Visions of wild things in the garden are attractive to some of us, less so to others. If the idea appeals to you, by now you may be feeling quite prepared to convert your backyard into a full-fledged nature sanctuary. You should be aware, however, that if you invite wildlife into your garden you cannot always be selective about the creatures you attract. An established, biodiverse native plant garden that offers food and shelter to some creatures is probably going to be an appropriate environment for a variety of others —some of them perhaps unwelcome predators. The first step in planning a wildlife habitat garden should be a decision-making one. Do you really want your backyard to be a wildlife sanctuary; is this an enterprise into which you can enter with real commitment?

Another drawback is the difficulty in implementing some of these wildlife-attracting ideas and projects. This is an ambitious venture to take on alone. Fortunately, there are public programs that lend support to gardeners wanting to cultivate an environment that helps restore and protect wildlife.

Naturescape is a program sponsored jointly by the British Columbia and Canadian governments and some not-for-profit societies. Designed to promote caring for wildlife at home, Naturescape provides tools to help us restore and protect the natural world. The idea is to encourage us all to take a few steps beyond recycling and composting in the interests of environmental conservation. When you join you receive a kit that contains instructions for wildlife habitat projects, such as building a pond or constructing wildlife nesting boxes; extensive and fascinating information about native plants and animals; and a regional resource booklet. The information package that is included with membership provided some of the resource material for this chapter.

For more details or membership information, contact Naturescape British Columbia, 300 - 1005 Broad Street, Victoria BC, V8W 2A1.

Another environmental program, Project Wild places an emphasis on education, offering workshops and activity guides designed to give hands-on experience and practical knowledge. For information, contact Project Wild Coordinator, Ministry of Environment, Lands and Parks, 300 - 1005 Broad Street, Victoria BC, V8W 2A1; telephone (604) 356-7111, or 1-800-387-9369.

In the United States, similar programs have been in place for awhile. The Backyard Wildlife Habitat Program, operating since 1973, encourages good wildlife management practices. Eligible members' properties become certified and are entered in the National Register of Backyard Wildlife Habitats. *A Gardening for Wildlife* kit is available. Contact the National Wildlife Federation, Backyard Habitat Program, 1400 Sixteenth Street, N.W. Washington DC, 20036-2266.

The Backyard Wildlife Sanctuary Program is administered by the Department of Wildlife in Washington State. The program offers information to help home owners become better habitat managers on their own property. Contact Washington Department of Fish and Wildlife, 16018 Mill Creek Road, Mill Creek WA, 98012.

6

 **WHO?**

The Human Connection

Our Land's Aboriginal Heritage

We think of this land as having remained unaltered from its natural state until European settlement, but that is not quite the case. The aboriginal peoples had an intimate relationship with the land and a significant impact on it. The northwest coastal peoples employed a system of land management which seems, from the present perspective, admirably in tune with the forces of nature.

By the controlled use of burning, aboriginal peoples were able to increase their harvest of important food plants. Selected woods and meadowlands were periodically burned to remove shrub species and keep the density of trees low. This kept the area in a state of secondary succession and prevented the forest from encroaching on the open meadows. Staple food plants such as camas (*Camassia quamash* and *C. leichtlinii*), other root vegetables, and some plants bearing fruit and nuts flourished in these open conditions, and so a continuous source of food was ensured. Some of the open meadow system that today remains in our coastal region is the legacy of this method of land management.

The relationship between early peoples and the land was deep and intricate. The life of each person was integrally connected with plants and depended on a knowledge of them. Plants offered an abundance of uses to these peoples, and one of the most important was food. Daily life revolved around the food cycle; during the growing season groups would set out from their villages on food-gathering expeditions, harvesting and processing foods for winter storage, and

in winter months food was a central focus of many feasts and festivals.

Although coastal peoples did not domesticate plants, they did manage and enhance the production of some foods. In some cases they owned certain productive parcels of land, trading the harvesting rights, and passing the land on through inheritance. As well as being cleared of encroaching shrubs and trees by burning, these patches of land were regularly worked to remove stones and weeds. When bulbs were dug, the earth was carefully peeled back in sods and only the larger bulbs taken, leaving the smaller ones to grow.

Today, our relationship with wild plants will perhaps deepen with some understanding of their importance to First Nations peoples.

The plants and their uses

These brief introductions to some coastal peoples' uses of a handful of familiar native plants are not intended as directions or suggestions. Because of the powerful properties of some of these plants—for example, devil's club (*Oplopanax horridus*)—attempts to replicate any of these plant uses without appropriate knowledge and experience could invite disaster.

Camas (*Camassia quamash* and *C. leichtlinii*)
The bulbs of camas were a staple food for many coastal peoples. Family groups would visit the camas fields from late spring to midsummer, the women spending long hours of backbreaking work digging the small onion-like bulbs with sticks designed expressly for the purpose. When the bulbs were not available in home territory,

they were procured by trade; camas was widely traded both along the coast and with peoples of the interior. Sometimes, rather than bulbs being traded, harvesting rights were bartered—camas fields were an example of land which was sometimes owned and inherited.

The camas was covered with leaves of sword fern (*Polystichum munitum*) and salal (*Gaultheria shallon*) and baked in large cooking pits dug in the ground, then dried in the sun and stored in baskets for winter use. The cooking process made this carbohydrate-rich vegetable sweet and digestible. Sometimes the bulbs were formed into loaves or mashed and pressed together like a cheese, then boiled in a stew with salmon. Camas was a favourite food at feasts and potlatches.

[The common, blue-flowering camas enjoyed by the coastal peoples is not to be confused with the creamy-blossomed death camas (*Zygadenus venenosus*), whose toxic bulbs, although similar in appearance to those of *Camassia quamash*, are potentially fatal.]

Other root vegetables cooked by a similar process included chocolate lily (*Fritillaria lanceolata*), tiger lily (*Lilium columbianum*), brodiaeas (*Brodiaea* spp.) and wild onions (*Allium* spp.).

Salmonberry (*Rubus spectabilis*)

A favourite food of northwest coastal peoples, salmonberry was valued for the sprouts as well as the berries. The children enjoyed the tender new shoots, or sprouts, which grow on the bushes in early spring; they would break them off, peel away the tender skin, and munch on them like candy. Gathered in spring and summer, the new shoots were also steamed and eaten as a green vegetable. The moist-fruited berries were eaten fresh, often with salmon. Salmonberry patches were sometimes owned, but the harvest was often shared.

Salmonberry was also valued for its medicinal properties, particularly its astringent quality. A salve of bark or chewed leaves was applied to burns, festering wounds, and aching teeth. A brew made of bark boiled in seaweed was used for the relief of labour pain, and for cleaning infected wounds and burns.

Salmonberry was an all-around useful shrub; as well as food and medicine uses, small implements were carved from the stems.

Salmonberries are one of the earliest fruits to ripen in this region. Their ripening period, from May to June, has long been associated with the song of the Swainson's thrush, known as the salmonberry bird in many First Nations languages.

Other fruit-bearing plants that were used extensively include gooseberries and currants (*Ribes* spp.), thimbleberry (*Rubus parviflorus*), wild strawberries (*Fragaria* spp.), huckleberries (*Vaccinium* spp.), salal (*Gaultheria shallon*), Pacific crabapple (*Malus fusca*), highbush-cranberry (*Viburnum edule*) and bog cranberry (*Vaccinium oxycoccus*).

Western red cedar (*Thuja plicata*)

All living things were traditionally viewed as having supernatural qualities, and the western red cedar was regarded as being particularly sacred. A plant of prominent importance to indigenous peoples, it was the most extensively used wood throughout the coastal region. In fact, the cultural boundaries of the northwest coast peoples can be defined by the large-scale use of western red cedar.

The uses of the wood were almost limitless; some of the items produced were house planks, posts and roofing materials, totem poles, canoes, fishing weirs, fishing floats, paddles, arrow shafts, spindles, harpoon shafts, spears, hooks, clubs, benches, cooking utensils, boxes, cradles, coffins, combs, rattles and masks. The bark was even more ubiquitous: it was used for a wide variety of cooking and eating utensils including dishes, platters and baskets, as well as mats, cord, tinder and torches; shredded finely it was used for towels, clothing and hats. The limbs were used for ropes and weaving materials. Even the roots were dug and used for a cording material.

Sometimes called the *tree of life,* cedar was also used for medicinal purposes. The buds were chewed and swallowed for sore lungs or toothache. Roots were sometimes boiled for a cold medicine; an infusion of the bark and twigs was thought to alleviate kidney problems; another infusion, from the limbs, was taken to relieve venereal diseases, and a brew of seeds and the ends of limbs was drunk to break a fever.

Although it was not eaten, cedar did have food uses. Food was cooked inside cedar baskets, boughs were used for catching herring spawn and for layering between drying seaweed, and the wood made a fine fuel for drying fish.

One of the cedar's most significant roles in the life of the coastal peoples was spiritual. The leaves and limbs were used for scouring the body in preparation for ceremonial occasions; whalers warded off bad luck in preparation for a hunt by placing branches under their beds; after the removal of a corpse from a house the walls were swept with cedar limbs; prayers for protection were sung to the tree before harvesting; even the simple act of standing with the back to the tree was believed to confer strength.

For all the use they derived from western red cedar, aboriginal peoples felled very few trees. Instead, they used fallen logs, or split planks off standing trees. When the bark was harvested, a wide strip was left so that the tree would not be killed.

Other culturally significant trees were red alder (*Alnus rubra*), Pacific yew (*Taxus brevifolia*), Douglas-fir (*Pseudotsuga menziesii*), Sitka spruce (*Picea sitchensis*), and bigleaf, Douglas and vine maples (*Acer macrophyllum, A. glabrum, A. circinatum*).

Devil's club (*Oplopanax horridus*)

This spiny perennial shrub of dense moist thickets has been an exceptionally important plant to west coast aboriginal peoples for its medicinal and spiritual qualities, and remains so today. Related to ginseng, it is one of the most important medicinal plants in the region. Infusions and poultices were made of the roots, bark and stems for the broadest imaginable spectrum of disorders: fever, stomach problems, arthritis, rheumatism, colds, coughs, tuberculosis, measles, lice, swollen glands, boils and infections.

Cosmetics were another application of devil's club. Aboriginal peoples used it for deodorant, talcum powder and hair conditioner. A more serious cosmetic function was ceremonial; it was used in making face paint and tattoo ink. The prickly characteristic of devil's club provided grounds for the belief that it contained protective powers; taken internally it was used to acquire strength, for purification, or to augment a shaman's supernatural powers. Devil's club sticks were used as protective charms, and its stems were hung over doorways to protect from supernatural powers.

Devil's club was also used to make fishing lures.

Vanilla leaf (*Achlys triphylla*)

An infusion made from the leaves of this beautiful little forest-floor plant was drunk for tuberculosis. The plant's uses were diverse: mashed and soaked in water it was drunk as an emetic; boiled, the leaves were used as a hair wash. Possibly its most popular use was as an insect repellent: the leaves were dried and hung from the ceiling in bunches to keep away flies and mosquitoes. Vanilla leaf is still used this way; the fragrant bundles perfume the air with their sweet vanilla fragrance (hence the common name) which becomes stronger as the leaves become older and drier—and, surprisingly, greener.

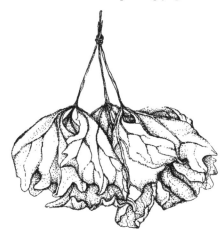

Kinnikinnick (*Arctostaphylos uva-ursi*)

The dry, mealy berries of this low-growing shrub were eaten by some, but not all, of the coastal peoples. There were various ways to eat the berries; one was to pop them, like popcorn, in salmon lard. A good source of vitamin C, the berries were also eaten fresh, or dried and stored, then mixed with oil or sometimes with salmon eggs. Sometimes the berries were boiled in soup, and the leaves were used in tea, or chewed as a thirst-quencher. Because the berries remain on the plants over winter, kinnikinnick could be regarded as an emergency food.

Food was a secondary function of kinnikinnick; the much more popular use was as a smoking mixture. The leaves were dried and pulverized and smoked alone until the introduction of tobacco, then mixed with it.

Medicinally, the leaves were used as a treatment for kidney diseases and urine infections. Canker sores, weak gums, broken bones and eye ailments were also treated by infusions from various parts of this plant.

In ceremonial and spiritual use, kinnikinnick branches were used as bedding for a bereaved spouse and the leaves were put into shoes for spiritual protection. The partner in mourning could not eat kinnikinnick berries for one year after the spouse's death.

Today the drug uva-ursi, derived from kinnikinnick, is used commercially as a treatment for bladder and kidney ailments. A brew from the leaves is drunk as a tea in Russia.

❧ ❧ ❧

Ferns and sea plants were two important plant food groups for the coastal people, but mushrooms, interestingly, were not—although some peoples ate the fungus growing on the leaves of the false azalea (*Menziesia ferruginea*).

These are just a few examples of the wealth of lore concerning the relationship between the aboriginal peoples, the land, and the plants they harvested. If this has piqued your interest in information about aboriginal peoples' use of plants, or the general subject of uses of wild plants, you may be interested in the following publications.

○ *Discovering Wild Plants: Alaska, Western Canada, the Northwest*, by Janice J. Schofield.

○ *Ethnobotany of Western Washington*, by Erna Gunther.

○ *Food Plants of the Coastal First Peoples*, by Nancy J. Turner.

○ *Northwest Native Harvest*, by Carol Batdorf.

○ *Plants for all Reasons: Culturally Important Plants of Aboriginal Peoples of Southern Vancouver Island*, compiled by students of the Environmental Studies Program, University of Victoria.

○ *Plants of Coastal British Columbia*, by Jim Pojar and Andy MacKinnon.

○ *Thompson Ethnobotany*, by Nancy J. Turner, Laurence C. Thompson, M. Terry Thompson, and Annie Z. York.

○ *Traditional Plant Foods of Canadian Indigenous Peoples: Nutrition, Botany and Youth*, by Harriet V. Kuhnlein and Nancy J. Turner.

Postscript

As a sad afternote to the above, here is an excerpt from the Garry Oak Meadow Colloquium (Proceedings), *held in Victoria in 1993.*

> *Aboriginal management ceased with European settlement. . . . Native peoples were displaced and their burning regimes interrupted. . . . Meadows were converted to fields and pastures and sheep and cattle introduced. As settlement proceeded, fires were seen as undesirable and actively suppressed. Exotic plant species were introduced for food, fodder, and amenity value, or by accident. As human population increased and land became more valuable, infilling and urban expansion destroyed or fragmented remaining areas of native vegetation.*

Today and Beyond

We can't turn back the clock, but it is never too late to shape the present for future promise. Habitat restoration is an interesting, fulfilling and productive project for an individual, a family or a neighbourhood. It is exciting and encouraging to see the concept generate so much interest, to observe so many native plant gardens appearing on the landscape, and to realize that indigenous plants are being used and appreciated on a scale that, in my own lifetime, has not occurred before.

Public use

One of the most promising signs is the emerging interest in native plants on the part of municipalities and public works departments. Still very much in its infancy, there is a movement toward a more naturalistic direction in municipal landscaping, and this often involves the use of native plants. In my home municipality, Douglas-firs (*Pseudotsuga menziesii*) are being used as part of massed natural plantings in large public parks; dogwood trees (*Cornus nuttallii*) are planted at woodland edges; Garry oak seedlings (*Quercus garryana*) grow on dry hillsides; the grounds of public utility buildings are landscaped with dense shrubbery borders of kinnikinnick (*Arctostaphylos uva-ursi*), snowberry (*Symphoricarpos albus*) and ocean-spray (*Holodiscus discolor*), and traffic islands display small beds of native flowers and shrubs. A few large parks now have functional and beautiful windbreaks planted in hedgerow style, using Indian-plum (*Oemleria cerasiformis*), Saskatoon (*Amelanchier alnifolia*), snowberry (*Symphoricarpos albus*), red-flowering currant (*Ribes sanguineum*), oceanspray (*Holodiscus discolor*) and nootka rose (*Rosa nutkana*). The municipality is also encouraging developers to save and protect existing old hedgerows.

This municipality (the District of Saanich

on Vancouver Island) is on the cutting edge of this new movement; it is receiving an enthusiastic response from local residents, and Saanich is encouraged to continue promoting the native plant concept. Perhaps its success will encourage others to initiate public native plant programs.

More and more native plants are being included in the landscaping surrounding town halls and municipal offices, and regional districts appear to be using them in greenways and connector corridors. Positive public response will encourage this trend, and as it gathers momentum it will provide an inspiring model for residential gardeners

Land reclamation

Indigenous plants play a key role in rehabilitating industrially damaged land. Mine tailings, metal extraction sites and old gravel pits become barren, devastated wastelands: dry, steeply sloped, and covered in sand and coarse rock. These disturbed areas are being reclaimed using plants that would have been there before the sites were disrupted.

In a sympathetic rehabilitation program, seeds are collected from the area, then propagated in a nursery environment and returned to the site, ensuring that the plant material is appropriate. Topsoil is sometimes salvaged and reused, substantial amounts of fertilizer are applied, and occasionally, but not often, the site is irrigated. Forage species—grasses, legumes, trees and shrubs—are planted and the vegetative cover that is reestablished becomes useful for wildlife. Steep slopes are modified and stabilized from erosion by the plants.

As well as being restored as habitat, the site regains aesthetic value. Green shoots begin to appear the first year after seeding, and within five to eight years the growth of trees and shrubs

has brought about a complete transformation to the site.

Plants are chosen from a wide range, dependent upon the location of the site. Some of the plants used in regional reclamation projects are arbutus (*Arbutus menziesii*), bunchberry (*Cornus canadensis* and *C. unalaschkensis*), Garry oak (*Quercus garryana*), juniper (*Juniperus communis*), kinnikinnick (*Arctostaphylos uva-ursi*), Indian-plum (*Oemleria cerasiformis*), mock orange (*Philadelphus lewisii*), Pacific rhododendron (*Rhododendron macrophyllum*), red osier dogwood (*Cornus stolonifera*), salal (*Gaultheria shallon*), salmonberry (*Rubus spectabilis*), Saskatoon (*Amelanchier alnifolia*), snowbrush (*Ceanothus velutinus*), thimbleberry (*Rubus parviflorus*), trembling aspen (*Populus tremuloides*), wild ginger (*Asarum caudatum*) and wild roses (*Rosa nutkana* and *R. gymnocarpa*).

Future generations

For my friend Leone, a poster provided the impetus in a serendipitous series of events. A schoolteacher in Victoria, Leone came across a beguiling native plant poster at a garden show. She was immediately intrigued, purchased it, and displayed it on the wall of her grade-three classroom. The children were soon asking about the plants, and Leone found herself researching the subject and becoming increasingly interested in indigenous flora. Her enthusiasm and the children's curiosity mutually ignited a spark that was quickly transmitted to some of the parents. Before long two of the students' mothers, through help from the school, were able to procure a small grant, enabling them to make a productive visit to a native plant nursery. Their next step was a few days of hard work in a neglected former garden, just outside a school window. Leone and her students now have a beautiful demonstration garden right under their noses, and native plant lessons are more interesting then ever.

This school is one of several that have introduced native plants into the schoolyard landscape, and it seems the perfect place to initiate an interest in these plants. Parent volunteers in many schools have established environmental committees, and while the focus of most of these groups is recycling and other aspects of environmental clean-up, native plants are fast becoming a subject of interest.

Children love learning about wild things and this eagerness can be encouraged by the wealth of children's literature—fiction and non-fiction—on the subject of creatures of the wild and their struggle for survival. (See the Regional Source Guide for a short list.) The hunger for knowledge can also be fed by giving children first-hand experience through wilderness outings—even though the wilderness you visit may be your own backyard!

For many of us, a considerable effort must be expended to acquire attitudes and information necessary to establish a new kind of landscape. For children growing up with this knowledge and these attitudes, we can only expect that the process will occur more easily and naturally.

Leone had the right idea; from primary grades to university levels, students are demonstrating that they want to learn more about their environment and how they can affect it. They carry into the future the hope that we can repair what we have so seriously damaged.

ꙥ Glossary of Terms ꙥ

Many of these terms have a botanical application. Most of them are used at least once in the text of this book.

Achene. A small, one-seeded, dry fruit.

Allelopathy. The adverse effect of one plant's chemicals on another plant's growth.

Alternate. Referring to leaf placement: arranged singly, not opposite.

Annual. A plant whose life cycle is completed in one year.

Basal. At the base.

Biennial. A plant requiring two growing seasons to complete its life cycle.

Bract. A modified or reduced leaf.

Catkin. A slender, spike-like cluster of small flowers, either male or female.

Chaparral. Semi-arid vegetation of dense, drought-tolerant evergreen shrubs.

Composite. A plant family (Compositae, or Asteraceae) with a head inflorescence consisting of many small flowers clustered into a flattened disk-shaped head, as in the daisy or thistle.

Compound. Divided into more than one part, as opposed to simple.

Coniferous. Cone-bearing; a coniferous tree is one whose seeds and pollen are formed in cones.

Corm. A short, swollen underground stem with buds.

Cultivar. Cultivated variety: a variety of a plant species originating in and persisting only under cultivation.

Damping off. A fungus disease which causes seedlings to die soon after germination.

Deciduous. Plants whose leaves fall at the end of the growing season.

Dissected. Deeply cut or divided into many parts.

Edge vegetation. Occurs where one habitat type joins with another.

Elliptic. A leaf form with an elliptical shape (flattened circle); longer than wide, broadest at the middle, and with curved sides.

Flora. The plants of a region.

Floret. Small flower, usually part of a cluster.

Forb. A non-woody, broad-leaved flowering plant (as distinguished from grass-like plants, for example).

Friable. Easily crumbled, as in soil.

Genus (singular), genera (plural). A group of closely-related plants containing one or more species; the first part of a plant's botanical name.

Hardening off. Gradually acclimatizing a plant raised under warm conditions to the outside environment.

Hardy. A plant that can live year-round without protection; in a cold climate this means it can withstand overwintering.

Herb. 1) Herbaceous plant. 2) A garden plant used as a medicine, seasoning, or flavouring.

Herbaceous plant. A non-woody plant.

Herbaceous perennial. A herbaceous plant living several years and whose stems die back to the ground each year.

Hip. The fruit of members of the rose genus, usually small, red and smooth.

Humus. Decomposed organic material in the soil.

Hybrid. A plant resulting from a cross between two different plants, occurring either in the wild or as a product of horticultural breeding.

Inflorescence. A flower cluster; any flowering system consisting of more than one flower.

Key. The winged fruit of the maple, which is a double samara.

Lanceolate. Lance-shaped leaf form narrowly elongated, tapering to a pointed tip.

Lateral. A leaf that is positioned on the side of the stem.

Leaflet. One of the parts of a compound leaf.

Leaf mould. Soil-enriching material composed of partially-decayed leaves.

Linear. Long and narrow with parallel edges.

Lobe. Shallow division on a leaf.

Microclimate. The climate, near the ground, of a small, specific area, as contrasted with the climate of the entire area.

Monoculture. The planting of only one species for a specific use.

Mycorrhizal fungi. Fungi which are intimately associated with the roots of certain plants, in a symbiotic union of root and fungus which benefits the host plant.

Node. Place on a stem that bears a leaf.

Nitrogen-fixer. A micro-organism that converts gaseous nitrogen from the air into a form that can be used for plant nutrition.

Oblong. Leaf form in which the length is much greater than the width and the edges are almost parallel.

Opposite. When used in reference to leaf arrangement, two leaves which occur directly opposite each other on a stem.

Ovate. Egg-shaped, with the broadest part at the base.

Oxygenation. The expelling of oxygen by green plants, a product of photosynthesis.

Palmate. Spreading like the fingers of a palm (as compared to pinnate), usually referring to the arrangement of leaflets of a compound leaf.

Parasite. A plant or other organism that obtains its nourishment chiefly from another live organism by penetrating its tissues.

Pedicel. The stalk of a single flower.

Pendant. Hanging.

Perennial. A plant with a life cycle of more than two years.

Petal. Usually the showiest and most colourful of the floral parts, attached below the central pistil and stamens.

Photosynthesis. The process by which green plants use the sun's energy to manufacture sugars from carbon dioxide and water.

Pinnate. Leaflets of a compound leaf, arranged along both sides of a central stalk (as in a feather).

Pistil. The central, seed-bearing organ of a flower.

Pollen. The yellow granular dust produced by the stamens, each pollen grain containing a sperm nucleus involved with fertilizing the egg cell in the pistil.

Pricking-out. Spacing out young seedlings while transplanting.

Prostrate. Growing flat on the ground.

Raceme. An elongated flower cluster in which the flowers are attached linearly along a central stalk and the lower flowers open first.

Rhizome. An underground stem that grows horizontally.

Rootstock. Underground rootlike stem.

Rosette. A group of leaves arranged circularly around the base of a plant.

Samara. A dry, winged fruit; the maple seed is one example (*See* Key).

Savanna. Semi-arid vegetation of widely spaced trees and with a ground cover of grasses and shrubs.

Scree. Rock fragments at the base of a rock wall or slope; also called talus.

Sedge. Grasslike plant often found on wet ground or in water, usually having triangular solid stems (which are edged rather than rounded), three rows of narrow leaves, and small flowers born in spikes.

Sepal. One of the outermost floral parts, attached below the petals, and often smaller than the petals, green and leaf-like.

Sheath. The basal part of a leaf that encloses part of the stem.

Shrub. A perennial woody plant with several stems, usually less than 10 feet (3 m) tall.

Simple. One piece, as opposed to compound (in leaves).

Snag. A dead or decaying tree which has been left standing, providing significant habitat to wildlife.

Spathe. A large leaf-like bract that encloses a cluster of flowers.

Spatulate. Spatula- or spoon-shaped.

Species. A group of genetically similar plants which are significantly different from other plant species; a subdivision of a genus; the second word in a plant's botanical name.

Spore. A microscopic reproductive cell, occurring in all the non-seed plant groups (ferns, mosses, liverworts, algae, fungi).

Spur. Saclike or tubular projection from either a sepal or a petal.

Stamen. One of the central floral parts, bearing the pollen.

Sterile. Not fertile; does not produce seeds or spores.

Stigma. Pollen-receiving part of the pistil.

Stolon. A long branch, forming a horizontal runner at ground level, that can root and develop a new plant.

Talus. *See* Scree.

Taproot. Main descending root.

Tendril. Slender coiling stem or modified leaf used by a climbing plant to support itself.

Tree. A woody perennial plant, usually over 10 feet (3 m) tall, usually with one main stem or trunk.

Umbel. A flat-topped inflorescence of flowers in which the pedicels all arise from the same point, typical of the parsley family (*Umbelliferae*).

Vascular. Plants containing conducting cells that convey water and nutrients.

Vegetative propagation. Plant reproduction by means other than seeds or spores.

❧ Regional Source Guide ❧

Native plants and seeds

Specialist nurseries

The best source for native plants is a reputable
retail nursery which propagates its own plants
or obtains stock from a known native plant supplier. Generalist garden centres are beginning to
stock natives, and will expand this service if the
public shows an interest. The onus is on gardeners to create the demand, so make your wishes
known to the store manager.

    The following wholesale and retail outlets
are good sources for native plants.

In Canada
O Alpenflora Gardens
17985 - 40th Avenue, Surrey, B.C. V4P 1M5
Telephone: (604) 576-2464
(Wholesale nursery.)

O Cardinal Gardens
13050 Cardinal Street, Mission, B.C. V2V 5X4
Telephone: (604) 820-0845
(Free catalogue.)

O C.E Jones & Associated Native Plant Nursery
Kanishay Road (off West Saanich Road near
Deep Cove), North Saanich, B.C.
Mailing address: 204 - 26 Bastion Square,
Victoria, B.C. V8W 1H9
Telephone: (604) 655-1374

O Fraser's Thimble Farms
175 Arbutus Road, Salt Spring Island,
B.C. V8K 1A3
Telephone: (604) 537-5788

O Gabriola Growing Co.
R.R. #1, Site 3CA, Gabriola Island, B.C. V0R 1X0
Telephone: (604) 247-8204
(Native seed and plant supplier.)

O The Green House
1340 Wain Road, Sidney, B.C. V8L 5V1
Telephone: (604) 655-4391

O Kimoff Wholesale Nursery
6656 Wain Road, Victoria, B.C. V8X 3X1
Telephone: (604) 544-2297
(Wholesale nursery with wide selection of mature
native plants.)

O Meadow Sweet
24640 - 16th Avenue, Langley, B.C. V2Z 1J4
Telephone: (604) 530-2611

O Mosterman Plant Propagators
43233 Lumsden Road, Yarrow, B.C. V0X 2A0
Telephone: (604) 823-4713
(Wholesale nursery.)

O Natural Legacy Seed
R.R. #2, C-1 Laird, Armstrong, B.C. V0E 1B0

O Nature's Garden Seed Company
P.O. Pox 40121, 905 Gordon Street,
Victoria, B.C. V8W 3N3
Telephone: (604) 595-2062
(Seed supplier.)

O Rainforest Gardens
13139 - 224th Street, R.R. #2, Maple Ridge,
B.C. V2X 7E7
Telephone: (604) 467-4218

O Reid, Collins Nurseries Ltd.
Box 430, 2396 - 272nd Street, Aldergrove,
B.C. V4W 2T9
Telephone: (604) 856-6408
(Native seed supplier and wholesale nursery.)

O Yellowpoint Propagation Ltd.
13735 Quesnel Road, R.R. #3, Ladysmith,
B.C. V0R 2E0
Telephone: (604) 245-4635
(Native seed supplier and wholesale nursery.)

In U.S.A.
O Abundant Life Seed Foundation
Box 772, Port Townsend, WA 98386
(Native seed supplier. Catalogues: $1.00.)

O Barford's Hardy Ferns
23622 Bothell Way, Bothell, WA 98021
Telephone: (206) 483-0205

O Boskey Dell Natives
23311 SW Boskey Dell Lane, West Linn,
OR 97068
Telephone: (503) 638-5945

O Colvos Creek Farm Nursery
P.O. Box 1512, Vashon Island, WA 98070
Telephone: (206) 441-1509 or 463-9776

O Cloud Mountain Farm
6906 Goodwin Road, Everson, WA 98247
Telephone: (360) 966-5899;
FAX: (360) 966-0921

O DeWilde's Nursery
3140 Northwest Avenue, Bellingham, WA 98225
Telephone: (360) 733-8190

O Ferris Nursery
415 SE 98th CT, South Beach, OR 97365

O Forestfarm
990 Tetherow Road, Williams, OR 97544-9599

O The Greenery
14450 NE 16th Place, Bellevue, WA 98007
Telephone: (206) 641-1458

O Wallace Hansen, Native Plants of the
Northwest
2158 Bower Ct. SE, Salem, OR 97301
Telephone: (503) 581-2638;
FAX (503) 581-9957

O IFA Nurseries
463 Eadon Road, Toledo, WA 98591

O Inside Passage
P.O. Box 639, Port Townsend, WA 98368
Voice Mail: (206) 781-3575
(Seed and native plant service.)

O Lamb's Nurseries
Rt. 1, Box 460B, Long Beach, WA 98631
Telephone: (300) 642-4856

O Madrona Nursery
815 - 38th Avenue, Seattle 98122
Telephone: (206) 323-8325

O   Maxwelton Valley Gardens
3443 E. French Road, Clinton, Whidbey Island,
WA 98236
Telephone: (360) 579-1770;
FAX: (360) 579-1496

O   MSK Rare Plant Nursery
20066 - 15th Avenue, Seattle, WA 98177
Telephone: (206) 546-1281

O   Mt. Tahoma Nursery
28111 - 112th E. Graham, WA 98399
Telephone: (206) 847-9827

O   Natives Northwest
190 Aldrich Road, Mossyrock, WA 98564

O   Northwest Native Seed
915 Davis Place S., Seattle, WA 98144
Telephone: (206) 329-5804
(Catalogue: $1.00.)

O   Plants of the Wild
P.O. Box 866, Tekoa, WA 99033
Telephone: (509) 284-2848;
FAX: (509) 284-6464

O   Russell Graham Nursery
4030 Eagle Crest Road, Salem, OR 97304
Telephone: (503) 362-1135

O   Siskiyou Rare Plant Nursery
2825 Cummings Road, Medford, OR 97501
Telephone: (503) 722-6846

O   Silvaseed Company, Inc.
P.O. Box 118, 317 James Street, Roy, WA 98580
Telephone: (206) 843-2246
(Custom seed collection and seed stratification.
Catalogue: $1.00.)

O   Soos Creek Gardens
12602 SE Petrovitsky Road, Renton, WA 98058
Telephone: (206) 226-9308

O   Sunrise Gardens
2401 Samish Way, Bellingham, WA 98226
Telephone: (360) 734-3091;
FAX: (360) 738-1767

O   Swanson's Nursery
9701 - 15th Avenue NW, Seattle, WA 98117
Telephone: (206) 782-2543;
FAX: (206) 782-1910

O   Watershed Garden Works
2039 - 44th Avenue, Longview, WA 98632
Telephone and FAX: (360) 423-6456

O   Wood's Native Plants
740 Berry Street, Parksdale, OR 97040

Seed exchanges and other seed sources

O   Heritage Seed Program
R.R. #3, Uxbridge, Ontario, L9P 1R3
(A grassroots seed exchange, concerned with the
loss of genetic diversity. Yearly membership.)

O   Seed Savers Exchange
3076 North Winn Road, Decorah, Iowa 52101
(Three yearly publications and colour brochure.)

O   Territorial Seed Company
Box 157, 20 Palmer Avenue, Cottage Grove,
OR 97424
(Excellent collection; wide variety of seeds in-
cluding natives to this region. Free catalogue.)

○ Territorial Seed Company (Canada)
Box 825, 8475 Ontario Street, Vancouver,
B.C. V5X 3E8
(Canadian outlet, separate catalogue.)

○ Canadian Wildflower Society
4981 Highway 7 East, Unit 12A, Suite 228,
Markham, ON L3R 1N1
Telephone: (905) 294-9075
(Membership indudes access to native wildflower
seed; yearly seed exchange.)

Plant and Seed Sales

Plant sales often include seed sales or seed exchanges. The following organizations have plant sales that include native plants.

In Canada

○ Alpine Garden Club of British Columbia
Box 5161, Main Post Office, 349 West Georgia
Street, Vancouver, B.C. V6B 4B2
(Seed exchange.)

○ Vancouver Island Rock and Alpine Garden
Society
Box 6507, Station C, Victoria, B.C. V8P 5M4
Telephone: (604) 477-2229
(Annual plant sale.)

○ VanDusen Botanical Garden
5251 Oak Street, Vancouver, B.C. V6M 4H1
Telephone: (604) 878-9274
(Annual spring sale.)

○ The Victoria Horticultural Society
Box 5081, Station B, Victoria, B.C. V8R 6N3
Telephone: (604) 381-4078
(Monthly plant sales; seeds sold at various times
of the year.)

In U.S.A.

○ Arboretum Foundation, Washington Park
Arboretum
University of Washington, 2300 Arboratum
Drive E., Seattle, WA 98112-2300
Telephone: (206) 543-8800
(Spring plant sale.)

○ County Conservation District Native Plant
Sales
Skagit Conservation District
214 - 2021 East College Way, Mount Vernon,
WA 306-42-4313
(Every county has a Conservation District
plant sale.)

○ Hardy Plant Society of Oregon
2148 Summit Drive, Lake Oswego, OR 97034
Telephone: (503) 635-2159
(Spring and fall plant sales.)

○ Northwest Horticultural Society
Center for Urban Horticulture, 3501 NE 41st
Street, University of Washington GF 15, Seattle,
WA 98195
Telephone: (206) 527-1794
(Fall plant sale in mid September.)

○ Nature Center at Snake Lake
Tacoma Park District, 1919 S. Tyler, Tacoma,
WA 98405
Telephone: (206) 591-6439
(Annual native plant sale. Catalogue mailing
list.)

○ Washington Native Plant Society
P.O. Box 576, Woodinville, WA 98072-0576

Organizations

Garden groups with an interest in native plants

In Canada
O Alpine Garden Club of British Columbia
Box 5161, Main Post Office, 349 West Georgia Street, Vancouver, B.C. V6B 4B2

O Native Plant Study Group (a sub-group of the Victoria Horticultural Society)
Telephone: (604) 381-4078

O Vancouver Island Rock and Alpine Garden Society
Roger Whitlock, telephone: (604) 477-2229

In U.S.A.
O Native Plant Society of Oregon
Jan Dobak, 2584 NW Savier Street, Portland, OR 97210-2412
Telephone: (503) 248-9242
(12 chapters in Oregon.)

O Washington Native Plant Society
Komo Kulshan Chapter: Joe Arnett, 1825 S. Nugent Road, Lummii Island, WA 98262
Telephone: (360) 758-2902
(Covers Whatcom, Skagit and San Juan Counties.)
Salal Chapter: Nancy Paine-Donovan
Telephone: (360) 856-2401
For other local chapters (South Sound, Olympic Peninsula, Central Puget Sound) contact Washington Native Plant Society, P.O. Box 576, Woodinville, WA 98072-0576.

Other organizations

For information regarding naturalist clubs or environmentalist organizations, contact:

British Columbia
O Federation of British Columbia Naturalists
321 - 1357 West Broadway, Vancouver, B.C. V6H 4A9
Telephone: (604) 737-3057

Washington
O State of Washington Department of Wildlife
16018 Mill Creek Road, Mill Creek, WA 98012
Telephone: (206) 775-1311

Oregon
O World Forestry Center
4033 SW Canyon Road, Portland, OR 97221
Telephone: (503) 228-1367

Nature sanctuaries

This list represents a sampling of the special wildlife habitats within the Pacific coastal region.

In British Columbia

Vancouver, Lower Mainland and the Sunshine Coast
O Boundary Bay Wildlife Management Area
Viewing sites: Blackie Spit in White Rock and Beach Grove in Tsawwassen.

O Burnaby Lake Regional Park
North of Highway 1, off the Kensington or Cariboo exit, 20 km east of Vancouver.
Telephone: (604) 420-3031
(The Burnaby Lake nature house is located on Piper Ave.)

O George C. Reifel Migratory Bird Sanctuary
Westham Island, 10 km west of Ladner, in Delta, B.C.
Telephone: (604) 946-6980
(Open year round.)

○ Lynn Canyon Park & Ecology Centre
3663 Park Road, North Vancouver, B.C.
Telephone: (604) 981-3103

○ Pitt-Addington Marsh Wildlife Management Area
Minnekhada Regional Park
From Lougheed Hwy. in Port Coquitlam turn north on Coast Meridian Road and follow the GVRD signs.

○ Serpentine Fen Wildlife Area
King George Hwy., just east of Highway 99, near White Rock, B.C.

○ Smuggler Cove Provincial Marine Park
15 km north of Sechelt, B.C. (west of Hwy 101).

○ South Arm Marshes Wildlife Management Area
Lower Fraser River, west of the Massey Tunnel in Delta
(Access to trails is off Ferry Road and at Ladner Harbour Park.)

○ University of British Columbia Botanical Gardens
6804 Southwest Marine Drive, Vancouver, B.C.
Telephone: (604) 822-3928
(Includes a native plant garden.)

Vancouver Island and the Gulf Islands
○ Freshwater Eco-centre
1080 Warncliffe Road, Duncan, B.C.
Telephone: (604) 746-6722

○ Goldstream Provincial Park
On Highway 1, 16 km North of Victoria, B.C.

○ Morrell Wildlife Sanctuary
Nanaimo Lakes Road, west Nanaimo, B.C.
Telephone: (604) 753-5811

○ Qualicum National Wildlife Area
At the mouth of the Little Qualicum River.

○ Royal British Columbia Museum Native Plant Garden
675 Belleville Street, Victoria, B.C.
Telephone: (604) 387-3701

O Sidney Spit Provincial Marine Park
Passenger ferries operate from May to September (or take your own boat from Sidney to the government wharf in the lagoon).

O Somenos Marsh
Wildlife area is located 1 km north of Duncan, B.C., on the east side of Highway 1.

O Swan Lake Christmas Hill Nature Sanctuary
3873 Swan Lake Road, Victoria, B.C.
(off McKenzie Ave near Highway 17).
Telephone: (604) 479-0211

U.S.A.

In Washington
O Ridgefield National Wildlife Refuge
P.O. Box 457, 301 North Third Street,
Ridgefield, WA 98642
Telephone: (206) 887-4106

O San Juan Islands National Wildlife Refuge
c/o Nisqually NWR Complex, 100 Brown Farm Road, Olympia, WA 98506
Telephone: (206) 753-9467
(Write for map and regulations.)

O Washington Islands National Wildlife Refuge
c/o Nisqually NWR Complex, 100 Brown Farm Road, Olympia, WA 98506
Telephone: (206) 753-9467

O Willapa National Wildlife Refuge
HC Box 910, Ilwaco, WA 98624-9707
Telephone: (206) 484-3482 (Naselle Exchange)

In Oregon
O Ankeny National Wildlife Refuge
c/o Western Oregon NWR Complex
26208 Finley Refuge Road, Corvallis, OR 97333
Telephone: (503) 757-7236
or: 2301 Wintel Road, Jefferson, OR 97352
Telephone: (503) 327-2444

O Baskett Slough National Wildlife Refuge
c/o Western Oregon NWR Complex
26208 Finley Refuge Road, Corvallis, OR 97333
Telephone: (503) 757-7236
or: 10995 Highway 22, Dallas, OR 97338
Telephone: (503) 623-2749

O Umatilla National Wildlife Refuge Complex
(Oregon and Washington)
P.O. Box 239, Post Office Building, Umatilla,
OR 97882
Telephone: (503) 922-3232

O William L. Finley National Wildlife Refuge
26208 Finley Refuge Road, Corvallis, OR 97333
Telephone: (503) 757-7236

Further Information

In British Columbia
Membership in Naturescape British Columbia (see page 131) will provide you with a resource booklet which includes detailed descriptions of these and other nature sanctuaries, and the wildlife you can view there.

Information is also available through:
Wildlife Branch, Ministry of Environment, Lands and Parks, Victoria, B.C.
Telephone: (604) 387-9717
and: GVRD Regional Parks, Burnaby, B.C.
Telephone: (604) 432-6350

In Washington and Oregon

A list of National Wildlife Refuges is available in a brochure titled *Visitor Directory, Pacific Region*, containing addresses of well over one hundred wildlife observation areas in Washington, Oregon, and other parts of the United States. To obtain the brochure, contact:

Visitor Directory, Pacific Region
U.S. Fish and Wildlife Service, Department of the Interior
911 NE 11th Avenue, Portland, OR 97232-4181
Telephone: (503) 231-6121

Current reading material

Magazines and Journals

Gardening with native plants is a relatively new, but rapidly growing concept, and popular journals on the subject are sometimes correspondingly difficult to find. For up-to-date information, local grass-roots organizations are among the best sources; environmental-awareness projects and community-based gardening and naturalist programs produce newsletters and educational pamphlets.

Covering a wider scope, the following publications discuss subjects of interest to gardeners, naturalists and botanists. They frequently include articles about native plants in this region.

Hortus Northwest: A Pacific Northwest Native Plant Directory and Journal, P.O. Box 955, Canby, OR 97013

Coastal Grower: Gardening in Coastal British Columbia, 1075 Alston Street, Victoria, B.C. V9A 3S6

Nature Canada, Canadian Nature Federation, 520-1 Nicholas Street, Ottawa, Ontario, K1N 7B7

Sunset: The Magazine of Western Living, 80 Willow Road, Menlow Park, California, 94025

Wildflower, Canadian Wildflower Society, 4981 Highway 7 East, Unit 12A, Suite 228, Markham, Ontario L3R 1N1

Wildlife Books for Children

Compiled by Naturescape British Columbia, the following is a list of some books that introduce children to wildlife issues.

The Fascinating World of Bees. New York, NY: Barron's Educational Series, 1993. (Also books on Ants, Butterflies & Moths, Spiders, Birds, Snakes, Frogs & Toads.)

Bumie, David. *How Nature Works: Fascinating Projects & Experiments that Reveal the Secrets of Nature*. Nevada City, CA: Readers Digest Association, Inc., 1995.

Bumie, David. *Dictionary of Nature*. Vancouver: Raincoast Books, 1994.

Burton, Jane and Taylor Kim. *Egg: A Photographic Story of Hatching*. Vancouver, B.C.: Raincoast Books, 1994.

Duensing, Edward. *Talking to Fireflies: A Parents Guide to Nature Activities*. New York: Penguin Books, 1990.

Earle, Ann. *Zipping, Zapping, Zooming Bats*. New York: Harper Collins Publishers, 1995.

Farris, Katherine. *Bee Hives & Bat Caves, Amazing Animal Houses*. (From the Editors of Owl Magazine.) Toronto: Greey de Pencier Books, 1990.

Farris, Katherine. *Singing Fish & Flying Rhinos, Amazing Animal Habitats*. Toronto: Greey de Pencier Books, 1990.

Hickman, Pamela. *Habitats*. Toronto: Federation of Ontario Naturalists. Kids Can Press Ltd., 1993.

Hillyard, Paul. *Insects & Spiders Picturepedia*. New York: Dorling Kindersley, 1993.

Love, Ann and Drake, Jane. *Take Action*. Toronto: World Wildlife Fund. Kids Can Press Ltd., 1992.

Lang, Susan S. *Nature in Your Backyard*. Brookfield, CT: Millbrook Press, 1995.

Mastin, Colleayn O. *Canadian Endangered Species*. Nature Canada Series. Kamloops, B.C.: Grasshopper Book Publishing, 1995. (Also *Canadian Wild Animals, Canadian Arctic Animals, Canadian Trees* and *Canadian Birds*.)

Micucci, Charles. *The Life & Times of the Honey Bee*. New York: Houghton Mifflin Company, 1995.

Morton, Sally. *Life in the Cities: Animals, People, Plants*. Richmond Hill, ON: Scholastic Canada Ltd., 1993.

Orenstein, Ronald. *How on Earth? A question-and-answer book about how animals and plants live*. Toronto: Key Porter Books, Toronto, 1994.
Potter, Jean. *Nature in a Nutshell for Kids*. John Wiley & Sons Ltd., 1995.

Sattler, Helen Roney. *The Book of the North American Owls*. New York: Clarion Books, 1995.

Swanson, Diane. *Sky Dancers: The Amazing World of Canadian Birds*. Vancouver: Whitecap Books, 1995. (Also *Coyotes in the Crosswalk, Squirts & Snails & Skinny Green Tails, A Toothy Tongue and One Long Foot*, and *Why Seals Blow Their Noses*.)

Taylor, Barbara. *Meadow: A close-up look at the natural world of a meadow*. Stoddart Publishing Co. Ltd., 1995.

The following booklets are directed to children at the grades four to six levels, and are published by Washington State Department of Wildlife; for information, contact 16018 Mill Creek Road, Mill Creek WA 98012, telephone: (206) 775-1311.

○ *Backyards for Birds*. (Introduction to bird habitats and instructions for building bird houses.)

○ *At Home Activities*. (Activities for learning more about nature; how to manage a backyard habitat.)

○ *Watching Washington Birds*. (Descriptions of birds, nests, eggs, habitat.)

❧ Bibliography ❧

Books

Archibald, David and Patton, Mary. *Water Gardens: A Harrowsmith Gardener's Guide.* Camden East, Ontario: Camden House, 1990.

Art, Henry W. *The Wild Flower Gardener's Guide: Pacific Northwest, Rocky Mountain, and Western Canada Edition.* Pownal, Vermont: Storey Communications, 1990.

Batdorf, Carol. *Northwest Native Harvest.* Surrey, BC and Blaine, WA: Hancock House, 1990.

Bennett, Jackie. *The Wildlife Garden Month-by-Month.* Devon: David & Charles, 1993.

Berrall, Julia S. *The Garden.* New York: The Viking Press, 1966.

Bittman, Sam. *Seeds.* Toronto and New York: Bantam Books, 1989.

Bovey, Robin; Campbell, Wayne; and Gates, Brian. *Birds of Victoria and Vicinity.* Edmonton: Lone Pine Publishing, 1989.

Brookes, John. *The John Brookes' Garden Design Book.* Montreal: Dorling Kindersley, 1991.

Brookes, John. *Planting the Country Way.* London: BBC Books, 1994.

Campbell, Susan. *Naturescape British Columbia.* Victoria: British Columbia Ministry of Environment, Lands and Parks, 1995.

Caros, Roger. *Treasures of Classic Nature Tales.* New York: Dutton, 1992.

Carr, Emily. *The Book of Small.* Toronto: Irwin Publishing, 1966.

Chatto, Beth. *The Green Tapestry.* London: Collins, 1989.

Clark, Lewis J. *Field Guide to Wild Flowers in the Pacific Northwest (series).* Adapted by John Trelawny. Vancouver/Toronto: Douglas & McIntyre, 1984.

Clifford, Derek. *A History of Garden Design.* London: Faber and Faber, 1962.

Cole, Brenda, ed. *Shade Gardens: A Harrowsmith Gardener's Guide.* Camden East, Ontario: Camden House Publishing, 1993.

Cox, Jeff. *Landscaping with Nature.* Emmaus, Pennsylvania: Rodale Press, 1991.

Daniels, Stevie. *The Wild Lawn Handbook.* New York: Macmillan, 1995.

Davies, Jennifer. *The Victorian Flower Garden.* London: BBC Books, 1991.

Druse, Ken. *The Natural Garden.* New York: Clarkson N. Potter, 1989.

Druse, Ken. *The Natural Habitat Garden.* New York: Clarkson Potter, 1994.

Ecosystems of British Columbia. Victoria: Research Branch, Ministry of Forests, 1991.

Environmental Studies Program, University of Victoria, Instructor: Nancy J. Turner. *Plants for all Reasons; Culturally Important Plants of Aboriginal Peoples of Southern Vancouver Island.* Victoria: University of Victoria, 1992.

Ewing, John and Stewart Bowen, Jill, editors. *Gardening Victoria: Tips and Techniques from the Victoria Horticultural Society.* Victoria: Gardenisle Publishing, 1995.

Feeney, Stephanie. *The Northwest Gardeners' Resource Directory.* Bellingham, Washington: Cedarcroft Press, 1995.

Feltwell, John. *The Naturalist's Garden.* Toronto & Montreal: McGraw-Hill Ryerson, 1987.

Gunther, Erna. *Ethnobotany of Western Washington.* Seattle and London: University of Washington Press, 1973.

Hansen, Richard and Stahl, Friedrich. *Perennials and their Garden Habitats.* Portland: Timber Press, 1993.

Harding, Lee E. and McCullum, Emily, editors. *Biodoversity in British Columbia: Our Changing Environment.* Ottawa: Environment Canada/Ministry of Supplies and Services, 1994.

Hardy, George A. and Hardy, Winnifred V. *Wildflowers in the Pacific Northwest.* Saskatoon: H.R. Larson Publishing Company, 1969.

Harris, Marjorie and Saunders, Tim. *The Canadian Gardener.* Toronto: Random House, 1990.

Hessayon, Dr. D.G. *The Bio Friendly Gardening Guide.* Herts, England: pbi Publications, 1986.

Hessayon, Dr. D.G. *The Garden Expert.* Herts, England: pbi Publications, 1986.

Hitchcock, C. Leo, and Cronquist, Arthur. *Flora of the Pacific Northwest.* Seattle and London: The University of Washington Press, 1974.

Hobhouse, Penelope. *Gardening through the Ages.* New York: Simon & Schuster, 1992.

Horn, Elizabeth. *Coastal Wildflowers of British Columbia and the Pacific Northwest.* Vancouver/Toronto: Whitecap Books, 1994.

House, Maria Newberry and Munroe, Susan. *Plantae Occidentalis.* Vancouver: The University of British Columbia Botanical Garden, 1979.

Imes, Rick. *Wildflowers: How To Identify Flowers in the Wild and How To Grow Them in Your Garden.* Toronto: Key Porter Books, 1992.

Innes, Clive. *Alpines: The Illustrated Dictionary.* Portland: Timber Press, 1995.

Jantra, Helmut. *Garden Pool Design.* Neptune City, NJ: TFH Publications, 1995.

Johnson, Hugh. *The Principles of Gardening.* New York: Simon & Schuster, 1979.

Keator, Glenn and Heady, Ruth M. *Pacific Coast Fern Finder.* Rochester, NY: Nature Study Guild, 1981.

Klinka, K.; Krajina, V.J.; Ceska, A.; and Scagel, A.M. *Indicator Plants of Coastal British Columbia.* Vancouver: University of British Columbia Press, 1989.

Kennedy, Des. *Crazy About Gardening.* Vancouver/Toronto: Whitecap Books, 1994.

Kruckeberg, Arthur R. *Gardening with Native Plants of the Pacific Northwest.* Seattle and London: University of Washington Press, 1992.

Kuhnlein, Harriet V. and Turner, Nancy J. *Traditional Plant Foods of Canadian Indigenous Peoples: Nutrition, Botany and Youth.* Philadelphia: Gordon and Breach Science Publishers, 1991.

Lacey, Stephen. *The Startling Jungle.* Boston: David R. Godine, 1990.

L'Anson, Mark and Bradford, Peter. *West Coast Rain Forest Kit Guidebook.* Victoria: Nature's Garden Seed Company, 1994.

Lyons, C.P. *Trees, Shrubs and Flowers to Know in British Columbia.* Vancouver: Lone Pine Publishing, 1995.

Marshall, Nina. *The Gardener's Guide to Plant Conservation.* Baltimore, MD: World Wildlife Fund, 1993.

Marshall, Peter. *Nature's Web: An Exploration of Ecological Thinking.* London: Simon & Schuster, 1992.

Menzies, Archibald. Letter to Sir Jos. Banks, from Nootka Sound, September 26, 1792. *Historical Records of New South Wales*, vol. 1, part 2. Sydney: Charles Potter, Government Printer, 1892.

Merilees, Bill. *Attracting Backyard Wildlife.* Vancouver/Toronto: Whitecap Books, 1989.

Mickel, John. *Ferns for American Gardens.* New York: Macmillan, 1994.

Monro, Michael. *Northwest Landscaping.* Seattle: Alaska Northwest Books, 1992.

Mosser, Monique and Teyssot, Georges, editors. *The Architecture of Western Gardens.* Cambridge, Massachusetts: The MIT Press, 1991.

Nichols, Beverley. *Garden Open Today.* London: Jonathan Cape, 1963.

Paterson, Allen. *Designing a Garden.* Camden East, Ontario: Camden House Publishing, 1992.

Pojar, Jim and MacKinnon, Andy. *Plants of Coastal British Columbia.* Vancouver: Lone Pine Publishing, 1994.

Pollan, Michael. *Second Nature: a gardener's education.* New York: Dell Publishing, 1991.

Robinson, Peter. *The Water Garden.* New York: Sterling Publishing, 1995.

Salt Spring Island Trail and Nature Club Book Committee. *Wildflowers of Salt Spring Island.* Ganges, BC: 1982.

Schofield, Janice L. *Discovering Wild Plants: Alaska, Western Canada, The Northwest.* Anchorage and Seattle: Alaska Northwest Books, 1989.

Schweitzer, Albert. *Reverence for Life.* San Francisco: Harper, 1993.

Sperka, Marie. *Growing Wildflowers.* New York: Harper & Row, 1973.

Scott-James, Anne and Lancaster, Osbert. *The Pleasure Garden.* London: Century, 1991.

Spurr, Joy. *Wild Shrubs.* Seattle: Pacific Search Press, 1978.

Stein, Sara. *Noah's Garden.* New York: Houghton Mifflin, 1993.

Stevens, Elaine; Hungerford, Dagmar; Fancourt-Smith, Doris; Mitchell, Jane; and Buffman, Ann. *The Twelve Month Gardener.* Vancouver/Toronto: Whitecap Books, 1991.

Strickler, Dr. Dee. *Wayside Wildflowers of the Pacific Northwest.* Columbia Falls, Montana: The Flower Press, 1993.

Sunset Books. *The Sunset New Western Garden Book.* Menlo Park, California: Lane Publishing, 1979.

Sunset Books. *Sunset Water Gardening.* Menlo Park, California: Lane Publishing Co., 1989.

Swan Hill Christmas Hill Nature Sanctuary and The Greater Victoria Water District. *A Guide to Backyard Water Conservation.* Victoria: Beacon Hill Communications Group, 1995.

Swindells, Philip. *Water Gardens.* London: Ward Lock, 1994.

Taylor's Guide to Natural Gardening. Boston/New York/London: Houghton, Mifflin, 1993.

Taylor's Guide to Water-Saving Gardening. Boston: Houghton Mifflin, 1989.

Tootill, Elizabeth, editor. *The Penguin Dictionary of Botany.* London: Penguin Books, 1984.

Turner, Nancy J. *Food Plants of the Coastal First Peoples.* Vancouver: The University of British Columbia Press, 1995.

Turner, Nancy J.; Thompson, Laurence C.; Thompson, M. Terry; and York, Annie Z. *Thompson Ethnobotany.* Province of British Columbia: Royal British Columbia Museum, 1990.

The Natural History of Thetis Lake Park. Victoria: Thetis Park Nature Sanctuary Association, 1974.

U.B.C. Guide to Gardening in British Columbia. Vancouver: The University of British Columbia Botanical Garden, 1990.

Underhill, J.E. *Alpine Wildflowers.* Blaine, WA and Surrey, BC: Hancock House Publishers, 1986.

Waldon, Bob. *A Guide to Feeding Winter Birds in British Columbia.* Vancouver: Whitecap Books, 1995.

Willis, A.R. *The Pacific Gardener.* Vancouver: Gray's Publishing/Whitecap Books, 1987.

Wilson, Jim. *Landscaping with Wild Flowers.* Boston: Houghton Mifflin, 1992.

Wilson, William H; McKinley, Michael; and Hildebrand, Ron. *Landscaping with Wildflowers and Native Plants.* San Ramon, California: Ortho Books, 1984.

Yocom, Charles and Dasmann, Ray. *Pacific Coastal Wildlife Region.* Happy Camp, California: Naturegraph Publishers, 1965.

Young, James A. and Young, Cheryl G. *Collecting, Processing and Germinating Seeds of Wildlife Plants.* Portland: Timber Press, 1986.

Periodicals, Journals and Magazines

Carson, Michael. "Birding Observations around Rithet's Bog." *The Victoria Naturalist* (January/February 1995).

Cullen, Mark. "The Basics: Cold, Hard Facts on Winter Composting." *Canadian Gardening*, October/November 1995.

Druse, Ken. "The Case for the Natural Habitat Garden." *Garden Design*, April/May 1994.

Hebda, Richard and Aitkens, Fran, editors. *Garry Oak Meadow Colloquium (Proceedings).* Victoria: Garry Oak Meadow Preservation Society, 1993.

Hebda, Richard. "Native Plant of the Month" (series). *The Island Grower* (August/September 1992 - October/November 1995).

Ingersen, Will. "The Impact of American Plants on British Gardens - Part II." *Hortus: A Gardening Journal* (Summer 1987).

Ingwersen, Ken. "The Native Question." *Wildflower* (Autumn 1993).

Kruckeberg, Arthur. "Native Plants for the Coastal Garden." *Wildflower* (Spring 1991).

McKeag, Michael. "A Natural Garden." *Pacific Horticulture* (Fall 1994).

Moore, J. Paul. "A Woodland Garden of Natives." *Fine Gardening* (June 1994).

Pollan, Michael. "Against Nativism." *Wildflower* (Spring 1995).

Riley, Robert B. "Analogy and Authority." *Landscape Journal* (Spring 1995).

Roemer, Hans, "Native Plants for the Rock Garden." *Vancouver Island Rock and Alpine Garden Society Newsletter*, January 1994.

Schneider, Dan. "Water Works." *Nature Canada* (Spring 1995).

Thomas, Donna. "A Meadow is a Meadow is a Meadow—or is it?" *Wildflower* (Summer 1994).

Wasowski, Andy. "Pro Nativism." *Wildflower* (Spring 1995).

Young-Berg, Kathryn and Berg, Dean. "Natives to Attract Wildlife." *Douglasia* (Winter 1994).

❧ Index ⚘

Main plant entries are in **bold**.

❧ About the Author ❧

April Pettinger has been collecting native plant information and expertise since she moved to Vancouver Island, where the rainforest inspired her to learn more about the region's unique vegetation. She has been involved in native plant gardening for several years and has contributed articles on the subject to *Gardening Victoria* and *Gardenry.* She lives in Victoria, B.C., where she is a member of the Victoria Horticultural Society and its Native Plant Study Group.